TEXTUAL INTIMACY

STUDIES IN RELIGION AND CULTURE

John D. Barbour and
Gary L. Ebersole, Editors

TEXTUAL INTIMACY

AUTOBIOGRAPHY AND RELIGIOUS IDENTITIES

WESLEY A. KORT

UNIVERSITY OF VIRGINIA PRESS

CHARLOTTESVILLE AND LONDON

First published 2012

1 3 5 7 9 8 6 4 2

Library of Congress Cataloging-in-Publication Data

Kort, Wesley A.
  Textual intimacy : autobiography and religious identities / Wesley A. Kort.
      p.   cm. — (Studies in religion and culture)
  Includes bibliographical references (p.   ) and index.
  ISBN 978-0-8139-3276-7 (cloth : alk. paper) — ISBN 978-0-8139-3277-4
(pbk. : alk. paper) — ISBN 978-0-8139-3278-1 (e-book)
  1. Spiritual journals—Authorship. 2. Autobiography—Religious aspects.
I. Title.
  BL628.5.K67 2012
  810.9′382—dc23

                                                                      2011048579

For Kai

CONTENTS

ACKNOWLEDGMENTS

SEVERAL OF my colleagues at Duke University read parts of this book at various stages of its development, and I thank them for their encouragement, suggestions, and corrections: Kalman Bland, Mark Chaves, and David Need in the Department of Religion and Tim Strauman in the Psychology Department. I also thank Ms. Jennifer Kryszak, my teaching assistant, for reading the manuscript and making several helpful suggestions.

In addition, I presented parts of this book as papers for guest lectures and conferences. One was at the Blaise Pascal Institute at the Free University of Amsterdam, and I warmly thank my host, Professor Albert W. Musschenga, for providing me that very informative occasion. Another was held at Durham University in England, and I thank my host, Professor John Barclay, and the other members of the faculty who participated in the session of the conference occasioned by my paper. Finally, I presented parts of the book as guest of the English Department at Calvin College, and I am grateful to Professor Brian Ingraffia, who was my host.

I also thank our daughter, Eva Deane, an able philosopher, who willingly responded to my queries, especially concerning personal identity theory. Wherever the book reveals awareness of the philosophical problems inherent in its topics, it very likely is due to her astute observations.

Finally, I am grateful to the chair of my department, Professor Richard Jaffe, for his personal and material support, and to my editor, Cathie Brettschneider, who from the very outset encouraged me in this project.

TEXTUAL INTIMACY

INTRODUCTION

INTIMACY IS crucial for autobiography because the force and significance of this kind of text depends primarily on a close relation between the reader and the teller. Intimacy is also a factor in religious self-disclosure because religious identity in American culture is a personal matter and not publicly displayed. This study exposes and explores the convergence of these two kinds of intimacy.

Intimacy arises in autobiographies because readers are led by such texts to levels of disclosure that lie beyond what can be expected both in other kinds of texts and in conventional live interactions. Indeed, autobiography generates appeal precisely for this reason. Readers are drawn to texts by writers willing to divulge matters not accessible in ordinary exchanges because readers themselves have lives that extend beyond the level of convention. Interdependent engagement arises between readers and writers when acts of self-disclosure are met by appreciative attention.

While autobiographical intimacy is located at a level distinct from ordinary and superficial disclosures, it also operates at a level distinct from intimacies of a more complete kind. Total exposure generally cannot be expected in autobiography. This means that the kind of intimacy about which we are talking arises in a space between superficial or conventional disclosures and those that require specialized audiences.

Something similar occurs with regard to religious self-disclosure. I am aware of conventional signs of the religious identities of people around me, such as religious affiliation. But public religious self-disclosures operate somewhere between such surface indicators and their contraries, fully established and finalized religious identities that assume or require agreement or are themselves religious acts.

The poles or contrary relations between conventional and complete open up a space between them that autobiography can occupy. This space is an ill-defined and uncertain realm of free-play. It is a space similar to that occupied by other social exchanges, such as an insider's tip. We are susceptible to giving and receiving tips about, say, investments or good wines, knowledge presumably of a kind that experts have, but that does not require the effort of becoming one. Or, intimacy in autobiography is similar in social standing to flirting, a personal interaction that takes place at a level below the ordinary but without the consequences of full involvement.

We read autobiographies because they give us knowledge not usually accessible, because they invite us into a relationship with the writer that is more candid than our usual relations with authors, or for both reasons. And we speak or write autobiographically because of what Janet Varner Gunn calls an "autobiographical impulse," the urge to share knowledge of some kind and/or something personal with the hearer or reader.[1]

By positing a space between superficial and complete as a field of play in which autobiography functions, I am aware that there is a school of opinion that not only legitimizes but encourages using autobiography to divulge extremely intimate matters. A complex version of this opinion focuses on the experiences especially of women who have been victims of various kinds of abuse and who are urged to end their silence. A good example is provided by Janet Mason Ellerby's *Intimate Reading: The Contemporary Women's Memoir.*[2] She writes about texts in which women describe intensely personal and often traumatic occurrences, and she does so out of her own decision to disclose secrets regarding her family and youth. One of her main points is that secrecy concerning experiences of victimization creates shame, and shame is crippling to a sense of self-worth. By telling the reading public what happened, the argument goes, the author is freed from the burden of secrecy and its poisonous results.

While I do not want to discredit autobiographical theory and practice of this kind, I think that such texts, rather than normative for or epitomes of autobiography, are exceptions to the usual degree of intimacy that autobiographies create between their authors and readers and that maximizes the form's potentials. As autobiographies that primarily convey knowledge do not go into the kind of detail that experts possess, so autobiographies that divulge personal matters do not usually grant the kind of disclosures that would be warranted by the care and trust of established interpersonal intimacy or professional expertise. The craft of autobiography lies, among other things, in knowing what and how much of the personal or informational to divulge in order to move from ordinary toward complete while remaining in what I have designated as a space between the two.

The limits of disclosure also affect the writing of autobiography because the "autobiographical impulse" can be very strong. Graham Greene's narrator in *A Burnt-Out Case* says of one of the characters, a priest, that the urge to confide grew in him like the pressure of an orgasm. This description, while graphic, is not wholly an exaggerated way to describe the impulse that some people exhibit to confide. This impulse to confide can be related to what Edgar Allan Poe calls the "imp of the perverse," since this impulse for Poe is also in part a reaction to the confinements and superficialities of the everyday, and Poe reminds us that the impulse can move toward extremes of self-injury. The appeal of disclosure is intensified by the fact that the everyday is often a locus of restraint, evasion, and posturing. While confiding involves risk and possible price, we are willing, for the sake of honesty, to take the risk or pay the price, and the impulse can lead to satisfying results. However, the impulse does not necessarily carry with it a dependable awareness of limit, and, I would think, most people have wondered, on reflection, if in some social situation they have spoken more candidly or in greater detail about a personal matter than they should have. Generally, however, we recognize in ourselves both a willingness and a desire to confide and an ability to assess what particular occasions allow us to divulge. Conversely, we respond immediately to the impulse to confide when it is displayed by others, including writers of autobiographies.

We generally think of personal self-disclosure as more related to relational and especially sexual matters than to religious identity. Indeed, a recent collection of essays on intimacy in literary culture treats sexual matters almost exclusively.[3] Also, our society does not have, as it does regarding personal, especially sexual intimacies, established limit markers and mores regarding religious self-disclosures in public that make clear when the boundaries of what is expected or permitted have been breached. In societies more determined than our own by religious authority and uniformity, the markers separating what is allowed or expected and what is unexpected and even risky are more readily distinguishable. This lack of clear markers may well inhibit religious self-disclosures because the hearer or reader may not know what kinds of things can be divulged or what the limits of the audience's patience or interest are. Despite the lack of social markers and the uncertainties created by that lack, general limits concerning public religious self-disclosures may exist. One such sign of limit is certainty or finality regarding religion. While specialized audiences, such as religion scholars or fellow communicants, may find fully established or finalized religious self-disclosures or disclosures that are themselves religious acts interesting or edifying to read, readers in general will not very likely enter the kind of intimacy with the teller or author that I have in mind. Religious self-disclosures that are likely to give rise to intimacy are those that are more tentative, complicated by other, often conflicting factors, and as much in process as in a state of completion.

The potential and real value of religious self-disclosures of this kind arises from the fact that they provide a healing alternative to the current division in our society concerning religion in public discourse. An entrenched opposition has arisen in American public life between assertive or dogmatic religious and equally assertive or dogmatic non- and even antireligious positions. On the one side, religious people, especially Protestant Christians, reacting to the increasing religious diversity and the secularization of American life and grasping the political platform offered by the demographic rise in importance of sections of the country dominated by them, commonly assert not only the relevance of their religious interests to public life but also the close relation of the Republic to the largely Christian religious identities of its founders. On the other side, there has arisen a correspondingly insistent voice, occasionally referred to as the New Atheism, that is opposed not only to the inclusion of religion in public life but also to religion itself on the grounds that it is divisive, regressive, oppressive, and intellectually unwarranted. While this divide is not new to American cultural history, it has created polarized positions. This polarization could suggest that autobiographies that include religious self-disclosures are either awkward or unseemly public acts that ought to be confined to religious locations. The position assumed by this study is that there is space between these contraries where Americans can disclose religious identities and, at the same time, gain or retain the interest of a public audience.

Despite the very visible, if not determining, polarization produced by the contraries of religion and non- or antireligion in American life, the central current of American cultural history regarding the role of religion in public life belongs to neither side but moves, as does this study, between them. While public spaces generally are taken as requiring both religious and non- or antireligious people to leave their views of religion behind or within them when they enter, this assumption or habit conceals the fact that American culture also allows for public acts of affirming and questioning religion. A major site of such occurrences is American literary culture. Commonly, American writers, rather than advocating religious or non- and antireligious interests, place their work in various locations between these poles where moral, spiritual, and religious issues are worked through in highly personal ways but also in ways that make doubt and affirmation sharable with and of importance for wide American audiences. The nine writers gathered by and examined in this study stand in that tradition. Like many of their predecessors and contemporaries, they locate themselves between the certainties that beckon on either side, and they forge their own ways of including religion positively in their self-accounts while anticipating, with more or less accuracy, perhaps, readers of their accounts who will be interested while also being different from them religiously or not religious at all. It will be our task, among other things, both to attend to their disclosures and to clarify how in various ways their religious and their American identities are brought or are held together in and by their accounts. In this way, a legacy central to American cultural history can be extended and strengthened, one that includes personal religious struggles and formations in public discourses.

In the hope that I have clarified a space that lies between superficial or ordinary interactions and intimacies of a fully developed form as a space in which autobiography operates and in which public religious disclosures can occur, it may be helpful to name this space. I call it "textual intimacy." I realize that little is nailed down by this name, since "textual" can mean many things and is put these days to many uses. What I hope it does in this case is to designate a location that lies between public and private, unfocused and resolved, inclusive and particular, or superficial and complete. Writers' impulses to confide and readers' willingness to be drawn into the space I am calling "textual intimacy" are served by the mutually enriching combination of autobiographical writing and religious self-disclosure.

The texts I have chosen are by writers who have professional writing careers distinguishable to varying degrees from their religious identities and disclosures. As professional writers, their careers do not fully coincide with their religious identities, and disclosing their religious identities does not necessarily advance their careers. Including religious factors in their self-accounts, especially doing so in a deliberate way, requires not only intention but also craft. I shall point out, when we examine these texts, how they have managed this problem by, among other things, relating the religious factors in their identities to American identify formation more generally.

By not including self-accounts of Americans who wholly and unequivocally identify themselves, either by personal conviction or institutional loyalty, as religious, I do not discredit them. However,

I find them less interesting because for them being religious and being American have nothing to do with one another or are the same thing. In my view, being American and being religious, while not contrary to one another, are also not identical, and this study is intended, along with other things, to make at least some contribution to understanding the complex project of bringing or holding these two identity factors together. Nor is it the case that, by omitting writers who treat religious factors in American culture negatively, I view people who are non- and even antireligious as personally deficient or less than American. There are good and honest reasons to reject religion and even to view it as injurious. But, as I shall try to point out, being American also exposes a person almost unavoidably to religion. And while not everyone can be expected to deal constructively and even appreciatively with the implications of that exposure, I am more interested in people who do than in those who do not.

The focus of this study serves also to explain why I have not included texts that reflect the strong contributions to American society and culture during the last few decades made by the many people coming to our shores, especially from Asian and African countries, who have lent greater visibility to minority religious identities. These religious people, although recognized participants in the formation of our society at least since Roger Williams, continue to form a very small part of the American religious scene. Furthermore, while their presence has, in recent decades, become more visible, we are still in a period when adjustments to the American context by such recent immigrants are only beginning to be made. This means that discernible patterns have not been established, and, since we should not assume that they will follow existing ones, we do well to await their clarification. In addition, there is a paucity of self-accounts by these Americans that reveal the effort of working out the implications of being religious and at the same time being American. As Sau-ling Cynthia Wong says, speaking primarily of Chinese Americans but of Asian Americans more generally, such autobiographies are "rather abruptly cut off soon after the author's arrival in the United States," and this characteristic means that they "do not chronicle the author's experience of encountering and coming to terms with American culture."[4] This is not surprising because the terms of adjustment require time for their formation and because the discourses in and by which negotiations and constructions that relate religious and American identities to one another have been largely shaped by Protestant, Catholic, and Jewish writers.

Treating the texts of these nine writers raised a question for me about what form my response to them should take. When I write critical studies of fictional narratives, I examine texts with only incidental attention to the persons who wrote them. But when a text is a self-disclosure that invites the reader into personal, though also textual, intimacy, it seems rude to respond the way one would to a less intimate kind of writing. While all nine are professional writers and are accustomed to having their work criticized, it is unusual that they have, so to speak, exposed themselves. How should one respond to such acts? I had thought of writing critical responses in the form of letters. But that seemed rather awkward and, perhaps, presumptuous. Instead, I decided to respond as I most likely would in a conversation. In a conversation I would respond to a personal confidence by disclosing something about myself. Indeed, the force or significance of a gesture toward intimacy can be measured by the degree to which it elicits a response in kind. An autobiographical gesture is, among other things, a gambit in a game of sharing. Consequently, in the final part I narrate and describe my own religious identity. But I also take this act as an opportunity to explore the potentials of another way of viewing identity generally and religious identity more particularly. Personal religious identity, I shall try to demonstrate, has three facets, one constituted by matters that are taken for granted, another by matters consciously formulated, and a third by matters looked for or aspired to. I group these three facets by placing them under a single term, namely, *assumption.* I engage in religious self-disclosure, then, both as a response to the writers who have done so and in order to provide an internally viewed religious identity and its components that complement the more external view of the autobiographical texts examined in the second part.

But we get ahead of ourselves. Before looking at recent autobiographies and religious identities, we must talk about self-disclosure itself, a subject vexed by confusion and even conflict. The unsettled, even questionable status of autobiography should be traced to its roots and broader context, namely, everyday acts of telling others who we are, something we are frequently expected and generally willing to do. In order to understand the complexities of self-disclosures within a space of textual intimacy, we need to recognize that saying who we are is always already a complicated act. We need to examine this act before we discuss particular autobiographies and religious self-disclosures. Also, since autobiographies are discourses that at least to some degree are narratives, we must ask about the relation of narrative discourse to personal identity, self-accounts, and

religious self-disclosures. Finally, since we will be looking at autobiographies that disclose religious identities, we shall have to look at
the place that religious self-disclosure holds in the context of today's
social landscape. The first part of this study deals with these three
basic matters, then: the act of saying who I am, the role of narrative in self-accounts, and what is involved when a contemporary
American publicly includes religion as a positive factor in his or her
self-disclosure.

The three parts of this study, theoretical, critical, and personal,
while related to one another, represent discrete acts and should retain their relative independence. This independence testifies as well
to their equivalence; the three kinds of acts imply one another, and
each of them is equally worthy of priority. While it is hoped that
the relations that exist or that I have drawn between the three parts
will not be lost on the reader, I hope that the integrity of each act
will also have been protected. The sequence given the three parts,
rather than priority, suggests a move from the general to the specific,
a sharpening, even a narrowing, of focus, from, to put it bluntly, all,
to some, to one.

I

THEORETICAL

1

TELLING YOU WHO I AM

The Two Sides of Self-Accounts

AUTOBIOGRAPHY ARISES from and is supported by everyday acts of self-disclosure. I often tell other people who I am, and I usually do so readily. However, when I perform these acts I often feel uneasy about and even unsatisfied with what I am doing. On reflection, my ambivalence, rather than resolved, increases. I frequently fault what I say and think it should be amended or corrected.

My ambivalence finds a counterpart in the standing that self-accounts have in contemporary, especially academic, culture. On the one side, self-accounts have become frequent, if not expected, parts of scholarship. Autobiographical passages often appear in scholarly writing. Impersonal scholarship has begun to wane in the face of writing in which scholars disclose why they are interested in the topic and approach it as they do. Personal location is less concealed, and this gives an autobiographical quality to much of academic discourse.[1]

However, while inclusion of personal matters in scholarship has become widespread and while self-accounts, whether as part of other kinds of writing or as freestanding, are on the increase in academic culture, doubts about self-disclosures have also increased in frequency and in their radical nature. I find, then, that my own ambivalence, both when I tell others about who I am and when I think about what I say on such occasions, has its cultural counterpart in the dual phenomenon of an increase in personal disclosures and a simultaneous doubt about the value and reliability of self-accounts.

I think that my own ambivalence and this dual phenomenon in academic culture arise from and reveal something about the act itself. There are good reasons why I am uneasy with the accounts of myself that I give and good reasons why doubt has been cast on performances of this kind. However, I also think that there are good reasons why I continue to perform such acts and why scholars in the academic world step out on the stage and introduce themselves. I think that these contrary reasons arise from what I call the two sides of self-accounts.

I shall look first at the side of self-accounts that gives rise to doubts about their standing and value. Then I shall look at the other side, at what prompts and warrants them. Finally I shall give an opinion about what we should make of the conflict and ambivalence arising from the two sides of self-accounts and how we should respond to them.

I

The most obvious reason self-accounts deserve to be met with skepticism is that any disclosure of who I am will be incomplete and inadequate. While a response may satisfy the requirements of the occasion in which the question of who I am arises, I know that my answer is an approximation. My life is too large, complex, and enigmatic to be grasped in and by a single account, and I will likely feel dissatisfied with what I say because it is partial, may convey inaccurate understandings, or may give rise to mistaken opinions of me.

Second, saying who I am does not only mean giving facts about myself; it also includes what I make of or do with them. Indeed, when I say who I am, it is important to include my attitudes and evaluations, since they have as much to do with who I am as does factual information. Jonathan Glover puts the matter more strongly when he speaks of "shaping our characteristics, even minor ones, in the light of our attitudes and values."[2] True, on some occasions it is sufficient simply to give information about myself, but when I begin more fully to disclose who I am, I include less exact matters, such as my attitudes toward my circumstances. These are more difficult to convey and not so readily justified as are their external counterparts, and my attempts to clarify how I view myself and why are likely to raise questions.

Third, I am aware that an account of myself will not do justice to the fact that I am constantly changing, if only by age. Saying who I am, then, is more of a process than a conclusion, as Michael Keith and Steve Pile point out.[3] This is why David Jopling suggests that saying who I am is "something that can *only* be had by working at it."[4] So, any account that I give of myself is an interim report of an uncompleted and only partially understood process.

Fourth, the accounts that I give of myself also vary because I give them for differing occasions. What I say depends on who asks the question or what I want to accomplish by what I say. This quality in self-accounts leads Roger J. Porter to treat them in terms primarily of intention and to refer to them as performances, a matter to which we shall return in the last section of this chapter.[5] This means that accounts of myself form a collection of utterances prompted by varying occasions and intentions. Consequently, they are in some state of disagreement with one another.

Fifth, since I want what I say to be to some degree coherent, I may well conceal disunity and even conflicts within myself. Disunity is already built into the very act of saying who I am, since, as Arnold Modell, echoing William James, notes, we become, when talking about ourselves, "both subject and object." A self-account, then, presents as a unity what is actually a divided state. If this weren't problematic enough, Modell adds that we are often not univocal concerning ourselves: "the self is hated and loved, punished and protected, aroused and inhibited, inspired and negated."[6] When I give accounts of myself, I must deal both with the ambiguities within who I am and with the ambivalent attitudes that I have toward myself. Indeed, divisions, tensions, and unresolved issues in my life may threaten to overwhelm my ability to say who I am. To avoid my self-accounts becoming bogged down by the confusion caused by internal conflicts and uncertainties, I tend to modify my presentation of such matters. However, such modifications may also leave me with the feeling that for the sake of coherence I have presented myself as more unified than I actually am.

A sixth reason why giving an account of myself is questionable is that I give information about and descriptions of myself while aware of norms as to who I ought to be. Who I am and who I ought to be are not necessarily the same thing, and who I ought to be is both something I have in my own mind and something that my hearers also have in theirs. Self-disclosures are acts that inevitably imply the question, as David Parker puts it, of *"What is it good to be?"*[7] Judith Butler points out that self-accounts are governed by "the social dimension of normativity."[8] My self-account will be affected very likely by my desire to present myself at least to some extent as the person I would like to be or the person of whom I expect my hearers will think highly. In addition, Charles Taylor points to cultural conflicts in norms concerning what it is good for persons to be. Until the end of the eighteenth century, the norm generally was attached to ordinary matters like vocation and family. However, this norm of "the good life" was challenged in the nineteenth century by a contrary need to distinguish oneself from what blended persons into the ordinary. It became equally important to be, at least to some degree, "our own persons," exceptional, what Taylor calls "epiphanic."[9] A conflict between norms consequently exists. When I say who I am, I likely want to combine a degree of normality with a degree of quirkiness. So, norms trouble what I say about myself both because I am aware that I am not including things that I am ashamed of or embarrassed by and because the contrary demands of being both acceptable and provocative may well play havoc with accuracy.

A seventh reason to question what I say about myself is that much of what goes into making me who I am I have forgotten or am unaware of. Indeed, my account is limited to what I remember and what I have been told. There is a gap and even tension between factors in my life of which I am aware and factors that I do not or do not want to remember or be aware of. Pointing to the example of Oedipus, Adriana Cavarero makes much of identity being less known to us than we may assume. She warns against autobiography as concealing rather than revealing who one is and against "the unreliability of every autobiography."[10] My self-account may make me aware that there is much about myself that I do not know, misconstrue, and conceal.

Finally, saying who I am arises not only from my willingness to talk about myself but also from the social and political requirement that I locate myself. It is not only an act of self-disclosure; it is also a response to a summons that I may well resent. It is an act affected by social and political forces to which, by virtue of my particularity, I would like to think I stand in contrast. When asked who I am, I may, then, feel challenged to defend myself, needing to deflect or pacify the attention being given to me. Traces of challenge and testing in the question of who I am are difficult completely to ignore even in supportive contexts.

This list of reasons why telling you who I am is a difficult and dubious act may not be exhaustive, but I hope it serves to clarify why, both when I am performing it and when I think about what I do on such occasions, saying who I am is questionable and disturbing. I also hope that this list provides adequate reasons for the skepticism about self-accounts that has arisen in academic culture. Doubts about the integrity and reliability of self-accounts can be traced to their very nature.

II

However, while the complexities and ambiguities that attend telling you who I am may undermine ease concerning the act, I continue to perform it. This is because, at least in part, I also view it positively. With good reason I even welcome occasions to perform it. A positive attitude toward saying who I am is also warranted.

One of the supports for the act derives from the fact that it counters the anonymity created in society by density and mobility. People who live in smaller and more stable societies are not asked who they are as often as I am. I encounter occasions that invite or require my saying who I am almost daily. Frequency fosters facility, and I consequently have come to think of such acts as normal and beneficial. They counter positively the lack of familiarity created in our society by its size and complexity.

Second, I welcome the question of who I am because in two ways it defers to me. The invitation implies that who I am is important or at least of interest not only to me but to others. The invitation also defers to me because it acknowledges that I am the best authority regarding the question of who I am. Not all people are deferred to in this way, most obviously suspected criminals or the mentally ill. But for most of us most of the time, a normality of circumstance is assured by our being asked to say who we are.

Third, I do not find questions about who I am difficult or threatening because when I say who I am, I stand in a privileged position that nobody shares equally. Opportunity to say who I am provides an occasion to exercise my authority on this matter, to respond implicitly to what others may say or think of me, and to prevent or counter misconceptions or uncertainties. There are few if any topics over which I hold more authority, and being asked to say who I am allows me to assert my privileged position relative to my identity.

Fourth, I welcome such occasions because they provide an opportunity to speak about something that interests me and about which I have given some thought. The question of who I am is familiar not only because I am asked it often but also because I ask it of myself. It is part of my self-awareness. So, the question of who I am provides an opportunity to share with others the conversations on this subject that I engage in with myself. Such occasions allow me to test and refine answers that may only have been inchoate, giving these answers, let us say, a textual status. Identifying myself, then, grants the satisfaction of furthering a process toward a goal—perhaps, though, an always receding one—of clarity or even completion.

Fifth, answering the question of who I am is a positive event because this topic is deemed by our culture to be highly important. Our culture places a premium on thinking of ourselves as having particular identities. The fact that I think that I have the best answers to the question of who I am is closely tied to the fact that I tend to think that in important ways I am unique.[11] This sense I have of myself aligns me with a characteristic of modern culture. From the seventeenth century to the present, this question, one that also goes back to the ancient philosophical and religious origins of our culture, has enjoyed a prominence that it did not previously have. An authoritative narrative of this cultural history has been provided by Charles Taylor, and his account has recently been augmented and corrected by Jerrold Seigel in his *The Idea of the Self* and by Raymond Martin and John Barresi in their *The Rise and Fall of Soul and Self*.[12] These studies trace continuity between thought concerning personhood in earlier periods and modern and contemporary thought, but, especially since the work of John Locke on personal identity, this topic assumes a major role in modern culture. When I give a self-account, then, I engage in a discourse that is a prominent characteristic of modern culture.

Sixth, saying who I am is a positive act because it protects or delivers me from the powerful effects of modern social constructions epitomized by technology and the city. The impersonal and homogenizing consequences of the massive constructions of modern life intensify the interest that I take in myself as a particular person. When I engage in this act, I join my contemporaries in resisting the obliteration of personal particularity and significance by pressures and controls that encompassing and powerful social, political, and economic structures and processes exert on us.

Perhaps more reasons could be given to explain why I also view positively the act of saying who I am. Moreover, as theorists since Locke have pointed out, important social, including forensic, consequences arise when we undermine confidence in self-accounts. If only for such reasons, it is vital, despite the complexities and uncertainties that mark my life, to think of and present myself as being, in some way and to some degree, a particular, continuing, and unified person. While a positive view of self-accounts does not put all that is questionable about them to rest, I hope that the reasons given here support the view that they should not be simply dismissed but should be given and received seriously and appreciatively.

III

It is fair to say that prior to the modern period persons were thought of primarily in terms of unity and continuity. According to Martin and Barresi, a shift, beginning in the seventeenth century and continuing through the nineteenth, to the negative side became prominent.[13] Today, consequently, we face a growing consensus, especially in academic culture, that self-accounts, when they are unified and suggest continuity in personhood over time, stand in a contrary relation to what persons really are like. It is widely assumed today that there is little if any continuity or unity in personhood that guarantees the coherence and truth-value of self-accounts.

The principal cause of this shift toward skeptical views of self-accounts is the loss of confidence in something substantial that grounds personal unity and continuity, the soul or the self. Martin and Barresi make a very good case that this confidence was shaken by Locke's shift of personal identity from a substance-based theory to a theory of mental acts, especially the act of recognizing deeds and ideas of the past as being my own. This shift to consciousness had the effect of undermining the status of immaterial substance as the basis for personal identity and discrediting the self as a stabilizing point in self-understandings and accounts. From Nietzsche to more recent thinkers like Michel Foucault and Jacques Derrida, the self and the unity and continuity in the face of complexity and change the self once provided are lost.

This loss of confidence in a stabilizing referent or sponsor of self-accounts sets them adrift in uncertainty. James Holstein and Jaber Gubrium, for example, argue that self-accounts continue because a complex society requires us to give them, and we are, consequently, conscripted by social requirements into self-disclosures that meet social demands and opportunities.[14] It follows, then, that being required or expected to say who I am should not lead me to conclude that I actually am a single and consistent person. I am simply engaged in an ongoing practice of producing varying self-constructions "at every turn of social interaction."[15] My self-accounts are acts of self-packaging, something like the social requirement that I dress myself in clothing that suits the occasion.

The current dominance of the negative or questionable side of self-accounts leads Stuart Hall, taking a cue from Jacques Derrida, to argue that the contingent, fragile, and arbitrary nature of self-accounts means that they should always be placed under "erasure." Personal identity is for him, then, not a matter of actuality or truth but of power. My self-account is a means by which I add force to my social position and utterances.[16] Kenneth Gergen seems largely to agree when he refers to self-accounts as instances of "voice warranting," of helping to give authority to what I say.[17]

A less radical position is provided by Martin and Barresi in a move that depends on David Hume. Self-accounts also have value because they often are engaging.[18] Although the unity or continuity of a self-account is a person's construction, it reveals something about the person and not only about the social occasion. David's Jopling's conclusion is even less negative as he tries to restore at least some truth-value to self-accounts. While they may be fabricated, self-accounts at least convey who I think I am.[19] My hearers can at least gain accurate knowledge of the person I take myself to be and choose to present myself as being.

Less skeptical opinions anticipate my attempt to take a more positive view of self-accounts. However, any positive view cannot arise at the cost of discounting the skeptical side. The questionable side of self-accounts and skeptical views of their reliability and value make it unavoidable that when I give a self-account I can or even will deceive others and even myself and that inaccuracies and duplicities always will pertain.

However, as Arnold Modell puts it, while we shape various accounts of ourselves to fit differing occasions, "there is a core of the self that remains the same."[20] He does not mean that there is an absolute sameness behind or below varying self-accounts, although his use of the word "core" easily reintroduces a language of substance that will cause trouble down the road. But I would also say that we retain a sense of who we are despite our knowing that we give various accounts of ourselves as external and internal changes occur. Lawrence Cahoone agrees, arguing that in every social occasion in which we identify ourselves there is "an *asocial* remainder."[21] Harold Noonan contends, furthermore, that a sense of personal identity over time, of my being to a significant extent the same person despite change and the variety of occasions, "is basic to our understanding of the world we live in and our emotional and moral relations in and to it."[22] My social and personal relations depend on the fact that I today am, to a significant degree, the same person I was years ago. Like forensic matters, engagements of everyday life such as contracts, financial obligations, and personal promises assume and require continuity of personhood over time.

The need for retaining or restoring unity and continuity in the face of radical skepticism concerning personal identity has produced a lively and complicated discussion in contemporary philosophy, especially in Anglo-American analytic circles where questions of truth and accuracy continue to have force. Harold Noonan puts the problem as presently debated succinctly: "The problem of personal identity over time is the problem of giving an account of the logically necessary and sufficient conditions for a person identified at one time being the same person as a person identified at another [time]."[23] This form of the problem, even though it peels away many of the complexities and ambiguities of personal identity, has not, despite its simplicity, produced satisfactory answers.

The unresolved status of the philosophical debate concerning personal identity gives rise to more proximate answers. Robert Nozick proposed, for example, that the best answer to the question of continuity in identity is a best candidate, or what he called the "closest continuer," answer. That is, people will and should take me as the same person I was in the past as long as there is no other candidate who fits that role better.[24] And Derek Parfit, a major voice in these debates, is well known for concluding that the question of identity is not all that important, that identity is not what matters in survival.[25]

The possibility that there can be truth and honesty in self-accounts rests on the fact that I usually know when I am being truthful and honest and when, on the contrary, I am employing an occasion in order to deceive someone or to advance some interest of my own at the occasion's expense. And the fact that I know the difference between trying to be truthful and honest and trying to manipulate a situation rests, in turn, on the fact that at least to some degree I know who I am and on the fact that this knowledge is, at least to some degree, reliable. Surely I deceive not only others but also myself much of the time, but it is also the case that I know what it is to be truthful and honest in self-assessments and in the accounts of myself that I give to others. And I assume that they do, too.

While considerations will be brought forward later on to substantiate my position further, I shall end for now by saying simply that the two sides of self-accounts should be retained and held in a mutually illuminating and corrective relation. A compromise between or a composite of the two would be mistaken. It also is not easy or, perhaps, even possible to affirm both sides at the same time. Although saying who I am is both a significant or rewarding and an unreliable or misleading act, I will likely be more aware of the positive side of a self-account at one time and of the negative side at another. Perhaps, given this situation, it is good to adopt the suggestion of Hubert Hermans and Harry Kempen when they tell us that self-accounts are marked by two forces or directions, centripetal and centrifugal.[26] This means that the sense I have of who I am is either in place or changing, either available or unavailable, either meaningful or questionable, and either unified or conflicted. I fluctuate between these two sides, able or needing at one time to affirm certainty and reliability regarding who I am and at another time able and needing to recognize confusion, duplicity, and self-deception, indeed, to be baffled by the question.

For reasons that will become clearer later on, we can say for now that extended self-accounts or autobiographies usually arise from a predominant confidence that there is a large enough degree of coherence and continuity in answer to the question of who I am to warrant my account. The intelligibility of the account itself requires focus on or foregrounding of matters that are or can be related to one another and understood. Even when puzzling and disconcerting ingredients are included, they likely will be contained by a framework or structure that gives to them, however dissonant they may be, at least partial resolution.

The Three Arenas of Self-Accounts

The complexity of saying who I am also arises from the fact that the accounts I give of myself are oriented to if not determined by three arenas. The three, while not unrelated, are distinct from and at times in tension with one another. These arenas are both external to what I say about myself, providing occasions for the act, and internal to what I say, affecting the content of my account.

One of these arenas is personal. I talk about myself in personal situations, and personal matters form a significant part of what I say about myself. The personal arena is quite different from a second arena, namely, the social. And characteristics of these two arenas are separable from a third, namely an arena created by the fact that I was born at a particular time and place, will die, have certain abilities, am of a certain age and gender, and the like, an arena that could be called ontological.[27]

I have understandings of myself as a result of relations in and to arenas of these three kinds, and my self-accounts are occasioned by one or another of these arenas. What I say will be affected by both the arena in which I am speaking and the attention I give in my account to one or another of the three. Consequently, there inevitably will be incompleteness in any account of myself that I give and differences between accounts. Surely there can be cross-referencing and overlapping between the arenas, but any account that I give can be located primarily within one of the three.

There are positive and negative, enabling and limiting qualities in each of the three arenas, and the qualities of one arena can affect those of another. We should look more closely at each of them, beginning with the personal.

I

My self-understanding arises in part from interrelations with other persons, relations that depend on and reveal differences and similarities between myself and them. This process of clarification is enhanced when the interactions I have with others include personal matters such as opinions, evaluations, and feelings. When I converse with someone in this way, I do so with the anticipation that I will encounter aspects of this person that are similar to and aspects that are different from those I take to go into who I myself am. I cannot begin a conversation with certainty regarding the relative percentages, so to speak, of difference and similarity or of the areas of life in which more of the one than of the other will appear, although I assume at least some answers to those questions before the conversation begins. Also, similarities and differences are not socially or culturally determined. When I engage in personal conversation with someone of a culture different from my own, I can anticipate that there will emerge in that conversation not only recognitions of how such a person and I differ, due to our differing cultures, but also how we are similar. Conversely, when I engage in a personal conversation with someone culturally very close to me, I can expect to encounter not only similarities but also differences, some of them, perhaps, sharp. All people are both different from and similar to me, and my personal conversations with others are, among other things, explorations and confirmations of that fact. The sense I have of who I am is prompted and enriched by interactions with other persons that reveal in what ways and to what extent I am like and unlike them.[28]

David Jopling emphasizes the role of personal conversations in identity formation by calling self-knowledge "dialogical." Dialogue for him is not merely one means by which persons develop knowledge about themselves; no, "the dialogical encounter of self with other is *constitutive* of self-knowledge," he says.[29] Jopling contrasts dialogical self-knowledge to detachment, what he calls the ironic stance of those for whom self-knowledge is "an activity *of* the self, *by* the self, and *for* the self."[30] He privileges dialogue, especially when the question of who I am is explicitly addressed: "In raising the question 'Who am I?' the self issues a call to the other, and addresses the other as a person who stands in the role of a moral witness."[31] In this paradigm case it is optimal, he adds, that both interlocutors are willing to give more attention to the ways in which they differ from one another than to the ways in which they are alike.

Without discounting the value of dialogue focused by the question of who I am, it should be said that I come to awareness of myself also indirectly in a conversation, such as realizing that my goals or values differ from those of my conversation partner. In addition, I think that Jopling's negative evaluation of solitary self-inquiries as ironic detachment and self-isolation is mistaken because the arena of personal relations also includes relations that I have with myself. Arnold Modell is helpful on this point when he argues that interactions with others in identity formation are far from the whole story; infants, for example, also require "private space," times when they are free to follow their own interests; "disengagement has a place of equal importance with engagement."[32] Modell suggests, in contrast to Jopling, that persons also need time for relations with themselves.

Paul Ricoeur, in his book *Oneself as Another*, makes this point about self-relations basic to his study of what he calls "*ipse*-identity." In contrast to "*idem*-identity," which stresses sameness, "*ipse*-identity" is dialectical. This involves the "other" in personal identity, and that "other" for Ricoeur includes not only other persons but also aspects of oneself. As his title suggests, this sense of oneself as being other is a dimension both of one's relations with other persons and one's relations with oneself. He concludes, in reference to Aristotle on friendship, that a person cannot have self-esteem without esteeming others because the self is also another. This means that we see others as selves because we see ourselves as other: "I cannot myself have self-esteem unless I esteem others *as* myself."[33] Arthur Aron and Tracy McLaughlin-Volpe, although they come at this matter from a different direction, agree with Ricoeur when they say that "there is considerable evidence that people at least experience close others as if they, in some sense, were included in the self."[34] In the personal arena, then, the relations that I have with myself need also to be included. I encourage, reprimand, and praise myself, and I carry on within myself conversations with other people.

The personal arena not only provides occasions in which I say who I am but also provides some of the content of what I say. My self-accounts can focus on personal matters. This does not mean that occasion and content need to conform. While I will tend to talk

of personal matters in personal situations, I also can cross the borders between arenas.

II

The second arena of self-accounts is social, political, and/or economic. This arena can be distinguished from the first because,
while it also is humanly constructed, it is not personal. It is marked
primarily by the structures and processes that order common life.
While it is true that some people are more personally invested in
the construction and maintenance of this order than others, these
structures and processes are to a large degree impersonal. Accounts
of myself that I give in social arenas will differ from those I give in
personal ones. Indeed, the two arenas can even be antagonistic to
one another, although they need not be. Finally, while self-accounts
in the arena of personal relations are marked by the play of similarities and differences in relation to other persons, self-accounts
prompted and focused by the social arena are marked by a play of
inclusion and exclusion in and by social, political, and economic
structures and dynamics.

We live in a time when people seem to have either too strong a
sense of their identity in relation to the social arena or too weak a
sense. The first extreme may come from the fact, as Charles Taylor
points out, that livelihood became in the modern period a major
norm by which judgments could be made about whether we are the
kinds of persons we ought to be. The evaluation of a person's identity in terms of social and economic criteria continues to be strong
in the present day. Who I am and whether or not I am the person I
ought to be are questions often answered by reference to occupation,
social standing, and economic strength.

While it is common to identify oneself with social and economic
placement, the contrary, treating the social arena as irrelevant or antagonistic to personal identity or integrity, is also frequently found.
This split between identification and alienation relative to the social
arena may well be unfortunate. As identity in the personal arena
should be marked by a play of similarities and differences with other
persons, so in the social arena personal identity should be marked by
both inclusion and exclusion.

Again, the social arena and my relations to and within it can provide both the occasion of my self-account and the content or focus
of what I say about myself. Although arenas are not watertight, there
are important differences between my relations to and within the

personal arena and my relations to and in the structures and processes of my social, political, and economic locations.

The social arena stands out among the three because it is the arena
that provides the terms by which most people know who I am: my
employment, residence, family situation, and the like. People in the
public arena also have opinions of me, but I do not know fully what
they are. These characteristics of the social arena can easily give an
unwarranted authority to it. However, because I do not fully know
what people think of me or whether what they think is accurate or
fair, I may easily be led to distrust and even resist the impact of the
social arena on my identity.

When questions of personal identity are raised in contexts dominated by social, political, and economic factors, they easily can swamp
or occlude the other two arenas. There is a remarkable tendency
in current cultural theory to take personal identity as an effect of
social, political, and economic conditions on me or as an effect of my
resistance to them. It is important to keep in mind that any of the
three arenas can be prominent and even dominant for saying who I
am, and it is not necessary that one of them will or ought to be more
important than the others.

III

The third, or ontological, arena of self-accounts is constituted by
conditions that also are impersonal but, unlike those of the social
arena, are not humanly constructed. This arena comes to focus for
me primarily by the fact of my mortality.[35] However, death, though
major, is not the only component of the nonhumanly constructed
arena of my self-accounts. I am also aware that my birth was dependent on processes over which I had no control. While the actions of
my parents were indispensable to my origins, my parents were stuck
with the outcome, as, in complex ways, am I.

The arbitrariness of my birth and the certainty of my death may
account for the eagerness with which I try to understand myself
or view my life as significant. The accounts of myself that I give,
then, personalize and particularize me in the face of these universal,
ultimately uncontrollable, biological determinants. In addition, the
quite arbitrary events of my conception and certain death prompt
me to see that other moments of my life, many of them crucial to
what I have turned out to be, were also unexpected and fortuitous.
In fact, what often makes my life interesting is that much of it
turned out differently from what was planned. Coincidences, chance

occurrences, and unexpected encounters—these are the things that give life its color and intrigue. What similarities and differences are for the arena of personal relations and exclusion and inclusion are for the social arena, so bad luck and good fortune are in the arena of ontological relations.

It is a curious thing about the ontological arena that it is constituted by factors that are both the most particularizing and the most shared. This arena sets me off from all other people and relates me to them. My birth and death, along with such other factors as my parents, my age, or experiences of illness and physical impairment, are uniquely my own, but they also establish, perhaps more than anything else, what I have in common with all other people.

Since, as I said, the three arenas provide not only the content of what I talk about in my self-accounts but also the situations that occasion them, the question arises as to whether there are interlocutors in this third arena. We saw how important, especially for some theorists, interlocutors are for the personal arena. Since the social arena is constituted primarily by impersonal structures and dynamics, interlocutors are not so obvious, although I do disclose things about myself at work, complain about government officials or the ineptitude of managers, and am glad to be on good terms with authorities. While the ontological arena provides no obvious interlocutors, we, in their absence, often create them. We thank our lucky stars, treat a disease as an antagonist, or say "the devil made me do it." This absence of interlocutors in the ontological arena may well reduce its significance in and for self-accounts. Religious people, however, since they tend to see especially ontological matters as related to divine agency and care, may more likely give this arena larger place in their self-understandings and accounts than do people for whom religion does not provide a language useful to the ontological arenas of their self-understandings and accounts. While religious language can appear in personal and social accounts as well, there is good reason why religious language in self-accounts deals so often with the unaccountable, with matters like good and bad fortune or the unexpected and gratuitous in life.

While more could be said about these three arenas, my principal purpose is simply to point out that giving an account of myself is a complex and vexed act because of the differences and possible tensions between these three arenas. Variation from one account to another is a consequence not necessarily of confusion or of attempts to manipulate others but is also or instead a consequence of richness. I am constantly in the business of negotiating understandings and accounts of myself focused by and appropriate to these three distinct arenas.

For reasons that will become clearer later on, it can be said for now that autobiographies, by virtue of being published texts, have an obvious location in the second, or social, economic, and political arena. It can well be the case that an autobiography interests readers when its content is also focused on and by the social arena; we may well like to learn, for example, how a celebrity went about fashioning a successful career. But often the interest of such texts lies in their bringing matters from the personal and ontological arenas into the social, and this is what autobiographies that disclose religious identities tend to do.

The Four Constituents of Self-Accounts

My self-accounts are complex not only because they have two sides and are shaped by three arenas but also because they combine multiple constituents. Four such constituents come quickly to mind: body, consciousness, language, and soul or spirit. We should look at each of them, beginning with the most obvious one, my body.

I

My body is constitutive because, for one thing, it provides the primary way by which other people identify me. While people know me for other reasons and by other means, these need to be warranted, at least potentially, by my body. Otherwise, my existence could be fictional. When I die, my standing as a person will, to put it mildly, be altered. And although doubts may arise as to whether I am who I claim to be, such questions can largely be settled in terms of my body—by pictures, fingerprints, and, now, DNA.

My body also determines many aspects of my identity: gender, age, race, abilities and handicaps, etc. Who I am and such factors, regardless of how I view or want to conceal or alter them, are viewed by others as inseparable from me. Whether as a burden or a blessing, my body is part of who I am. One of the reasons why my body is not more fully a part of my self-accounts is that it is so much *there,* so taken for granted. Indeed, Locke includes the body in personal identity only when and to the extent that I am conscious of it. But, it seems to me, I am not conscious of it also because it is so basic. If I am conscious of my body and include my body in a self-account, it likely is due to something negative, some illness or embarrassing physical characteristic, for example. Indeed, there is a large and growing autobiographical literature that narrates illness and its effects on the writer.[36] Usually the body is implied in a self-account by means of abilities, age, gender, physical pains, and pleasures.

In addition, as Jacques Lacan points out, my body gives me a sense that I am single and unified. Lacan ties the fascination of children for their mirror image to their being confirmed as particular persons.[37] It could be suggested, then, that I look at myself in mirrors not only to be sure that my hair is combed but also to assure myself that I am, despite many distractions and multiple interests, one person. As Stuart Hall puts it, the body emerges in identity theory as counter to the fractures and dispersions of identity. He refers to the body, therefore, as an almost "transcendental signifier."[38]

However, my body, while it provides a base that can be prominent in my self-understanding and account, cannot be adequate. For one thing, some parts of my body are more important for my identity than others—my face, for example. Second, it is true, as David Jopling says, that my body is also socially constructed.[39] Women and members of racial minorities, for example, know more fully and frequently than white males that their bodies are not simply taken as they themselves present them but are also social constructions imposed on them. Third, it is not so clear that the body is a single thing rather than an assemblage of some kind. Singularity and unity are also images, although important and useful ones. Fourth, the body, however reliable a constituent it may be, changes. I can relate more readily to the memories that I have of my earlier self than I can to the body that I see in pictures taken of me decades ago. Fifth, the body as a constituent raises the question of how much of my body can be replaced by artificial or donated organs and still be my own. Whole-face transplants put a sharp point on this question. Finally, the body is limiting. It is subject to locality, fatigue, and illness, and this seems negative in relation to the kind of freedom or expansiveness that can be associated with the other constituents of self-accounts, such as mind or spirit.

For these and other reasons, the body in personal identity has been as much a problem as a positive base. In our culture, the body holds a prominent place partly because Romantic attention to sensations, feelings, and energies gave the body a strong position in understandings of identity. The interest of high modernism in so-called primitive or pagan cultures also reinvested Western art, culture, and religion with an emphasis on physicality, including sexuality. The view that young rather than old people epitomize humanity may well be traced to identifying personhood with physical vitality. Despite limits and cultural determinants to its role as a constituent, the body remains an important factor in self-accounts, and it can be primary.

II

A second constituent of accounts of myself is, as already suggested, mind or consciousness. While this basis comes into prominence with Descartes, it assumes a primacy in modern identity theory through the work of John Locke. But while mind and consciousness are preoccupations of modernity, they had from ancient times a high standing in views of what it means to be a person. This very likely is because having a sense of who I am is also a consequence of thinking about the question and trying to answer it. Giving an account of myself depends on thought. Acts of mind and consciousness—interpreting and evaluating myself, forming intentions, recalling memories, and exercising self-control—are important aspects of my sense of who I am. For Plato and Aristotle, reason is crucial to the ordering of life and the actualization of personal potential, and for Jews and Christians the principal acts of identity formation are tied to remembering and promising, communal and particular acts of consciousness and mind. Mind's position among the constituents of personal identity is long-standing, therefore, and not only the consequence of modern interests.

Mind has a privileged position despite the fact that it is difficult to pin down. In order to sidestep the intricacies of a philosophy of mind, let us posit "mind" in terms of contributions to self-understanding such as awareness, ideas, intentions, memories, and beliefs. As Raymond Martin and John Barresi point out, Locke's contribution to identity theory was to shift attention to consciousness from attention to the soul. He thereby also, they argue, shifted the question of identity from survival of the person after death to the endurance or continuity of a person over time. They attribute Locke's shift from soul to mind or consciousness to a move made in 1690 by William Sherlock, who described the divine Trinity not in terms of substance but in terms of consciousness. Locke followed this move and based human identity not on an immaterial substance, such as soul or spirit, but on consciousness, primarily on the ability to recognize that things that occurred in the past occurred to me.[40]

In the modern period, then, personhood is closely identified with the ability not only to think and to remember but also to be conscious of oneself. As Jonathan Glover puts it, "a person is someone who can think I-thoughts."[41] Galen Strawson contends that "the central or fundamental way in which we . . . experience ourselves . . . is as a mental unity" and "our conscious mentality is a huge, astonishing, absorbing, and utterly all-pervasive fact about us."[42] And Harold Noonan asserts, "Identity of consciousness determines identity of persons as identity of life determines identity of organism."[43] While attention to mind, consciousness, and self-reflection is not unique to modernity, modernity is marked by a heavy emphasis on mind and consciousness in identity theory. While it need not be dominant, as it frequently is in modern discussions of persons, mind and consciousness certainly form, along with body, one of the constituents with which we construct accounts of ourselves.

Mind, despite its prominent, often dominant, position in identity theories, however, cannot be established as exclusive or adequate. For example, "mind" is difficult to distinguish from the brain and its functions and is traceable, then, to the body. In addition, what must we say of people whose mental capacity has become limited? Do they at some point cease to be persons and, if so, when? Third, does it place too great an emphasis on self-consciousness? Could it be said that self-consciousness is a form of arrest, of withdrawing from the ordinary interactions and engagements of life to reflect not only on them but also, even more so, on oneself? Is it not true that I am more myself when I am concentrating less on myself and more on my everyday relations and activities? And what would happen to our thinking about ourselves if we lacked language? And, since language is a social/cultural construction, isn't the emphasis on mind and thinking really a concealment of the determining role of social and cultural factors, especially of language, in self-understandings and accounts?

III

A third constituent of self-accounts, then, is language. The most obvious form this takes is my name. I and my name are closely tied. Indeed, as Oscar Wilde humorously establishes in *The Importance of Being Earnest*, name can trump person.

In the twentieth century a new kind of attention has been given to language for self-understandings and accounts. The shift was occasioned by the reorientation in the human sciences commonly referred to as the "linguistic turn."[44] That is, language came to be viewed largely as a social system that is already in place into which individuals are inducted and thereby, it can be assumed, become persons. Also, the structure of language became viewed primarily as determined by the relations of terms to one another, relations primarily of similarity and difference. This placed the meaning-effect of language on the relations and interplay between terms in the system rather than on the relation of words to something outside the system, entities and events, on the one side, and ideas or feelings on the other.

This understanding of language as a synchronic social system and of signs within the system as related to one another rather than to something outside them forms the background for current theories of personal identity that give primacy to language. An important additional factor for the linguistic turn is Jacques Derrida's denial of presence. For Derrida the world in which we live is not only linguistic but also, to keep presence out, textual.[45]

As a result of the linguistic turn and the textualizing of the world, identity theory can be divorced from the question of that to which the word "I" refers. Rather than by something prior to or apart from it, the "I" is constituted by the language system and texts of which it is a part. Something strange and frustrating happens, then, when a person, understandably interested in the referent of that word, looks behind "I" for something to which it refers. Nothing is there because the meaning of "I" derives from the force and role conferred on it by its place in the linguistic system and its uses in discourse. As Emile Benveniste stresses, the meaning of "I" is derived from its relations to other terms in the system, particularly to "you."[46]

Contemporary identity theory focuses on language in a second way, namely, by "interpellation." This term indicates that a person is called by language to take or play what a person thinks of as a particular place or role in society. Language, while it brings persons into relations with one another, also individuates them. Louis Althusser calls this effect of language, its being a medium by which a person is called out as particular, "ideology." It is the function of ideology in language to constitute individuals as subjects and to do that in such a way that a person's place, calling, and, therefore, identity seem to the person to be not imposed but natural or chosen.[47]

Most theories that make language primary in and for identity do not rest with language as a neutral system. Behind most of these theories is the assumption, as can be seen with Althusser and Foucault, that there are regimes of power that use language to control persons. While language is not thought to arise from or to be controlled by referents, it is thought to be controlled by social and political interests.

These interests are often construed, relative to personal identity, as malign. Identity, therefore, becomes something imposed, and it is imposed for purposes that serve the interests of power regimes more directly and fully than those of persons.

Certainly justice needs to be done, in giving an account of myself, to the fact that I live in a society and a culture that provide me with the language that both shapes who I am and gives me the means for understanding myself and for conveying to others a sense of who I am. Self-accounts are determined forms of discourse, draw on social and cultural conventions, and conform to linguistic norms. Language not only is a constituent of and for self-accounts; it also serves to determine their shape and content.

However, I think that it is important to contend that when I say who I am, I construct my own account, one that stands out from, while it also is related to, the linguistic, social, and cultural repertoire. The importance of language as a constituent of self-accounts does not necessarily dissolve them into socially controlled constructions. The reason why it is difficult to make this point is that the linguistic turn, when adopted by social and political theorists, often is grounded in philosophical materialism, and materialism usually is deterministic, thereby eliminating human agency. Although it is difficult to make the point in the face of the generally materialist and determinist qualities of much current identity theory, I think that it is crucial to maintain that I am not only conditioned and determined as to who I am by language but also that language provides me tools for constructing or articulating who I am. Persons are not simply puppets controlled by language and by the regimes of power that stand behind or dominate the use of language. Speakers are also agents.[48] While avoiding the metaphysical problems inherent in any theory of agency and choice, it is important to maintain that, while aware of the fact that I am who I am because of social/political factors over which I have little control, who I am is not simply an imposition but is also a process of my differentiating and particularizing. Not all of this process is conscious or willed, but some of it is.

We can draw from the linguistic turn the conclusion, then, that language is a constituent for constituting and accounting for who I am and not an exclusive or necessarily dominant one. As neither body nor mind can be posited as exclusive or necessarily primary for self-understandings and accounts, so also language cannot be so deployed. However, like the other constituents, it can be dominant in any self-understanding or account.

IV

Although not relied on very much these days, soul and spirit have a distinguished history of grounding personal identity and shaping self-accounts. Indeed, the question of personhood was answered from Plato on down well into the modern period primarily by reference to the "soul." The term was used mainly in two ways: to refer to a unifying constant in persons and to substantiate the belief that persons in some respects endure not only over time but also, especially with Plato, after death. Reference to the soul served to answer two questions about personal identity that continue to set the terms for the discussion: Can it be said that I, at this moment, am, despite my many parts, a unified being? And can it be said, despite the many changes that mark my life, that I am the same person that I was years ago and will be the same person in the future that I now am?

When the role of soul or spirit for personal identity lost cultural prominence, questions of unity in present time and continuity over time became problematic and controversial, very likely because the other constituents lacked the resources for answering these questions that had been provided by soul or spirit. This adequacy in the resources of soul or spirit as a basis for self-understanding may account in part for the present resurgence of interest in religion and spirituality, since such interests can focus on personal integrity and continuity.

It is worth noting some recent gestures toward restoring the soul to identity theory apart from positing an immaterial substance. One is by the well-known literary and cultural theorist Terry Eagleton. Eagleton argues that the body, which has become so important in contemporary identity theory, provides an inadequate resource for personal identity because the body is vulnerable to torpor, illness, and death. Indeed, the body is more a negative check or limit, a critique or constraint, on personal identity than a positive basis for it. He argues that, as reading a text gives life and meaning to the marks on the page, so, as Aristotle and Aquinas taught, the soul is the inner form of the body. Rather than something a person has, soul "is the way that human beings are always somehow in excess of themselves, always in the process of becoming. The soul was supposed to be about the unity of the self; in fact, it is a way of suggesting how we are never identical to ourselves."[49] Using a formulation more Aristotelian than Platonic and depending more on Aquinas than on the Platonist tradition in Christian thought, Eagleton wants to restore soul to identity theory not at the expense of body but as an equal partner with it. He concludes, then, that "the Platonists and idealists who deny the body has anything to do with the self are just as mistaken as the reductionists and materialists for whom this inert lump of flesh is all we are."[50]

There is some similarity between Eagleton's contribution and the nonsubstantive concept of a "core" self that Albert W. Musschenga attempts to bring into focus. He defines it "as what we think we essentially are and what we want to be or become or think we need to become."[51] Musschenga goes on to present this self as a goal that relates identity and personal integrity closely to one another. The person searches for and aspires to identity and integrity as to something ahead or above: "For those who strive for personal integrity, it is part of their *ideal identity*."[52] Augusto Blasi seems to support this point when he says that "we understand identity . . . minimally as the experience of an inner self on which one's special individuality is established. . . . According to its description, the central experience consists of the discovery of an inner psychological quasi-substance that is taken to be one's true or real self."[53] This self, a "quasi-substance," beckons the person to seek it as a desired truth or wholeness. This sense of my truer or more real self also reveals, by contrast, actions and attitudes that are phony or self-betraying.

An engaging addition to this line of thought is provided by Adriana Cavarero. She ties the question of identity to a desire for personal particularity, even uniqueness. This is a desire not for something that is obvious or fixed but for something yet to be determined. It is a desire related as well to a desire for unity in one's life, unity both in the present and over time. This unity is not monolithic, not an *idem*, but is multivocal, an *ipse*. One finds this unity in the relation of what is thought of by the person and what is said of the person by others. This unity, which coincides with the awareness of particularity and uniqueness, is not a projection or hypothesis but a reception, a gift. The principal occasion for this reception is story, both told by the person and told of the person by others. Personal identity, then, although it is also much more, primarily is, for her, recognition of one's life as unique, a uniqueness found in or giving rise to unity.[54]

I take these attempts to restore the soul as intriguing indications that in identity theory we must also come to terms with something elusive and outstanding that the other bases cannot adequately take into account. Although I do not reinstate soul as an immaterial substance, there is an aspect of ourselves not taken into account if important matters that can be grasped by these uses of soul are ignored. Desire, intuition, imagination, aspiration, hope—the list could go on—are important aspects of who we are, and they seem to point to something about ourselves that remains outstanding and yet to be received, a particularity and a unity as much conferred as achieved. One of the things that make me who I am is that, while I know who I am, to some degree I am not who I can, desire to, or should be, and my self-account, among other things, is oriented to and by a search for reception or fulfillment. Rather than as an internal immaterial substance or as something already and always there, soul on this understanding becomes something yet to be recognized or received, and it directs identity theory not so much inwardly or toward the past as outwardly and toward what is yet to come.

V

We have, then, four distinguishable but also related constituents that form a repertoire upon which self-understandings and self-accounts draw. Perhaps, however, a fifth should be added, namely, will. David Jopling implies, in his treatment of Sartre, that this should be the case, since for Sartre and others, persons are authors of their identities and they author them by will and action.[55] Some agreement with this position has been implied by the fact that I tie self-identity and the decision to give a self-account closely together. It is the emergence of the person as an agent in self-accounts that, in my opinion, most immediately supports the candidacy of will as a constituent.

The inclusion of will as a constituent, however, raises the question, first, of whether a distinction equal in importance to those that distinguish the other constituents from one another can be discerned between will and consciousness. And, if agency is related to impulse and drive, we have the second question of whether a distinction equal in importance to the others can be made between agency and body.

A recent attempt to relate identity to agency is interesting enough to be noted.[56] David Kim, bringing together Charles Taylor and his tendency toward idealism and Judith Butler and her tendency toward materialism, posits agency as prior to identity and as combining both intention, with its idealist suggestions, and desire, with its materialist suggestions. Kim seems to say, to paraphrase Derek Parfit, that identity is not what matters in agency. But intention and desire are sufficiently unlike one another to question positing them as unified by "agency" as a primordial category. It is not clear that agency has a position prior to and even separable from identity. And, as I have said, intention seems very much to be a matter of mind, and desire a matter of body.

I think that we complicate the question of self-accounts unnecessarily if we attempt to establish will or agency as a constituent separable from and equal to the other four. I think we can include will and agency as aspects of the others, as I have defined them. As Harry Frankfurt says, in his identification of the limits within which will operates, these limits are set most fundamentally by "what a person cares about, what he considers important to him,"[57] by what above I included under "soul." Without goals a person lacks basis or direction upon or toward which to act, becoming "amorphous, with no fixed identity or shape."[58] At least it can be said that there is good reason not to give volition and agency equal place alongside the other four constituents

My principal point, however, is not to establish once and for all what the constituents for personal identity and accounts are but to emphasize that who I am and what I say when I give an account of myself are complex matters also because they bring and keep together at least four horses in harness. Each of the four has the potential not only to go its own way but to dominate the others. Not only am I ambivalent about saying who I am, at times knowing and at times not knowing what I am doing, and not only are my self-accounts vexed by the fact that who I am is affected by three separable arenas, but also I constitute my account by drawing in and on at least four constituents. These three sets of complexities create problems; they may even intimidate the attempt. But variety and instability also suggest richness. I am intrigued by the act of saying who I am because it is for many reasons not so much a daunting as a challenging, engaging, and rewarding thing to do. A self-account is an achievement, a working with and through the complexities and ambiguities to an at least partial resolution. It is helpful that I am not the only one who attempts it.

The Unifying Intention of a Self-Account

Having some of the tensions, complexities, and richness of self-accounts before us, it is good to conclude with what it is, in the face of all these divisions and uncertainties, that gives at least some unity to self-accounts. By doing so we return to a point made earlier in reference to the work of Roger Porter.

Enough has been said about identity to foreclose the option that the unity of a self-account is sponsored by or testifies to the unity of the life. While at times my life may seem unified and directed, at other times it does not. And, as we have seen, although I am the single sponsor or owner of accounts of myself that I give, those accounts are varied and partial.

What gives unity to a self-disclosure primarily is its intention. It is a performance. When we address in the next chapter the relation of self-accounts to narrative discourse, we shall see that narrative also provides, albeit in a formal way, coherence and unity. But given the fact that we are talking now more generally about self-accounts and the fact that when we address narrative self-accounts we will emphasize the narrative language of teller, it is fitting to say, in a quite general way, that intention is largely the source of unity or direction in a self-disclosure.

The intention of a self-account may be determined from within or from without. I may direct what I say toward a personal goal, I may try to meet the requirements or expectations of the occasion, or both. While the intention may not adequately be realized, the unity of my disclosure arises largely from its motivating intentions.

This does not mean that all of my self-disclosures differ from one another because my goals change and occasions vary. I may well have overriding intentions in the ways that I present myself that create continuities between performances and offset the variety that changes in moods or conditions may prompt.

Nor is it the case that intentions play fast and loose with accuracy. They may. But it can well be, and I think it usually is, the case that what I want to accomplish in a performance and who I actually am or think I am have a good bit to do with one another. True, a job applicant or a young man trying to impress a woman at a party may alter actuality radically to fit the intention, but there is no necessary incongruity between what I want to accomplish in a self-account and who I actually am or think myself to be.

Intention grants unity to autobiographies as well. While some unity to a life narrated is provided both by the life itself and by the narrative form, autobiographies also carry forward intentions and are aimed at goals. Sometimes intentions are stated, while at other times they are only implied, as we shall see in the texts examined later.

Who we are and how we present ourselves are neither the same nor contrary things. Certainly I can deceive others and myself in the accounts of myself that I give, but that also says something about who I am. The presumption in self-accounts favors truthfulness, but we assume in them as well that not everything can or will be told. Selection and shaping are as indispensible as reliability, and the unity of the act arises, among other things, from the intentions that motivate, direct, and conclude it.

2

NARRATIVE AND
SELF-ACCOUNTS

The Role of Narrative in Self-Accounts

A FURTHER question about self-accounts that is worth raising concerns the importance of narrative discourse for self-accounts. This question takes two forms. The first and more particular form is whether or not giving a self-account requires narrative. Does the act of telling you who I am and narrative discourse have a natural or necessary interdependence? The second form of the question, which arises from the first, is the cultural standing of narrated self-accounts. Are they, for example, specific to our own culture, or can they be thought of as constituting a more general human phenomenon?

I

There is wide divergence in answers to the first form of the question. Some theorists think that story and self-accounts are in large part identical, while others think of story as, at best, optional for saying who I am. I think that the truth lies somewhere between these contrary opinions.

One theorist who argues for a close relation between narrative and self-accounts is Paul Eakin. He tells us that "narrative is the sine qua non of identity formation, and there is important clinical evidence to support this view; when the capacity to construct narrative is impaired—or never acquired in the first place—then identity itself is damaged."[1] I think this overstates narrative's importance for self-accounts. I have two reasons for this opinion.

For one thing, this view assumes too sharp a distinction between narrative and non-narrative discourses. It is safe to say, for example, that a narrative self-account implies, at least partially, some description, evaluation, or intention that the narrative supports. So, I may narrate my life in support of my opinion that I am a wretched person. It is not clear, then, which is the more important, the evaluation or the narrative. Both narrative and non-narrative discourse tell you who I am, and this suggests that it is good not to privilege one over the other but to recognize a reciprocity between them. However, non-narrative accounts tend to group me with other people; I have company in the category of wretched persons. Narrative, in contrast, can particularize what form of wretchedness my version of it takes. In addition, narrative discourse can complement non-narrative descriptions by presenting me as a more complicated and unified person than a simple descriptive would suggest that I am. I suspect, then, that self-accounts rely on both narrative and non-narrative discursive forms.

Second, if we were to make narrative discourse essential to self-accounts, as Eakin does, it would mean that people who, like me, are not noteworthy storytellers have less interesting, significant, or developed lives and identities. I envy good storytellers, people who can make quite ordinary material engaging and revealing. I'm on the other side. While I have had a rich life and many interesting experiences, my narration of them usually fails to do them justice. I need to bolster my narratives with comments on what in them is important or interesting. If we take Eakin's word for it, we would have to assume that inept storytellers like me necessarily have less of an identity or are less realized persons.

While we should avoid assigning excessive importance to narrative discourse in self-accounts, we should also give narrative discourse its due. Narrative is a primary and generative form of discourse and not secondary to or derived from non-narrative discourse.[2] And its particular value for telling you who I am, as Cavarero emphasizes, is to surface the particularity and unity of my life. Indeed, these are not small matters, since establishing or clarifying at least a degree of particularity and unity in my life lies among the principal problems for and ingredients of personal identity. I think, then, that narrative, while neither exclusive nor, relative to descriptions, primary, is a valuable and even necessary form for telling you who I am.

I therefore question Galen Strawson's claim, which contradicts Eakin's, that I can do without narrative when I tell you who I am.[3] He allows that narrative may be useful for some people, but for himself it plays no necessary or significant role. He views his life as "a (stringless) string of pearls," a series of unrelated mental states.[4] Strawson can dismiss narrative in part because he has an inadequate understanding of it. He assumes, as do many narrative theorists, that temporality, the coherent ordering of events and actions, is definitive of narrative, and this, as I shall point out later, is simply not the case. There is also a question as to of what each of Strawson's "pearls" consists. While unrelated to one another, except sequentially, they themselves seem to have a coherence that allows them to stand out as identifiable wholes. This coherence, I would think, is not entirely free from narrative. Strawson, incidentally, does not stand alone in this position. David Jopling also seems to conclude that narrative, while one of the forms in which responses to self-inquiry appear, is optional.[5]

What should we conclude, then, about the importance of narrative for our self-accounts? Shall we agree with theorists who say that "getting a life means getting a narrative, and vice versa?"[6] Do we need to agree with Paul Eakin, who asserts that "self-narration is the defining act of the human subject, an act that is not only descriptive of the self but *fundamental to the emergence and reality of the subject*"? (emphasis in original).[7] Or should we side with Strawson and Jopling and discount the role of narrative? I would rather say that narrative plays an indispensable but not necessarily a dominant role in self-accounts. As Arnold Modell says, it is not the only means of achieving and communicating the particularity and coherence of one's self.[8] However, it is, with good reason, important for self-accounts.

If narrative provides my life particularity and unity, the question arises whether these are produced by the narrative or are already inherent in my life. As John Sturrock points out, there are some who "assume that the contours of their past are already sufficiently definite simply to be transcribed," while others assume "that there is as yet no sort of story to tell, no contours to reproduce, self-knowledge being the end of autobiography and not its source."[9] Sturrock, by making narrative the source of unity and particularity, concludes that the value of narrative self-accounts lies not so much in the life that is narrated as in the narrating skills revealed, so that we read such accounts in order "to know more about a certain kind of writing."[10] Jerome Bruner agrees with him: "A life is created or constructed by the act of autobiography."[11] On this view, the particularity and unity that narrative provides are not already a part of my life but reside in the story into which I turn my life by telling it.

There are factors that commend this skeptical view of the relation of my life to the narrative that I tell of it. Many differing stories can be told of the same set of events and circumstances, for example. And it can well be the case that my life yields so readily to story because I know stories about other people and shape my life as much by these models as by what is actually there. Narratives have culturally derived characteristics, and these shape my story as much as, if not more than, the actual contours and dynamics of my life.

Given this skepticism, the best thing to do is to follow Shari Benstock, who tells us to address the question of the relation of story to life, "at the crossroads of 'writing' and 'selfhood.'"[12] This implies potential compatibility between my life and a narrative of it. If so, my narrated self-account is not simply imposed on my life but also supported by it.[13] There is mutuality between the life I am living and the narratives of it that I craft, material already there and what I make of it. Folkenflik puts the matter suggestively, I think, when he compares a narrative self-account to Lacan's mirror stage, an image of myself as particular and unified.[14] While it is only an image, a narrated self-account is also not simply a fabrication.

The relation of narrative to non-narrative discourses in accounts of myself that I give should not be resolved, I think, by saying that by means of non-narrative discourses I tell you *what* I am and by means of narrative discourses I tell you *who*. Adriana Cavarero's study of storytelling and selfhood employs this distinction. What is most appealing about her position is her identification of unity with uniqueness. What is particular about me is the unity that I sense in myself despite the diversity in my life. Narrative discourse elicits the uniqueness that provides unity.[15] However, as there is reciprocity between non-narrative and narrative discourses in self-accounts, so also *who* I am can be suggested by descriptive terms. In addition, the particularity that narrative provides is not clearly unique, since narratives draw on cultural conventions and other shared components.[16]

We are left, then, with a rather complex view of the role of narrative for the accounts of myself that I give. First, narrative does not necessarily precede or trump non-narrative forms of self-accounts. Second, narrative, although not exclusively, attends to and provides particularity and unity to my self-account. Finally, the particularity and unity of my life are both incipiently there and provided by the narrative. This complex view means that my narrative self-account should be taken by me and, if of interest to them, by others both as reliable and revealing and as constructed and partial.

II

We turn now to the standing of narrative self-accounts in modern Western culture. Texts of this kind command an increasing amount of attention, and I may well have distorted the actual situation when I moved from the question of saying who I am to the question of narrative. The contrary may be true: We so often reflect on who we are because we so frequently encounter stories of their lives told by other people.

This raises the question of whether autobiography is a distinctively Western or modern phenomenon or is shared by human beings across cultures and history. Some assert, for example, that "autobiography is non-existent in primitive societies nor is it found in societies of non-bourgeois ideology."[17] Georges Gusdorf argues that a focus on personal particularity is absent from other cultures because "lives are so thoroughly entangled that each of them has its center everywhere and its circumference nowhere."[18] But others point to a "widespread use of self-representation in both preliterate and literate non-Western cultures" and contend that this fact "contradicts the allegation of an earlier generation of literary critics that 'autobiography' is a uniquely Western form and a specific achievement of Western culture."[19]

This debate is complicated by our ambivalent attitudes toward premodern societies. Involved is a mixture of superiority, as toward people who have not developed a sense of personal freedom and value as we have, and of envy, as toward people who enjoy a more communal sense of identity than do moderns. Although I shall not attempt closure on this question, I think it is fair to assume that people in other and earlier cultures are or were aware of themselves as particular persons, although this awareness may not be so important or troubling to them as it seems to be for us. People in smaller and less mobile societies than ours know one another and need not, so often as we do, identify themselves or narrate their lives. Self-accounts will perform fewer, different, and, perhaps, more focused functions in such societies.

The particularity of persons, while a modern preoccupation, is not a modern invention and was important for the ancient societies that shaped modern Western culture. In addition to classical philosophy and literature, biblical texts are replete with references of subjects to themselves, particularly the Psalms, and, while isolation may have been taken in ancient cultures less as definitive of human life and more as a misfortune, there is a strong sense of the wonders and discomforts of being a particular person. St. Paul also refers often to himself, seeing his life both as illustrative of faithfulness to be emulated and as a site of frustration and a cause for excoriation. St. Augustine, whose *Confessions* is one of the principal models of narrative self-accounts in Western cultural history, is driven to inward-turning not only to discount himself but also to find where and how a personal relationship with God can be found.[20]

Self-awareness, both as something positive and as a cause for uncertainty and distress, is well-founded in Western culture by its biblical and classical sources, and these go a long way toward explaining why self-awareness, while not unique to our culture, has an important standing in it. However, this awareness was certainly intensified and altered in the modern period. Robert Folkenflik argues that it was not until the end of the eighteenth century that narrative self-accounts began to gain the separate attention and cultural importance that they have today, and he designates the mid-1820s as the time when "an institutional recognition of the term [autobiography] and a budding canon" arose.[21] Folkenflik attributes this rise to Romantic emphases on origins, human internality, and the erosion in authority of more established genres.[22] In addition, political revolutions and reforms gave space and validation to a growing cultural awareness of personal integrity and freedom. And, I would add, autobiography becomes important in the nineteenth and twentieth centuries because it counters the other defining aspect of late modernity, namely, urbanization. Autobiography holds an important cultural position, then, as a "specific achievement of Western culture at a moment of individuation in the wake of the Enlightenment," as a marker of newly created political and economic spaces, and as a contrary to the other side of late modernity, namely, the homogenizing force of anonymous and massive urban spaces.[23]

While the role of self-accounts in American culture cannot be separated from general descriptions of modernity, particular aspects of American life are relevant to the present high standing in our culture of writing of this kind. One of these was the desire of people who formed this society not only to fashion new collectives but also to treat the new land as a place to actualize personal possibilities. Benjamin Franklin, for example, presents a strong exemplar of one who thought of his own life as a project, and he set a pattern for how one could go about making the most of his or her life, as though forming raw material into something distinctive, significant, and successful.[24] However, we should also keep in mind Lawrence Buell's point that, while autobiography marks American writing from the start, it takes the form that we are now familiar with only in the nineteenth century.[25]

Rather than abating, the rise of self-accounts continues, and they have become major texts in contemporary American culture. They hold a potential interest for literary studies that stands as a counterpart to the interest New Critics a few decades ago took in lyric poetry. For other scholars, they provide useful material for identity theory, cultural studies, and, for my purposes, the study of religious self-disclosures in contemporary American society.

Autobiography as a Kind of Narrative

There are three questions that require answers if we are to gain a firmer hold on the importance of narrative discourse for telling you who I am. The first is how to distinguish narrative from non-narrative discourses; the second is how to distinguish autobiographical from others kinds of narrative discourses; and the third is what relation narrative discourse holds to an ongoing life. I will take up each of these questions separately.

I

There is no clear and widely accepted answer to the question of how to distinguish narrative from non-narrative discourses. This may be because we think of narrative as so easily recognizable that no serious attention needs to be given to the question of what gives it recognizability. We should see, however, that narrative discourse is not recognizable for obvious reasons and that narrative is a complex and variable and not a simple and constant discursive form.

The argument could be made that no clear line separates narrative from non-narrative discourses. For example, declarative sentences can be concentrated or incipient narratives. We can use E. M. Forster's famous example: "'The king died and then the queen died of grief' is a story," he says.[26] The sentence is a simple statement, but, since it contains characters and events, it could also suggest, if it is not one already, a narrative. Another way to argue against a clear distinction between narrative and non-narrative discourses is to point out that the sentences that make up narratives are not generally distinguishable from the sentences that constitute non-narrative discourses. Since many sentences in non-narrative discourse are narrative-like and since sentences in narrative discourse generally have a non-narrative nature, one can conclude that a clear distinction between narrative and non-narrative discourses cannot be made.

It may be possible to argue that narrative discourse, if not distinct at the level of sentences, becomes distinct at the point of delivery. There are conventional signals, especially at the outset, that may announce to readers or hearers that narrative discourse is occurring. There may be other signs, such as shifts in verbal pace and in body language. Finally, there are socially determined times when narratives are expected and times when they are out of place. Such conventions do cluster around the act of narrating and without doubt help make the distinction between non-narrative and narrative discourses clearer. However, an argument for the recognizability of narrative discourse based upon them is unconvincing, since one can conceive of a recognizable narrative discourse lacking all such signals.

I think it is wise, when approaching this question, not to look for some point of separation between non-narrative and narrative discourses but to look at discourses that are recognizable as narratives, since few would say that they have never heard a story and do not know what encountering such a thing might be like. The question directs attention to how stories are constituted, to their defining characteristics. My answer to the question, then, is that stories stand out because they bring together four interests or, to put it differently, are constituted by four related but distinguishable languages.

So, for example, we expect to encounter characters in a narrative, and we are engaged by narratives that bring to life memorable characters. A second kind of narrative language is that of action and event, and we expect actions and events to be related to one another. The third language of narrative is that of place or context. We have some idea where and when what is narrated is taking place. The fourth language of narrative is that of the teller. We are also aware, as we read or hear a narrative, that we are in the hands of someone who is narrating. All four of these languages of narrative are always present in a narrative discourse, although they need not be, and usually are not, of equal importance in and for a particular narrative discourse.

This last point, namely, that the importance of the four languages of narrative varies from one narrative discourse to another, is largely missed by theorists and critics of narrative. This is because they come to narrative with prior commitments to one or another of the four languages and read narratives with primary attention to that language. Any of the four can dominate. Although it may occur that all four languages in a given narrative are of equal importance, one of the four is likely to be dominant in a particular narrative and to deform the other languages to itself.

II

Having proposed an answer to the question of how narratives are constituted, we now can ask how autobiographical narrative is distinguishable from narrative in general. My answer to this question is that in autobiography the language of the teller is primary. While characters will appear, actions and events and their relations to one another recounted, and locations described, for autobiography the language of the teller is prominent, if not dominant.

There are three factors in the language of the teller that help to establish its position and draw the attention of the reader to it. The first is material choice, what the teller chooses or feels obliged to tell about. Although it can be the most important factor, it need not be. We naturally think that autobiographies and memoirs are interesting when they are written by people who have participated in highly unusual or significant events. While the autobiographies of celebrities or of prominent political figures have an obvious appeal and ready market, it is not the case that only autobiographies of this kind hold interest. Material is not necessarily the most important factor for the force and significance of the language of the teller in autobiography.

A second, and perhaps more important, factor in the language of the teller is the stance or attitude assumed by the teller in relation to the material narrated, especially the teller's interpretive or evaluative relations to what is narrated. Is the material commendable or regrettable, for example? Implied or stated attitudes or judgments go a long way toward accounting for the attention that the language of the teller draws to itself. Important for this aspect of the teller, when it comes to autobiography, is the unifying intention of the teller. The reader or hearer of a self-account will be aware of implied or explicit goals toward which the material is directed, of interpretations and evaluations that turn the material toward, and even select and shape material to accord with them.

The third and, perhaps, most important factor in the language of the teller is the most difficult to identify or locate. It has to do with style or voice. We all know people who have achieved important positions, have had unusual experiences, or hold provocative views but are unable to narrate them in engaging ways. We also know people who can narrate something as ordinary as a trip to the supermarket and whose views of things are fairly conventional who can engage, delight, and even edify us. Given the fact that the teller's attitude toward the material is revealed, at least in part, by the intention or goal of the narrative, the quality of the narrator's voice or style becomes very important. If we become aware while hearing or reading a self-account that we are expected to end with a certain impression of the teller or to draw a certain conclusion from what is presented to us, the teller will need to have our confidence and regard. The desired or expected response requires an engaging and confirming style, one that aligns the reader or hearer with the teller's designs.

Although the factor of style or voice is, I think, the most important, all three factors serve to make the language of the teller engaging and rewarding. A teller who relates interesting and unusual things, who expresses or implies convincing interpretations, evaluations, and intentions, and who has an engaging way of narrating will give us autobiography that most rewards its reading. The reader's response will resemble that of Holden Caulfield, who remarks somewhere in *The Catcher in the Rye* that what he likes is a book that when you read it you wish the author were some terrific friend of yours that you could call up anytime.

John Sturrock comments most directly on the potential of autobiographical writing to convey the personal qualities of the teller. He says that we expect to encounter autobiography as "inhabited by a living person," by a person who "was peculiarly present to himself while he was writing" and is "now present to us as we read."[27] Autobiographical writing is, he says, "an invitation to intimacy."[28] Sturrock concludes that "autobiography is unquestionably an appeal to us as its readers to progress in intimacy with the autobiographer."[29]

The conclusion we reach, then, is that the decisive function of the language of the teller for an autobiographical narrative is to occasion a degree of intimacy with the willing reader. In other words, autobiography is a form of narrative that emphasizes an aspect of narrative that always is present. As Paul Eakin says, "narrative is the mode in which relational identity is transacted," and this relational potential is fundamental to autobiography "in its origins and in its practice."[30] Larry Sisson adds that reading an autobiography, because of its relational potential, can well influence the reader's "own life and spiritual condition."[31]

This is not to say that people do not compose autobiographies for other reasons: to set the record straight, to condemn or to praise someone or something, to give an insider view of public events, even simply to gain attention or make money. Nor is this to say that we do not read autobiographies for other reasons—to get the inside scoop, to satisfy a voyeuristic interest in personal behaviors, or to find how someone else has handled a personal problem similar to our own. It is simply to say that the primary factor accounting for the power and significance of autobiography is a relationship between the teller and reader, one that can be called, to use Sturrock's term, intimacy.

Sturrock argues that a major ingredient of autobiographical narratives that serves to create intimacy is "truth-telling."[32] This emphasis on honesty and candor is complicated. As we already have seen and as Linda Anderson points out, recent theory has caused us to be "skeptical about the claims that the personal can ever automatically guarantee authenticity."[33] The teller cannot ground autobiographical writing in herself as in something that will warrant veracity, since the teller is as much the product or effect of the discourse as its source. Mary Evans supports this view by commenting that the person is "in any case a fiction, a belief created by the very form of autobiography itself."[34] Smith and Watson concede that recent autobiographical theory has reconceived "self-referential narratives not as sites of the truth of life but as creative self-engagements."[35] As a result of this emphasis on performance, truthfulness becomes a questionable basis for teller-reader intimacy.

While giving such skepticism its due, I think that it assumes an unwarranted disconnection between historical and fictional narratives. While Aristotle, in his treatise on tragedy, distinguishes the two, it is not that historical narrative is subject to the criterion of truth and fictional narrative is not. The question of truthfulness applies to both, although the standard for determining truthfulness shifts from a sense of what actually happened to a sense that this is the kind of thing that does happen to this kind of person. Autobiography, by virtue of the dominance of the teller, is subject to the question of truthfulness in both of its forms, of giving us in the material of the narrative what is reliable and of giving us material and evaluations that are apt and justified.

Truth telling, then, is relevant to the reader's sense of whether this teller is someone with whom the reader can and wants to have what in the introduction I call "textual intimacy." As Jean Starobinski stresses, truthfulness is crucial to autobiography's style.[36] However, we also need to be assured that the material given is reliable in order to judge that the expressed evaluations of that material are justifiable and honest. Judith Butler combines these two kinds of reliability in her attention to what she calls "the truth of the person."[37]

We are in a position now to make good use of a narrative theory that holds a potential that has not yet fully found its place. I refer to Wayne Booth's theory of the ethics of fiction. His principal point is that a narrative teller not only creates a self-image, what Booth calls the created or implied author, but also that the teller creates and projects an image of a desired or anticipated reader. A successful reading is one in which the implied or created author and the implied or created reader develop a sense of agreement and rapport.[38] The metaphor that Booth uses for a positive relation between the implied or created author and the implied or created reader is "friendship" (170). He appeals to Aristotle, for whom friendship has moral content (174). Booth employs the term "intimacy" in his description of this relationship (191). The key question for a reading is this: "Is the pattern of life that this would-be friend offers one that friends might well pursue together?" (222). Texts most to be admired are those whose value resides "in the irresistible invitation they extend to live during these moments a richer and fuller life than I could manage on my own" (223).

Booth is aware that his theory of narrative implies a relational view of self-formation, a view that counters the prevailing modernist belief that persons form identities in isolation, a belief implicit in much modernist literature (251). For Booth, however, the self is formed primarily in relation to others, and narrative is crucial to this process because in narrative we are invited to live in another's world. Living, however briefly, within a world other than one's own is an act in which "our most exhilarating personal prospects lie" (257). The most valuable result of such experiences is to create in us a "desire to improve our desires—to desire better desires" (271).

Like all quality or Longinian theories, Booth's theory of narrative is a bit elusive. I trust that my locating the potential for intimacy in the narrative language of teller and primarily in one of the three factors of that language at least partially offsets Booth's less formal account. Also, Booth tends to devalue what could be called confrontational texts, texts marked not by invitation but by assault. Norman Mailer is a good example, and Booth has no use for him. But selves and values are also formed in and through negative encounters, and room should be given to the value of a narrative whose teller contends with the reader. Third, I think that Booth's theory is not suited to all narratives, as he implies it is, but to narratives in which the language of the teller is dominant. Since this is a defining character-istic of narrative self-accounts, Booth's theory finds its fullest role in relation to them. Narrative self-accounts provide occasions for honesty and truthfulness, for friendship and trust, for the arousal of desire—in a word, for textual intimacy.

Having settled on the term "intimacy" to designate the principal characteristic and effect of autobiographical narrative, we should note that this does not warrant unguarded bluntness or full expo-sure. Coyness, selection, and posing may well be part of the rheto-ric of narrative intimacy. Also, intimacy does not mean immediacy. Indeed, narrative has its other languages, and the reader is engaged not only directly by the teller but also by means of the temporal processes, characters, and locations to which the teller directs at-tention. Finally, intimacy is not without design. As with any self-portrait, the teller in autobiography poses. Intimacy occasioned by autobiography is intimacy of a particular and intentional kind, and it is affected by the teller's purposes and goals. I have tried to imply these qualifications by my use in the introduction of the designation "textual intimacy."

III

The third question concerns the relation of narrative discourse to my life. Is there compatibility between life and narrative? While, as we have seen, some theorists are skeptical concerning such a relationship, I think that there is correspondence between a person's life and narrative discourse. This correspondence implies, I think, the strongest argument for the value of narrative discourse for self-accounts.

The compatibility or correspondence between narrative and a life rests on the fact that the four languages of narrative match what is required for or implied by my living in a world. The four languages of narrative, as I said, are character, plot, location, and tone or the presence of the teller in the tale. It can be argued, I think, that these four languages of narrative parallel the necessary constituents of a workable or viable personal world.

My world is constituted, first, by other people, and that relates it to narrative at the point of the language of character. My world is in part constituted by my encounters with, relations to, and dis-tance from other people and by my understandings and evaluations of them. Other people, positively and negatively, are constitutive of my world.

My world is also constructed by the processes in which I am involved, natural, social, and personal. The natural processes include, among other things, aging, drives, and diurnal, seasonal, and annual rounds. Social processes are constituted by my interactions with other people, whether close or casual. Personal processes are those by which I have some sense of personal development, of overcoming problems and actualizing my particular potentials. The nature and complexity of human temporality can be conveyed by musical metaphors, natural processes being rhythmic, social processes polyphonic, and personal processes melodic.[39] As with my relations to other people, my involvements in these processes are affected by and produce in me evaluations that cause me to affirm, resist, or attempt to alter them and their effects on me.

Location is a third constituent of my world. I am situated by a variety of factors. This means that far more is involved than, so to speak, my geographical location, although that is important. It also involves my location in terms of many social, economic, political, and other conditions. Again, my location presents me with a range of opportunities or possibilities as well as limitations and oppositions and can be a source of irritation and resentment as well as an occasion of delight and gratitude. As with other people and processes, I will also have some sense of what in my location is unalterable and what can be changed.

Finally, my world is constituted, as already indicated, not only by other people, processes, and locations but also by my recognition and evaluation of these matters. It is possible to imagine two people who live in similar situations but in quite different worlds because their attitudes toward and evaluations of their situations differ from one another. My evaluations, understandings, and attitudes, in other words, are not only responses to or consequences of my world but are also constitutive of it.

Because there is a formal correspondence between narrative discourse and life, narrating my life is revealing to me. The languages of narrative force me to flesh out or become aware of my world or my life in these four constitutive directions or dimensions. However, I do not want to go so far with this point as to make narrative discourse the exclusive or necessarily primary discourse for self-accounts. Narrative discourse and self-accounts are constitutively but not exclusively related.

The second reason why narrative discourse and my life are compatibile to one another is that both narrative and my life are grounded in and shaped by beliefs. Let us first see why this is true of narrative.

Characters in narratives are distillations or embodiments of beliefs about other people. They imply answers to such questions as whether people are basically good or evil, what makes a person good or evil, whether people can change, or whether people should be viewed primarily as individuals, as members of groups, or as types. We differ in our answers to questions such as these, and such differences are seldom resolved by argument or evidence. If I think that people are inherently good, it will not alter my belief very much if you point out that I have suffered many things at the hands of others. The converse is also true. Our evaluations of other people are based less on argument or evidence than on belief.

A similar situation exists regarding the temporal processes which affect our lives or in which we are involved, natural, social, and personal. Are these processes good and deserving of support, or do they spell doom and deserve resistance and defiance? Is one helpless in the face of them, or should one attempt to make alterations? Again, we differ in our responses to such questions, and our answers are not necessarily supported by arguments or evidence. Some people view these processes negatively and others positively. Some people are convinced that changes need to and can be made in the course of events while others feel resigned to and determined by these processes. Such evaluations rest primarily on beliefs.

We see this as well regarding location. We will differ in our assessments of limits and potentials, the negative and positive conditions of our locations or situations. We also will differ as to whether negative conditions can be altered. And these differences, because they are based primarily on beliefs, may well resist argument and evidence.

Finally, the language of the teller also is affected by belief. This time the beliefs concern what is important and should be brought to attention, whether my interpretations of what I encounter are adequate or accurate, and how I should evaluate the entities and events of my world. The principal tasks of the teller—to select, depict, and evaluate material—are tasks grounded in beliefs as to what is worthy of attention and what makes something admirable or deplorable.

Narratives, then, are really webs of beliefs. When we designate the four languages of narrative, we really are saying that there are four distinguishable kinds of beliefs that are to be found in and are constitutive of narratives.

Something like that, mutatis mutandis, can be said of my life or personal world. I would not be able to get up in the morning and go about my activities if I did not have beliefs in place regarding the people I will encounter, the processes in which I am involved, the locations or situations in which I find myself, and my sense of what in my world requires or deserves my attention and how it should be evaluated. My answers to these questions affect what I take to be arguments and evidence that support or challenge my beliefs. My beliefs, although usually slowly, may change, but I need to have beliefs in place when my day begins.

While we are interested in narratives for other reasons, one reason why they engage us is that in narrative we encounter beliefs that confirm and/or challenge our own in all four of the constitutive ingredients or dimensions of our worlds. And, it would seem, we are most engaged by narratives that display some combination of confirmation and challenge to our own beliefs.

Narrative discourse and a life, then, are compatible because both are built on four sets of beliefs. This is why I can be personally engaged by narratives that have otherwise little connection with my life, stories placed in the distant past, in other cultures, or in other parts of the universe. Although remote in other respects, a story relates to my life in both ways, the four constitutive corners, so to speak, of my own and the narrative world and the fact that both my life or world and a narrative are grounded on or constructed by beliefs.

Autobiographical narrative, since it is shaped primarily by the dominance of the teller, is particularly interesting regarding the question of belief because attention is drawn to the teller's act of selecting, interpreting, and evaluating material. The teller comes out onto the stage and identifies him- or herself. I as reader am invited into the very act of the teller's choosing and justifying what deserves attention, what merits praise and blame, and is true. My own values and opinions are confirmed and/or challenged by my encounter with the teller in an autobiographical narrative, and I develop a close relation with the teller not necessarily because I agree but because I am persuaded that what is important for the teller and how it is evaluated merit the standing that they are given and that the way in which the teller negotiates these questions and exposes beliefs in response to them encourages me in my own struggles and illuminates directly or indirectly my own world.

The Hazards of Autobiography

Having assessed the importance of narrative for self-accounts, having disclosed the nature of narrative discourse and of autobiography, and having exposed the relation of narrative discourse to a lived world, it may be helpful to point out that autobiography, while it is vexed by the complexities and uncertainties of personhood, is also in itself a hazardous form of discourse. Several reasons why this is so come to mind.

First, autobiography solicits attention and implies that its author thinks of him- or herself as worthy of notice. Celebrities and people who have been involved in public events are partially delivered from this problem. Otherwise, the teller faces the task of establishing why his or her life merits attention. As John Sturrock says, an auto- biography "is the story of singularization, or of how the autobiogra- pher came to acquire the conviction of uniqueness that has impelled him to write."[40] Diminishing this problem somewhat, Sturrock sug- gests that offering an unsolicited self-account implies that each life is in some way unusual and deserving of attention. If nothing else, the reader is invited by autobiography to support the teller in the struggle to be liberated from "the great mass of the anonymous."[41] The problem may also be diminished if the teller calls attention to something of importance outside him- or herself that imparts sig- nificance. Larry Sisson claims this advantage for spiritual autobiog- raphy: "Whereas autobiography generally has tried to be a 'mirror of the self,' spiritual autobiography tries to turn the self into a mirror of something else: a record or reference to the Bible or Providence; a sensible reflection of some larger order."[42] This move, we should note, may also increase the problem. If as a reader I am hesitant to grant the teller that his or her life merits attention, I may be even more hesitant to do so if the teller claims that the particular- ity and importance of his or her life are divinely conferred. Finally, the fact that autobiography calls attention to the person may cause havoc with the reliability of the account, since its author may well be tempted to select and even to amplify material that is unusual or defend his or her decision to offer a self-account.

Also, self-accounts, because they require selection and construc- tion, can easily slip into fabrication. Fabrication has its appeal, however, particularly for reasons of economy. The criterion is truth- fulness, but truthfulness need not be established only by the rela- tion of what is narrated to what actually occurred; it can also be established by the relation of what is narrated to what the teller's life really is like. However, since the relation between the teller and the reader is one of trust, even intimacy, it may be best for the reader to be told when something in the account has been altered or, for purposes of clarity or economy, even fabricated.

Since autobiography is not only a self-narrative but also includes other people, truthfulness regarding depiction and evaluation creates problems. Relationships, especially if they are crucial to a person's self-account, are as often negative as they are positive. If negative relationships are narrated, they beg the question of what the other party would say in response about the relationship or about the teller. As to positive relationships, especially involving intimacies, it may not be possible to narrate them as fully as their importance in the teller's life would warrant. The boundaries of what earlier I called the "arenas" of self-accounts are being transgressed by publication, and material more suited to a personal arena is presented in a social arena. Such crossing of boundary is hazardous.

It is also difficult to handle the contraries of a divided or uncertain and a unified or goal-oriented life. This falls on the divide between the sense persons often have of their lives as both scattered and unified, both possessing an inherent unity or having a unity imposed on them. A narrative self-account will include such contraries. There is something questionable if not off-putting about an account that charts a straight line of certainty and goal or that is told from a position of unequivocal finality. Conversely, there will be something puzzling about an account that altogether lacks personal unity in the present and over time. Conversion narratives tend to sort out this problem by casting the preconversion period primarily in terms of disunity and confusion and the postconversion period primarily in terms of stability and direction. This is why, I should think, John Sturrock takes all autobiographies to contain an element of conversion, since narrating one's life as meaningful and unified suggests a redeeming of that life from confusion, randomness of purpose, or being forgotten.[43]

The question of the unity and meaningfulness of a life reveals another hazard. Meaningfulness, at least in part, depends on relations of similarity with, as well as difference from, cultural patterns or exemplars. Implied or explicit temporal patterns and character types are elicited in and by any narrative, including autobiography. Jerome Bruner points out that the culture gives patterns to self-accounts: "In ours, for example, it is chronological, oriented around emblematic events and 'stages' of life, focused on the voyage from the private to the public domain . . . voluntaristic, and marked by the 'life crisis' made so familiar by Erik Erikson."[44] Mary Evans cites other patterns: "overcoming specific hardships or illusions, living through difficult times in finding personal happiness," and the like, all having, she suggests, something in common, however faintly, with *Pilgrim's Progress*.[45] Autobiographies participate in the culture of narrative, and writers and readers will use and expect recognizable figures and patterns. These both enhance and threaten the sense that the writer conveys or the reader expects concerning the particular significance of the narrated life.

Another thorny matter is the writer's relations to political conditions, social class, or cultural capital. Does the sense one has of oneself as a person whose life warrants an unsolicited narrative serve a larger political and ideological agenda that encourages persons to think of themselves in that way? Does autobiography warrant the economically or culturally advantageous position the writer holds relative to other people and the leisure it provides to craft uniqueness in the form of a narration? Or, conversely, are self-accounts political or social protests against reigning assignments to persons of how their identities should be shaped? As Linda Anderson points out, women have a political imperative "to constitute themselves as subjects if they are to escape being never-endingly determined as objects."[46] This could also be said of minority or other oppressed members of the society. Whether in opposition to social and political determinations or, as with Althusser's theory of interpellation, in compliance with ideology, autobiography, in its crucial role of presenting a life as in some way singular and meaningful, cannot be divorced from its dependence on social, economic, and ideological conditionings. Since attention is on the particular life, the broader but perhaps more important matters of political or ideological context may easily be slighted.

The play between positive and negative self-estimations can also create difficulties. In general, it is to be expected that published autobiographies will carry more positive than negative evaluations of the teller because we tend to own attitudes and behaviors that are positive and to dismiss our negative attitudes and behaviors as anomalies. This selection may be intensified by our need to defend or justify ourselves. Judith Butler makes much of the fact that self-accounts are responses to real or anticipated accusations.[47] If self-defense and self-justification are goals of an autobiography, the account may well be slanted. If it is the case, as Georges Gusdorf says, that it is "to do away with misunderstandings, to restore an incomplete or deformed truth, that the autobiographer takes up the telling of his story," autobiography is not so much my telling my story as my telling my side of the story.[48] That intention threatens reliability.

Problems also arise from the role of the teller's early years. It is questionable that youth is in some way "a privileged source of

meaning" or "the 'natural' ground of identity."[49] Early years, however, do suggest what a person is given and what the person has
chosen, the hand dealt and how it was played. Youth has at least
three other autobiographical functions. It provides a benchmark, the
sense one has of one's present self as needing to be narrated beginning with a certain event or point in time. Second, early years are
often presented as a measure of what one has accomplished and of
how surprisingly one's life has turned out. Third, while youth need
not be cast as determining the adult or containing the potential that
adulthood actualizes, it is one's own, and some ties with it can be
made. Indeed, the matter may be deeper than that. We tend to have an
affectionate attitude toward our young selves, and we narrate them
because we want to make a place for them.

Present time, like the past, also raises questions for writing self-
accounts. While they can arise in adverse conditions such as serious
illness or states of grief, they usually are written not in the midst of
life's storms but in relative calm. The crisis has been weathered; the
destructive behaviors have been altered; the wrong has been righted.
The present is usually higher ground. Wisdom has been gained;
health has returned; vocational goals have been reached; a long-
standing internal or external conflict has been resolved: the time
of narrating is relatively a good time. In addition, a degree of confidence and sense of coherence is crucial for the teller if the reader
is to form a relation with him or her. A conflicted, fragmented, or
self-excoriating self-account will not provide a basis for intimacy
between teller and reader. However, their opposites are also not
productive of intimacy. While I do not think that we are "always
fragmented in time, taking a particular or provisional perspective
on the moving target of our past, addressing multiple and disparate
audiences,"[50] I also think that the teller needs to incorporate, along
with confidence and coherence, at least some degree of perplexity
and instability, and it is best if these negative and positive qualities
are not relegated to separate aspects of the account, the problematic
to the past or to the outside and the resolved or unified to the present
or to internality.

Future time also raises questions. If the present is slighted in self-
accounts relative to its importance, this is even truer of the future.
The future is generally a more major factor in our lives and self-
understandings than our self-accounts reflect. As Hubert Hermans
and Harry Kempen put it, "personal narratives represent internally
consistent interpretations of the past as presently understood, the
experienced present, and the anticipated future."[51] But the teller in

self-accounts usually gives little of the future. Conversion narra-tives, for example, are usually long on the preconversion period and short on the life resulting from the conversion. When the future does not get its due, its role as prompter of the self-account is slighted. As Kathleen Woodward says, anxiety and desire are significant causes of self-accounts, the fear of losing the present sense of well-being, for example.[52] There are other threats and fears, such as being unknown or misunderstood. Desire is also a stimulant to writing, the desire to be recognized and confirmed. Sidonie Smith and Julia Watson write of autobiographical acts that "move the 'I' toward the collective and shift the focus of narration toward an as-yet virtual space of com-munity, across and beyond the old boundaries of identification."[53] The purpose of self-accounts is also to establish firm ground for the future and to project into that future an identity that looks for fulfill-ment. As Hubert Hermans and Harry Kempen put it, "the notion of 'story' or 'narrative' assumes the existence of a person who tells and an actual or imagined person who listens."[54] The dialogical situation initiated by the narrating points toward continuation. The narrative is a gambit in a projected process, and the relationship formed by autobiography between the implied author and the implied reader is future-oriented. This may be why it is not unusual for people who write autobiographies to write more than one.

These many hazards—and there may well be more—make clear, I think, that narrating our lives, while something we might take on readily and consider natural, is a risky and not easily performed act, one usually unsatisfying to the teller and at times not favor-ably received. Indeed, we are often put off by people who talk about themselves, and it may not be too much to say that the writer of autobiography can anticipate at least some degree of skepticism or even resistance on the part of the reader toward what will be said. If the telling is to result in a degree of what I call textual intimacy, that achievement must be earned. The art of autobiography lies both in negotiating the hazards of this kind of discourse and in maximizing its potentials for textual intimacy.

3

DISCLOSING A RELIGIOUS
IDENTITY

WE SHOULD not be surprised, while reading the autobiographies of fellow Americans, to encounter religious self-disclosures. After all, roughly 85 percent of Americans self-identify as religious. In addition, religion is so pervasive in our society that the life of any American is likely to include references to religion in some form and degree or other. American autobiographies that include religious disclosures are not exceptional, then. Conversely, autobiographies that include religious self-disclosures are potentially engaging to American readers because they themselves are likely to have had to deal with religion as part of their pasts, their current interactions, or their thoughts as to what kind of persons they want to be or are becoming.

We also should not be surprised to find religious self-disclosures in autobiographies because, as we saw earlier, a person's life is structured by beliefs, and narrative accounts require and rest on beliefs. Autobiographical narratives draw attention primarily to the beliefs of the teller as to what is assumed to be important, how things are to be evaluated, and to what he or she aspires. Since beliefs of this kind are bound to occur, it is not surprising that their sources, reinforcements, or warrants should also be included, and these easily can be religious. Moving in a self-account from being candid about what matters, to making value judgments, and then to disclosing religious beliefs or identity, while not inevitable, is a somewhat natural progression.

Also, religious self-disclosures in American autobiographies are not unexpected because religion and being American are interwoven.

The settlement of this land and the founding of the Republic, although they also form a political, social, and economic history, are important chapters in the history of religion in modern culture. Religion continues to be a constant and visible part of American life. We are surrounded by religious institutions, exposed to religion in and by the media, and rallied by political speeches with rhetoric readily laced with detectable religious language. The prominence of religion in American life and the continuing relevance of religion to American culture, although now also attenuated and contested, mean that including religion in a self-account is not an odd thing to do.

Finally, it is not surprising that most Americans think of themselves, at least to some degree, in religious terms because they do so in resistance to a determining characteristic of modernity, namely, the modern city and what is epitomized by it: incorporation of people within vast material constructions, mobility, density of populations, impersonal bureaucracies, networks of mass transportation, industry, commerce, and the like. The accelerating pace of urban growth in America has granted urgency and significance to the act of establishing personal identity, and religion is one way of doing that. Feelings, a sense of particularity, personal spirituality, and human internality as a locus of or point of access to spirit, transcendence, or the divine: these interests along with urban expansion become prominent in the nineteenth century and continue today. Religion, while it plays other roles in the lives of contemporary Americans, provides a resource for people to substantiate the worth, particularity, and integrity of their personhood in the face of realities that have homogenizing and depersonalizing effects. While religious languages and their uses vary and while many Americans do not use religious language at all, religious self-disclosures are recognizable as particular forms of a more general American concern and practice.

While there is, for reasons such as these, a remarkable compatibility and interpenetration between being American and being religious, the two kinds of identities also stand in real or potential tension with one another. Self-identifying publicly as a religious person is also a complex and, recently, an even awkward act that calls for discretion and justification. Indeed, while Americans freely include religion in their public self-accounts, they also must be aware of the context of these self-accounts. We should look at reasons why American and religious identities, while related, also question and even challenge one another.

The Current Context of Religious Self-Disclosures

There are at least three factors that determine the current context of religious self-disclosures in American society: the normalization of being nonreligious in American society; being religious in relation to nonreligious persons; and being religious in relation to differing religious people.

I

While it is easy to underestimate the importance of religion for American identities, it is just as easy to fail to take adequate account of the force and results of secularization in American life. Secularization can be tied primarily, although not exclusively, to the urbanization of the American population. While American political and economic institutions and processes were from the outset largely dissociated from religion, the disestablishment of religion in American public life occurred more quickly and completely in urban than in rural and small-town settings. The momentum of an economy increasingly dissociated in the early nineteenth century from domestic and rural settings and located in cities contributed strongly to the pace of secularization in urban life, but it was also hastened by the increasing diversity, especially during the closing decades of the nineteenth century, of religious identities and affiliations. A social and economic system related to a particular religion could not operate. The city provided the frontier for the diminishment of religion in public life.

The normalization of the nonreligious in American society was marked by what José Casanova calls the three stages of religion's disestablishment in American public life. The one most commonly recognized is political and is epitomized in and by the First Amendment. The second, a more gradual, subtle, and cultural form of disestablishment, took hold during the second half of the nineteenth century and was fueled by the Darwinian revolution in scientific thought. It produced a growing separation of intellectual inquiry and higher education from the influence and norms of religion. The third, which can be detected from the ending of World War I but becomes obvious after World War II, especially in the 1960s, was the separation of personal, sexual, and reproductive values and behaviors from religiously sponsored directives and restraints.[1] While all three disestablishments continue to create uncertainty and contestation, they mark a progression, if not an acceleration, in the weakening of religion's influence in and over public life. These three stages, along with other developments such as an understanding of the economy as operating by laws and dynamics of its own, the application of Darwinian theories to social development, and the diversification of religious identities in cities, helped support the perception, one that persists today, that there is a contrary relation between the city and personal, that is, moral and spiritual, well-being.

The major consequence of the disestablishments of religion in American public life has been the increasingly and, by now, generally secularized nature of its inclusive social and cultural container. Casanova describes the results of this change well: "If before it was the religious realm which appeared to be the all-encompassing reality within which the secular realm found its proper place, now the secular sphere will be the all-encompassing reality, to which the religious sphere will have to adapt."[2] While there are differing opinions concerning the extent of secularization in American life and while American society may well be less secular than Casanova's comment makes it out to be, I think the point cannot be gainsaid that the general container of American public life is more secular than it once was. And movement toward the normalization of that secularized container continues.

Focusing more on academic culture, Charles Taylor also refers to the general cultural container when he describes the secularization of the structure or frame of American society. What he means is that the primary assumptions of the culture are detached from, if not contrary to, traditional religious beliefs. We have moved, he argues, from secularity understood as a separation of some areas of public life from religious influence and even from secularity as a waning of religious language and practice in public life to what he calls "secularity 3," a set of governing assumptions that throw religious beliefs on the defensive. The framework that structures intellectual discourses today, he concludes, is immanent and even materialist, excluding, thereby, the transcendent and the spiritual. The increasing irrelevance of "the beyond" for intellectual inquiry and debate makes the exclusion of religion no longer a matter of deliberate effort but something assumed as part of cultural conformity.

While one of the noticeable changes in American culture over the past two decades has been the increase in the number of Americans whose religious identities are other than Christian or Jewish, a more striking change has been in the number of Americans who self-identify as nonreligious. Roughly 15 percent of Americans, according to the recent "American Religious Identification Survey," now self-identify as nonreligious, and it can be anticipated, given the close relations between cultural assumptions or practices and personal identity, that this percentage will increase. For many Americans, especially for those in urban and academic settings, religion has become outmoded and plays no role in personal identity.[3]

The growing secularization of the general container or cultural frame of American life and the increasing number of Americans who self-identify as nonreligious help normalize the "nonreligious." Nonreligious identity has become not only an acceptable way of being an American but also has become or is becoming increasingly assumed and, perhaps, even normative. You can now assume that the person sitting next to you on an airplane, lacking signs to the contrary, is nonreligious. This means that there is an implicit if not noticeable dissonance between disclosing oneself as a religious person and normal social interactions, affected as they are by increasingly secular mass media, social, economic, and political processes, academic culture, and the increasing normalization of the nonreligious American. Giving explicit and positive place to religion in a self-account, then, counters the general direction in which many Americans and American culture are moving.

Largely in reaction to these changes, Americans with more specific religious identities, particularly Christians, have tried to tie American identity more specifically to religion. This has created a counter-reaction, the deliberate effort to expunge vestiges of religion from public life altogether. As Robert Putnam and David Campbell point out, "Americans are increasingly concentrated at opposite ends of the religious spectrum—the highly religious at one pole and the avowedly secular on the other."[4] This polarization is abetted by the agreement on both sides that the existing remnants or vestiges of religion in American public life are of little if any importance. The religious ingredients in American public life, then, rather than provide a common ground between the two camps, tend to be discounted, if not disdained, by both religious and nonreligious Americans.

It can be argued, I think, that the disregard on both sides for the lingering religious ingredients of American public life is unfortunate. Those ingredients, while vague and somewhat random, potentially, if not actually, contribute something positive and important to American identity. They mean, for example, that American identity has a moral and spiritual and not only a material quality. Also, since the reference of that religious language is to all human beings and not only to Americans, it is not nationalistic but, rather, affirms the well-being and rights of people both within and without our national borders. It suggests, third, that the rights of citizens are not conferred on them by the state but are constitutive of their beings. Finally, it implies that the loyalty of citizens extends to norms and goals that transcend their loyalty to the state. However, attempts to call Americans to a unified appreciation of the traditional religious components of American identity built into the formation of the Republic and still active, despite attenuation and contestation, in the present day seem bootless in relation to the conflict between those religious people who continue to characterize the Republic as having been and as needing once again to be more specifically Christian and, on the other side, people who advocate the elimination of religion from public life altogether and its consignment to private interests and religious institutions.

The most important inhibiting factor to the increasing normalization of a nonreligious identity in American society, in my opinion, is that religion continues to provide Americans with resources for identifying and clarifying personal particularity and internality. All Americans, although in varying degrees, share the problem of having to maintain a sense of particularity and moral integrity in the face of massive, incorporating, and determining forces resident in and exerted by the general and impersonal container of their lives. What binds religious and nonreligious Americans together is that both are engaged in the common enterprise of actualizing their own personal identities, especially in resistance to the homogenizing and depersonalizing effects of urbanization and mass media.[5] This commonality creates a bond between religious and nonreligious Americans.

II

The normalization of the category "nonreligious person" in American society creates a new context for understanding the status of its contrary, "religious person." When the cultural context is determined by nonreligious discourses and characterized by the increasing normalization of nonreligious American identities, self-accounts that include a significant role for religion begin more sharply to stand out.

Several consequences arise from this situation. The first is that the normalized, perhaps increasingly normative, status of "nonreligious person," because it clarifies its contrary, allows us to impute content and specificity to what it means to identify oneself or someone else as a religious person. Indeed, it opens the possibility that it may be more productive to talk about what we mean when we refer to someone as a religious person than what we mean when we refer to the more abstract category of "religion." It is well known that defining "religion" is a treacherous task, and attempts to do so seem to create more problems than they solve.[6] But some difficulties of definition are reduced when attention shifts from religion itself to the characteristics of self-disclosed religious persons. We may not know what we mean by "religion," but we may well know what is meant when a person self-identifies as religious or when we refer to someone as a "religious person."

Because it will be increasingly assumed that persons are nonreligious unless they identify themselves as religious, what they say or do to identify themselves as religious gives content to that designation. Furthermore, we draw inferences from observing various religious persons and hearing their accounts, and these allow us to place religious persons in relations of similarity to and difference from one another. While we may also use the adjective loosely, we tend, given the present situation, to mean something quite specific and significant when we say that so-and-so is a "religious person." The designation has a midlevel standing. It is different from calling someone a Catholic, let us say, because institutional affiliation, while more specific, may not mean that religion is a positive and significant aspect of that person's identity. And when we want to move above this midlevel designation, we refer to someone as very or dogmatically religious. "Religious person" is for us somewhere between these two levels, someone for whom religion plays a positive role in the description or narration of his or her personal identity.

Cities, while they form a principal site for the secularization of American public life, should not so easily be viewed as contrary to the formation and clarification of religious identities. While cities oversaw the weakening of religious authority over the public lives of people, cities also became frontiers of personal liberation and self-formation. They still are. The vitality and expansiveness of American life are the consequences not only, or even so much, of the Western natural frontier as of the cultural frontier opened by cities. While they created anonymity and depersonalization, cities also released people to cultivate their lives personally and particularly. This cultivation easily included religious components. For one thing, people coming into cities from other parts of the country and from foreign lands valued group identities highly, especially those provided by shared religious identities. Religious group identities stood, buffer-like, between a person's individual identity and an identity conferred by being a denizen of the metropolis. In addition, since being religious was not something required or imposed by the social environment, people were free to appropriate religious resources as they deliberately chose to and in ways that meaningfully addressed their needs. These dynamics at least in part account for the fact that "many Americans—at least one-third and rising—nowadays choose their religion rather than simply inheriting it."[7] These dynamics gave rise to or emphasized the common location of personal identities as between those granted by religious association or affiliation and those granted by the larger social setting, a location requiring a person's interpretation of the relation between these two, at least to some degree always differing, connections. When we refer to someone as a "religious person," using this midlevel designation, we refer to someone engaged in that interpretive and negotiating project.

Self-identifying as a religious person is affected today not only by the fact that the increasing presence of nonreligious identities gives greater force and clarity to religious identity and by the fact that cities, despite their reputation as sites of secularization, foster religious identities but also by what José Casanova refers to as the "deprivatization" of religion. Casanova argues that beginning in the 1980s, religious people increasingly refused to confine their interests to the privacy to which it had been thought that religion had been relegated.[8] "Like the unconstrained exposure of one's bodily parts and emotions," he writes, "religious confessions outside the strictly delimited religious sphere were considered not only a degradation of one's privacy but also an infringement upon the right to privacy of others."[9] What we have seen in the recent rise of attention to and interest in religion, then, is less an attack on the increasingly secular nature of the general container of social and academic life and more a defiance of the assumption that there is no place for religious self-disclosures and for the furtherance of religious interests in that increasingly secularized arena.[10] While this breaking out of religious interests and disclosures in the public realm is not an evenly pervasive and always smooth development, it is a noticeable and important change.

The deprivatization of religion in American society may also be abetted by a phenomenon that Charles Taylor calls "expressive individualism." People have come not only to value highly their personal take on things but also to think it legitimate if not gratifying to display their personal opinions and behaviors in public. People feel free to do their own thing in the presence of an audience. "It matters to each of us as we act," he says, that "others are there, as witnesses of what we are doing, and thus as co-determiners of the meaning of our action."[11] Talking on cell phones in crowded places may be one example. Blogs and other means of publicly expressing personal opinions may be another. There is, to put it differently, a growing urge to create or seize coincidences between personal interests and public display or, as he puts it, "between solipsism and communication."[12] Taylor's point may well explain an otherwise puzzling event reported in the news during the summer of 2006. A group of teenagers in Brattleboro, Vermont, took to the practice of gathering in the parking lot of a shopping center in the nude. The incentive seems to have been neither the desire for full-bodied exposure to sun and air nor the erotic possibilities of nude exposure to one another, since both purposes could have been served in more secluded or comfortable settings. No, the purpose seems to have been to experience a coincidence of opposites, the exposure of something highly private to public notice and reaction. Having said this, however, it seems fair also to say, using the Brattleboro example, that religious self-disclosures that are in-your-face and attention-getting will very likely not be disclosures we refer to, in a midlevel way, as those of "religious persons" but, rather of persons who are very or dogmatically religious.

Indeed, religious theatricality may stimulate its contrary, namely, greater reserve concerning religious identity. For many Americans, religious self-display will appear unseemly. For those we refer to as religious persons in a midlevel way, the motivation for self-disclosure will less likely be exhibitionism and more the need to do justice to the positive role of religion in one's life and its relations to other factors constituting personal identity. If it is the case, as it appears increasingly to be, that people will assume that I am a nonreligious person, it may become increasingly important for me to counter that assumption by disclosing that the contrary is true. Religious self-disclosures, then, arise somewhere between a culturally warranted theatricality, the urge toward religious exhibitionism, and the reserve that religious exhibitionism may well create in those religious persons not so inclined.

There are, then, forms of religious self-disclosure that will put off a general audience, such as the desire to convert others, to claim a higher moral or spiritual ground, or to identify oneself with dogmatic or institutional exclusiveness and authority. In contrast, three forms of religious self-disclosure may well be engaging and helpful to many contemporary American readers: the clarification of particularity that comes from setting oneself off from the determining effects of the society on personal identity, the need to work out the increasingly unclear, sometimes even contrary, relations between the religious and the American components of one's identity, and the need to be honest, to counter the imposition of the increasingly normalized assumption that one is a nonreligious person.

III

The third thing to point out regarding the current context of religious self-disclosures in American society is that being a religious person not only sets one off from the increasingly secular culture and the growing number of people who self-identify as nonreligious but also serves to distinguish oneself as a religious person from religious institutions and other religious people. Religious identities stand in tension not only with their nonreligious contraries but also with religious identities of other kinds.

To begin with, it can be said that the category of "religious person" seems to have gained force and substance in our society at the expense of the more specific connotations of particular religious affiliation. This works out in two ways. First, to say that someone is Christian or Jewish is not any longer the same as to say that that person is religious. People who identify themselves with religious categories may not necessarily think of themselves as religious. There are nonreligious or cultural Protestants and Catholics, for example, as well as nonreligious or cultural Jews. We often clarify our reference by saying that not only is so-and-so a Christian or Catholic but also that this person treats his or her religion positively. Second, there are Americans, an increasing number of them, who do not identify with an established religion but consider themselves to be religious nonetheless. As Putnam and Campbell say, "a large portion of those who demur from indicating a formal religious affiliation believe religion is important, pray regularly, and even attend a given congregation on occasion."[13] For both reasons, the designation "religious person" often has more force and content than traditional, institutional categories.

In addition, it is common to encounter Americans who self-identify religiously by means of affiliation but who hasten to add that they are not in full accord with the religious institution or with other members of it regarding beliefs and practices. What is particularly interesting here is not so much that people are distinguishable from the institution with which they identify but that it is important for them to state that fact. Very likely there always have been members of religious institutions who took private exception to the beliefs and behaviors expected of them, but it seems today important for many people who identify with a religious institution to make the distinction.

This act of distinguishing oneself from the institution with which one is affiliated seems to be replacing other forms of religious self-identification by opposition. Saying that you are religious meant in the past and for many still today that you are religious in one way and not in another—Protestant, say, and not Catholic, Episcopalian, say, and not Baptist. This has, at least in part, been displaced by taking exception or distancing oneself from religious people in the institution with which I identify. So, when I meet someone of another faith or another branch of my own, rather than distinguish myself from that person I may well assume that he or she is as fully engaged in the process of clarifying differences with his or her institution as I am and that we have, due to this similar location and despite other differences, more in common with one another than we do with those members of our differing institutions who fully identify with them.

A second reason for the tendency of religious people to put some distance between themselves and the institution with which they are affiliated is the voluntarism of American life. This means, among other things, that Americans tend to appropriate things on their own terms. This tendency, if not habit, is tied to identity by possession. If I think of my identity as my own construction, I imply that it is not conferred on me by an institution. While religious identity may also be something I inherit or something conferred on me by affiliation, these determinations are countered by the act of distinguishing myself from them, taking at least partial exception: "Yes, I'm Catholic, but I don't agree with the church regarding. . . ." There is, one could almost say, an imperative implied by being American, namely, that I determine for myself what I think of as valuable or valid among the religious components of my upbringing or the institution with which I am affiliated.

A third reason why Americans who affiliate religiously also distance themselves from their institutions is that, primarily because of increasing mobility, they are exposed to a variety of religious beliefs, practices, and identities. In extreme forms, this gives rise to marriages between people with differing religious identities. But it also takes more casual forms. People have college roommates, friends, or colleagues at work who are religiously different from them and with whom they have personal relations. This exposure to and acceptance of differing religious orientations makes people susceptible to affirming a variety of religious options and even being influenced by them. This is why Putnam and Campbell can say that "most Christian clergy see salvation as exclusively Christian, while most Christians have a more—if not completely—inclusive view of who will be saved in the hereafter."[14] This creates what is sometimes called a "salad bar" approach to religious identity; people find a variety of religious beliefs and practices helpful in constructing their own religious identities. This approach puts the construction of religious identity even more fully in the hands of the person. Affiliation is nonexclusive. I can be Catholic and also appreciative of my friend not in spite of but including the fact that he or she is religiously different from me.

A fourth reason why religious people often distinguish themselves from religious institutions is that religious institutions, because of disestablishment, do not have the force in public life that is generated by groups and movements made up of various religious people. These groups, such as political action groups, combine religious people of differing kinds, as do groups opposing the death penalty or those involved in the ecological movement. While there are important exceptions, such as some African American churches, the point is that religious institutions are less important in American public and political life than are groups of religious people, often of differing kinds, acting together to further social or political goals. Such groups and movements create associations that may rival the importance of affiliation with religious institutions.

A final reason why religious people distinguish themselves from the religious institutions with which they affiliate is that they widely give validity to some of the consequences of religion's disestablishment. Scientific and technological assumptions play their part in the self-understandings of many religious people, and, while these people may attempt to integrate differing sets of interests, they also live with them and do not feel fully identified with their religion because of its felt distance from current intellectual assumptions. In addition, many religious people today condone or even affirm personal attitudes and behaviors regarding sexuality and procreation that their religious institutions at least officially continue to proscribe. While there are American religious people who resist the effects of these two forms of disestablishment, many American people who possess religious identity hold their religious beliefs and practices in some kind of personally constructed relations with culturally emerging and prevalent behaviors and assumptions. Americans so involved will likely view the institutions with which they are affiliated both as components in or contributors to the construction of their religious identities and as less up-to-date regarding cultural assumptions and developments than they themselves are. They may even think that those more closely identified with the institution, such as its clergy, are not exposed, as they are, to the real world in which dissonant assumptions and behaviors prevail and the need to adjust to and accommodate them is unavoidable. When it comes to social and cultural change or to newer awareness about a wide range of things, from race relations and sexual identities to theories of evolution and technologies of reproduction, religious people may well think of their religious institutions as slow to respond. This means that who they are religiously is not simply acknowledging an affiliation but describing, perhaps narrating, an ongoing process that may include but is not identical with an institutional affiliation.

The Content of Religious Self-Disclosures

Having looked, however briefly, at the current context of self-identifying as a religious person in America, we can turn to the content of religious self-disclosures, to the kinds of things we mean by referring to ourselves or to someone else as a "religious person." There are several matters that we should address. The first is the question of whether or to what extent religious content gives stability to personal identity. Does the content of religious identity provide ballast, so to speak, to what we have seen as the otherwise complex or variable dynamics of personal identity?

I

Given the complexity of self-accounts—that they are two-sided, shaped by three arenas, and inclusive of at least four constituents—it could be thought that narrating a religious identity would counter the uncertainties and ambiguities of identity formation more generally. Putnam and Campbell assert that religious identity stabilizes: "Compared to other aspects of ourselves—our attitudes, values, identities, habits—our religious outlooks are, in fact, highly stable."[15] We should look at what gives rise to the expectation that religion stabilizes identity in order to see that this expectation is not well grounded.

The first reason why we may think that religion stabilizes identity is that many conversion narratives describe the path from a nonreligious to a religious identity as a move from confusion and uncertainty to clarity and conviction. Moral quandaries, a lack of direction in life, a sense of meaninglessness: these are often replaced in conversion narratives by a stability and certainty that religion has provided. There tends to be a sharp before/after structure to conversion narratives: Once I was lost, but now I am found or have found my way. But, as was suggested in the previous chapter, this plot structure of contrast is characteristic of autobiographical narratives more generally. The position of a teller is often at a point of arrival or clarity from which the person's earlier life is viewed as comparatively troubled or unresolved. While this common characteristic of autobiographies may be more noticeable in narratives of religious conversion, it is a characteristic shared with self-accounts by nonreligious people and therefore not clearly an attribute specific to religious self-accounts.

A second reason why we are led to assume that the content of religious identity provides certainty and stability is that many people think of religion as giving answers to the great uncertainties of life and value religion for doing so. The assumption or expectation that religion gives answers to life's major questions is strengthened by the high value that our culture imputes to answers. We have such a high view of answers because we think of the value of a thing in terms of our ability to possess and use it. Answers are, like commodities, things that we can possess, put in our pocket, so to speak, and use when needed. People seem often to view religion as a set of answers that apply when nonreligious answers are overstretched and break down. The assumption that religion grants stability to personal identity because it provides answers to the quandaries of life is fortified by the assumption in our culture that people do not do anything unless they are rewarded for it. People are religious, then, because they get something out of it, and what they get, among other things, is a set of answers to questions that otherwise would distress them.

It can be argued, however, that people are often not religious because religion gives answers to questions that otherwise are unanswerable. Stewart Guthrie, for example, rejects the thesis that people are religious because religion gratifies such needs. He argues that religion raises as many, if not more, questions and uncertainties than are created by nonreligious understandings of and orientations to life.[16] While religion may grant people some assurances in the face of uncertainties and answers to some questions, religion also creates questions and causes uncertainties. Mystery, the unexpected, the disconfirming—these are also aspects of religious experience and life. And they have a role equal to, if not surpassing, that of certainty and stability. While we may expect religion to give people answers to the difficulties and enigmas of life, one will find that religious self-accounts do not always reveal such certainty and stability. It may be better to say that religious people live with or within questions and answers that differ in content but not necessarily, so to speak, in size or gravity from those with or within which nonreligious people live.

Also, it will not be clear from the narratives we shall examine that people are or become religious because they get something out of it. Perhaps they do get something, but that is in the presence of something that they also lose or forfeit. This is not to say that religious people do things without an eye to personal gain while nonreligious people are selfishly motivated. I would say that there are religious people who, one would think mistakenly, are in it for what they get out of it, and there are altruistic and self-sacrificing nonreligious people. In other words, people are capable in general of acting unselfishly, although religious people may well be exposed, given the nature of religious languages and disciplines, to attitudes that direct attention to things more important than the satisfaction of their own needs.

A third reason why we tend to think that the content of religion lends stability to personal identity is that group identity, especially affiliation with a religious institution, seems to provide it. Indeed, religious institutions construct specific and stable identities and need to. In the market economy that characterizes the American religious scene, religious institutions must be aggressive in getting their identities known, and vagueness and variability do not sell.[17] Label recognition is important. Religious institutions, then, tend to have specific and stable identities and to confer the same on those affiliated with them.

While there is no doubt that willingness to self-identify as a member of a religious institution gives clarity and stability to what a person means by accounting for him- or herself as religious, we should remember, as already mentioned, that the self-accounts of American religious people reveal that many who are not affiliated consider themselves to be religious and that many who do affiliate with a religious institution qualify that identification. An ingredient in this phenomenon may be that religious affiliation is, as Gauri Viswanathan points out, "a subcategory of social composition," and people, especially contemporary Americans, are uneasy with being categorized, lumped together with others.[18] In addition, there are, as we have seen, strong incentives to being religious that come from the modern American desire to clarify particularity. As Charles Taylor comments, "For many people today, to set aside their own path in order to conform to some external authority just doesn't seem comprehensible as a form of spiritual life."[19] A religious self-account, indeed, will be prompted, perhaps in large part, by the need to clarify one's own religious identity not primarily in relation to a religious institution but to some degree in contrast or exception to it.

We should keep in mind, however, that religious identity, while often not identical to institutional affiliation, will very likely also not be purely individual. While there may be persons who think of and present their religious identities as wholly self-derived, it is safe to say that religious people learn to be religious from other people. This source may be the family of origin, a group with identifying beliefs and practices, or a person chosen as a model to emulate or a seer from whom to learn. People who develop their sense of being religious persons without institutional affiliation as a significant factor, will, however, have learned the language and practice of their religious identity from someone else. The popularity of books that serve as guides for spiritual development is not surprising since people look to guides of various kinds to improve or to alter their lives. In this case, the reader defers to someone who already has arrived or is further advanced in these matters. So, being a religious person means identifying at least in part with something in one's past, with a group in the present, or with some guide or program worth following.

Although institutional affiliation is a common aspect of American religious identity, disestablishment put religious institutions on a level field of competition. This means that they have had to be adaptive to the changing needs and interests of actual and potential members, to the individual consumer in a buyer's market, so to speak. Indeed, institutions, rather than requiring their members to conform strictly to the institution, may easily be ready, in order to retain their members, to tolerate a range of ideas and behaviors among the individuals within the group or institution.

Given these factors, it is important, when considering religious affiliation, to avoid the widespread use of the term "community" as a substitute for group or institution. "Community" imputes a certain quality to religious groups and institutions that they do not have, so to speak, in and by themselves. A "community" is not an entity. It is the assumed sum of beliefs concerning agreement and acceptance felt by the individuals who constitute the group. As Claire Mitchell argues: "Community is based on individuals' feelings that they belong to a larger group. People could feel this way because they share certain things with one another, perhaps a language, a location or a regular activity. In all these cases, however, communities only actually exist because individuals believe them to be real. Communities are not entities in their own right, but rather live in the minds of groups of people."[20] To refer to religious groups or institutions as communities confers a unity on them that they do not themselves necessarily possess.

Due to the mobility and variety of backgrounds among its members, especially in urban settings, a religious institution will likely not be unified. There will be interest groups within the institution that may have more identity-granting potential, in terms of assumed agreement and acceptance between persons, than the institution as a whole provides. Churches are increasingly obliged to provide their members with a variety of possible interest groups that they can join, and the identification of a person with one of these groups may be more significant and confirming than identification with the institution as a whole.

Discussions of religious identity and institutions are also muddled when religious "tradition" is used, as it often is, as a substitute for group or institution. "Tradition" seems preferable to institution because it suggests significant content. In addition, "tradition" carries with it a suggestion of a content or complexity greater than what the institution embodies. "Tradition" becomes a repertoire from which participants can variously draw. Sophisticated adherents can know enough about the tradition of their faith to select moments in the tradition with which to identify that may have minimal importance in current institutional practices or have been forgotten. "Tradition" can justify the sense of difference that a religious person can feel between personal and institutional religious identities.

In addition, use of "tradition" instead of institution suggests a coincidence between the narrative that seems implied by the term "tradition" and the narrative of a person's, family's, or group's history. This use of tradition has an important philosophical warrant in the work of Alasdair McIntyre, who argues for the importance of tradition and the incompatibility with one another of traditions culturally operative today.[21] This position leads to the conclusion that everybody operates within some tradition or other. When framed in this way, religious identity by tradition becomes very attractive. The narrative of one's life and of the religious tradition appear to have formal and substantial compatibility, and identifying with a religious tradition is placed in the broader cultural context established by the fact that everyone operates in a tradition of one kind or another.[22]

Though attractive, this position has problems. First, as we saw earlier, it is not clear that personal identity and narrative are coexistent. This is also true of a religion. It cannot be assumed, then, that persons and institutions are joined by their both having their identity basis in narrative. Second, it is not clear that a tradition is a narrative. While a tradition can be narrated, this narrative is as much a construction as it is a given. When tradition becomes a narrative, it does so under certain conditions and for certain aims. There are many ways to narrate a religious tradition. Indeed, one could argue that not only are there many real or potential narratives but also that there are conflicting narratives under any religious label. It is not the case that there is one neutral, comprehensive narrative that contains and unifies the many, often conflicting, parts. Indeed, it is not too much to say that when tradition is made synonymous with narrative, we likely are presented with a ruse by which an institution's or group's narrative of the tradition is being passed off as the tradition itself. Third, tradition has more appeal and authority for some religious people than for others. Religious people with strong institutional orientations are likely to treat tradition more seriously than those who are more oriented to spontaneity and the future. Conservative more than Reform Jews, Catholics more than Calvinists, those who adhere to priestly forms of religion more than those adhering to prophetic forms will find the term "tradition" useful and meaningful. Tradition, while it may always be operative, is not a term that can be used evenly across all kinds of religious people. Some venerate tradition; some resist it.

We should, I think, be wary about the widespread uses of "community" and "tradition" as substitutes or euphemisms for institution or group. Their use carries unwarranted assumptions and undisclosed agendas. While "institution" carries some implications that do not apply evenly across religious options, that problem can be relieved by joining "institution" with "group." Religious people often identify with a religious institution or group, but this identification will very likely be modified or attenuated by a strong sense of personal selection and appropriation. Consequently, it is not clear that religious affiliation or group identification, any more than conversion narratives and the assumption that religion gives answers to life's major questions, provides clarity and stability to personal identity.

II

Now that we have questioned the assumption that religion grants stability to personal identity, we should also look at characteristics or content of religious self-disclosures that cause but also restrict variability and complexity. These factors produce differences not only between various kinds of religious people but also between religious people of the same faith.

Religious identities are varied and complex because people are religious in one of three ways: by reason of their beliefs, practices, or feelings.[23] While all three can be expected to play a role in the constitution of religious identity, not all will be equally important, and one of the three may dominate a person's religious self-understanding. More than that, one of the three may be taken to be definitive of religion in general. This is why people who study religion often do so with the assumption that one of these three ways is or should be always dominant. Richard King makes clear why until recently religions were studied primarily in terms of the beliefs that constituted them.[24] However, now the study of religion focuses less on beliefs than on religious practices. In response to this shift of dominants, we should protect the principle that all three are actually or potentially in play and that any one of them may be dominant in and for both particular religious persons and for religious groups. Indeed, one of the three factors can serve as the basis for the objections that one kind of religious person can level at another, even within the same faith: "all doctrine and no action" or "practices that are purely formal and lack feeling," for example. Consequently, branches of a religion may differ according to whether one or another of the three is dominant, and it may be easier for members of one branch to understand and relate to religious people of another faith for whom their own form is also dominant than to people in other branches of their own faith whose form differs.

A second reason why religious identities are varied and complex is that there will be, for religious persons, a range of attitudes toward and evaluations of the larger world around them, both natural and cultural. There are what Casanova calls "public religions," that is, religions that lead their adherents to take an interest in and participate in the larger natural, cultural, and political world and religions that lead their adherents to negative judgments of or nonparticipation in that world. And negative attitudes may take the form of attacks on that context, with the goal of changing or displacing it, or of a withdrawal from it into separate groups or personal isolation. This is not, as Casanova implies that it is, a distinction to be made only between kinds of religions. It also forms a set of options within particular religions and, consequently, also creates ambiguities for stabilizing religious identity. There is an unsteady affirming/rejecting relation that religious persons can have to their larger natural and cultural locations, including their own bodies. This vacillation or ambivalence can lead to inconsistency and inconclusiveness, a lack, in any case, of stability and certainty.

A third reason why religious identities are not fixed is that they can have differing attitudes toward people with other religious identities. For some Christians, for example, the gods of other religions are actually demons in disguise so that, for them, it is better that another person be nonreligious than of another religious identity. However, there are Christians who are very affirmative toward people of other faiths and who recognize large degrees of similarity and common interests with them. To put it differently, religion can sponsor an attitude or even a culture either of civility or of identity, to use Terry Eagleton's terms, either a sense of continuity with or of antagonism toward other religions.[25] Major religious traditions contain ample warrants for attitudes that vary along a wide spectrum in this regard. In contemporary American society, marked, as I have said, both by a nonreligious social container and by the importance of religiously based groups, it is likely that American religious people will see themselves more or less allied with religious people of other kinds in contrast to the increasingly nonreligious environment. In addition, there are strong historical incentives, as we already have seen, to understand American life as both supportive of religious identity and as accommodating religious diversity. Given these incentives, there may be more similarity between differing religious people who agree on an affirmative attitude toward other kinds of religious people than between them and others of their own affiliation who are antagonistic and exclusive in their attitudes toward other religions.

A fourth reason for variability caused by the content of religious self-disclosures is that religious people are marked by three orientations, any one of which may, even will, be dominant in relation to the others.[26] One of the three orientations is toward what I shall call "that which cannot be understood or controlled." Second, religious people are oriented, either directly or by mediation, toward a form of relation to or with that which cannot be understood or controlled, a form present here and now, in the past and needing to be recovered, and/or in the future and anticipated. Finally, that which cannot be understood or controlled has, by means of relation to this real or potential form, important, if not crucial, consequences for human well-being.

It is possible to argue, I think, that in particular religious institutions or groups, for particular religious persons, and for a religious person at any one time, one of these three characteristics of being a religious person will dominate the other two and deform them to itself. It is possible, then, to discern three kinds of religious people or moments in religious life. When the first of these orientations—namely, toward what cannot be understood or controlled—is dominant, we have what could be called, for lack of a better word, a "prophetic" form of religion. When the second orientation—to a mediating form of what cannot be understood or controlled—dominates, we have a "priestly" religion. And when the third—the consequences of this relation for human well-being—dominates, we have, again for lack of a better term, a "sapiential" form of religion. Further, I think that it can be anticipated that relations between kinds of religious people and identities, even within a single faith, will be troubled because when a person of one of these three kinds encounters a person of another kind, he or she will find that what is dominant in and for his or her own religious orientation and identity is subordinate to and deformed toward the differing dominant in the other religious orientations and identities. Since it is safe to say that all three forms of religious identity and orientation can be found in major religions, it easily can occur that a Christian, let us say, of a "priestly" orientation, may be more understanding of and sympathetic toward people with a "priestly" orientation in another religion than toward persons of the same religion who have differing orientations and, consequently, identities.

III

I may now have brought forward so much that challenges the notion that religion grants stability and certainty to personal identity to have forced the conclusion that the category of "religious person" has no stabilizing content. This is not the case. For one thing, to call someone "religious" is to say that the person gives religion a positive, constitutive place in his or her self-account. This distinguishes that person from people who are non- or antireligious and from people who are very or dogmatically religious. Second, since religious identity entails group or institutional relations, it places a person at least to some extent in identifiable associations. Third, with the disclosure of that person's religious identity, it will be possible to measure the person's identification with or distance from that institution, group, or cohort. Finally, it will become possible to identify that person with one or another of the options in the sets of options that I have cited. We have, then, a map of religious identities so that when a person self-identifies as a religious person and begins to say what that means, the person will be locatable on this map. Indeed, placement or location on this map may well be as important for identifying and comparing religious persons in our society as are common designations like Protestant, Catholic, or Jew.

The Act of Religious Self-Disclosure

The act of self-identifying as a religious person is complicated by a number of conditions and considerations. Some of these would seem to inhibit the act and others to encourage it.

First, disclosing oneself as a religious person occurs in a society that has become increasingly conflicted over the question of religion's appearance in public arenas. On the one side are Americans, most commonly evangelical Protestants, who want religion, especially Christianity, to play more important roles in public American life. On the other side are Americans who want to remove what are thought to be outmoded or inappropriate vestiges of religious language and observance from American public life. While I believe that the general and inclusive religious factors in American public life are more viable and valuable than either of these sides assumes they are, it is true that they tend to pale in relation to the two sides that stand, for opposite reasons, against them, the more specifically religious, especially evangelical Christian, Americans on the one side and the nonreligious and even antireligious Americans on the other. The traditional religious content of American public life has lost much of its force today not only because many religious and nonreligious people join to oppose it but also because it has lost connection with the sapiential form of religion that was prevalent in the early modern period and helped to sponsor the Republic's rise. Its weakened position is due, finally, to the fact that American public religion, like all mediating and accommodating positions, looks less like a position than like a compromise or strategy. In contrast to the inclusive quality of American public religion, the positions standing in opposition to it, one pushing for a more specifically religious America and the other for the nonreligious quality of American public life, seem in contrast to carry the clarity and conviction of viable

positions. Consequently, the conflict is not likely to be resolved by
restoring the standing of the more general and inclusive religious factors built into American identity by its founding culture and public
observances. Since the two sides are opposed both to the tradition
of general and inclusive religious factors in American identity and
to one another, the sides are sharply distinguishable and mutually
intensifying. Given this sharp division between people concerning
the place and role of religion in American life, self-identifying as a
religious person means exposing oneself in an arena of contestation.
It will be seen as actually or potentially abetting one or the other side.

In addition, declaring oneself to be a religious person has an inevitable group-identity effect. To say that I am a religious person
tends to align me with other religious persons and to suggest that I
am more like them than like their nonreligious counterparts. Since
there are religious rights that need to be protected in an increasingly
secular context, especially the right to express religious concerns
and values in public discourses, this alignment with other religious
people is important. However, it may also be the case that a religious person has more in common with many nonreligious people
than with many religious people and, indeed, that such a person may
well be put off by the behaviors and attitudes of many religious people. This consequence of self-identifying as religious, being grouped
with other religious people, may be part of the reason why one so
often meets people who self-identify as "spiritual but not religious."
Religious self-identification carries a strong group-identifying consequence that requires of many people, it seems, an equally strong
measure of distancing from or taking exception to other religious
people.

The third consideration is that disclosing a religious identity
is more and more likely to be viewed as countercultural. This is
because recent American cultural history, as briefly described earlier, is one of the increasing secularization of the general container
of American life and of the frame of American culture as well as
the normalization, even the increasingly normative status, of the
category of "nonreligious person." This tendency or direction of
American society places religious self-disclosures at least to some
degree in the position of being a critique or act of resistance to prevailing cultural currents. As Viswanathan puts it: "Because conversion's [and, I would add, disclosure of religious identity] alliance
with cultural criticism is so apparent, especially when accepted as
an activity rather than a state of mind, there is an obvious tempta-
tion to read conversion [and religious self-disclosure] in general as

originating in motives of critique."[27] While particularity and differ-ence are positive ingredients in the formation of personal identity, identity disclosures that buck what increasingly is assumed by the culture makes that act dissonant. There is, in other words, an ac-cepted repertoire of possible ingredients in the construction of one's identity, and the place of religion in that repertoire is weakening. Of course, this is far truer in some quarters than in others, and it is nowhere more the case than in secular academic settings that have been for generations conditioned by what Casanova describes as the second moment in the disestablishment of religion, namely, the freeing of intellectual and academic life from the interests and directives of religion.

Finally, declaring oneself to be a religious person is fueled by the personal need to be honest with others and with oneself. It is a way of saying, in effect, "while you assume that I am a non-religious per-son, there is something I should tell you." Disclosure is exposure, making oneself vulnerable. There is little if anything to be gained and likely something to be forfeited. Being a religious person sug-gests not fully fitting in, and that may have a negative effect on others. It is motivated, then, by a desire for candor, for honesty. It gets matters straight; it challenges the assumption. It is a way of saying, "This is who I am, and it likely makes me different from you in a way that you cannot fully relate to or understand and in a way toward which you may well have negative attitudes." It is an act by which the desire for truth or candor disrupts the harmony of cultural practices and expectations. It's easier to keep religious identity to oneself or to appear nonreligious. But, despite these restraints, the urge to get it straight, to honor something that deserves to be said, has the upper hand. Given the fact that self-accounts are often, if not usually, constructed to fit occasions or to accomplish a goal, it is noteworthy that self-accounts that give significant place to religion can be taken as motivated not so much to accomplish something as to be truthful. While there may not be anything that is purely hon-est and wholly unmotivated by selfish impulses and aims, it can be said that religious self-identification introduces something unusual to identity theory, namely, the factor of truthfulness in the face of the common interpretation of self-accounts, that is, that they con-form to social expectations or are deployed to advance social stand-ing. In addition, since the force and significance of autobiographical narratives rest, as we have seen, on the relation or rapport between teller and hearer, and since honesty is one if not a major ingredient in this sense of relation or rapport, it seems also possible to say that autobiographies that include positive religious ingredients in personal identity may very well achieve a high level of significance and force, since they will be narratives that attempt to be, to a noticeable degree, honest.

Michel Foucault gives particular attention to the dissonance and cost inherent to telling the truth about oneself. In his analysis of Christian forms of what he calls "technologies of the self," he relates telling the truth about oneself to testifying against oneself, to subverting the continuity between what people think I am and what I actually am. Telling the truth of who I am, then, is an act of self-betrayal and self-punishment. This means, as he says, that "self-punishment and the voluntary expression of the self are bound together."[28] Self-disclosure is tied to the larger belief that the truth of oneself can be told because "the self is that which one can reject."[29] What seems to follow, then, is that self-identifying religiously can become, as to personal identity, an act that at least in part serves to help establish what it means to be both religious and a person.

José Casanova relates what he calls the "deprivatization" of religion in America to the feminist movement, particularly in that both events transgress the boundaries that had been well established in American society between the private and the public arenas. As women emancipated themselves from their confinement to the home and other personal or private arenas, so also religious people have increasingly identified themselves in public as religious and expressed their religious views and values in public discourses.[30] The analogy is a good one, especially because it reveals how separate movements and changes in American life can be mutually stimulating and supportive. I would like to take his lead and suggest that there are also similarities, however faint, between the self-disclosures of American religious identities and the gay and lesbian movement. Because self-identifying as a religious person occurs in a context of social contestation concerning religion in public, because it aligns one with a group with which one may otherwise have little in common, because it implies a social and cultural critique, and because it is an act of truthfulness that is not required and may well have costs, religious self-identification resembles to some degree characteristics and consequences of "coming out" in terms of sexual orientation.

Positioning the Religious in Self-Disclosures

While I hope that the preceding gives helpful background to what lies ahead, a further clarification anticipates the structure of the next part of this study. That clarification concerns the position or location that the person grants religion in a self-disclosure. That position or location is revealed by the fact that religious self-disclosures place religion in the past, in the present, or in the future. So, a person, by way of saying why and how religion is part of who that person is, may point to youth, to matters like home and upbringing, to the present, such as conclusions reached or an affiliation acquired, or the future, to discoveries yet to occur or aspirations yet to be fulfilled.

These three orientations provide the structure for the second part of this study. We will find that fellow Americans who give religion a positive place in their self-accounts reveal a primary orientation to one or another of these three directions. I shall point out, when introducing each of these directions, that the three also relate religious identities to American identities more generally because Americans recognize religion as part of American identity in one or another of these three ways. First, they recognize that religion was an important ingredient in the settling of this land and for the formation of the Republic. Second, they recognize that religious movements, groups, and institutions are visible and consequential components of the contemporary American social landscape. Finally, when we find religious self-disclosures directed toward the future, as though toward the goal of a journey or quest that is still ongoing, this positioning is similar to the general American emphasis on goals that have not been achieved, on missions that are as yet unaccomplished, and on values that have not been realized. While acts of self-disclosure are particular and while they distinguish religious people both from their nonreligious countrymen and from religious Americans of other kinds, they also clarify ways by which being American holds religious and nonreligious and religious people of various kinds in relation to one another.

These three orientations are more external than internal. That is, the reader or hearer of a religious self-disclosure will be able to identity one or the other of these three orientations as prominent or even exclusive in an account. A second, related set of distinctions is more internal than external. When I raise for myself the matter of my own religious identity, as I shall in the third part of this study, the positioning of religious factors will be somewhat different from the ones we just viewed. The first, while oriented to the past, concerns what remains with me due to the influences on me of a religious home and upbringing. What assumptions or beliefs do I retain from that religious past? The second question concerns the present, but it takes the form of decisions made, conclusions drawn, or affiliations clarified. Finally, I look forward to things not as yet realized to which I aspire, and this that is outstanding may well be not so much something to be achieved as it is something desired, particularly a kind of reception or acceptance. It is possible to unify these three internal orientations in religious identity by giving them a single term, namely, *assumption*, a term that includes, along with other meanings, all three of these. Assumption, then, in these three meanings of the term—what is taken for granted, what is constructed, and what is looked or hoped for—will structure the third and final part of this study, the personal account or religious self-disclosure.

II

CRITICAL

4

RELIGIOUS DEBTORS

WE TURN now to nine contemporary American autobiographies, all of them by professional writers for whom religion plays a positive role in their self-accounts. I have put them into three groups not as to what they tell us about religion but as to where they locate it in their accounts. This placement reveals the differing ways in which religion contributes to their identities, and it reveals how religious identities relate to aspects of American identity more generally shared.

I relate texts to one another and to American identity according to whether the writers place religion as a significant aspect of their pasts, as an engaging component in the present, or as a project that looks toward the future. Those who locate religion primarily as part of their past I have grouped under the heading "Religious Debtors." Those who include religion positively as part of the present I have put under the heading "Religious Dwellers." Those for whom religion is oriented primarily toward the future, as a project directed toward a goal yet to be found, I have named "Religious Diviners." This does not mean that these three locations are mutually exclusive. A text can contain more than one, but if so, one of the three locations is more important than the others.

We turn first, then, to the texts by Religious Debtors, a group of Americans who, when they tell us about their lives, include indebtedness to a past that has continuing value for them because, among other things, of its religious content or quality. Religion was a formative aspect of youth, and it has continuing, even if also attenuated, importance. The commendable attributes of parents and other adults, the content of the life of their communities of origin, the early aspirations that shaped their maturation, values they continue to hold, and other significant matters cannot be adequately described without including religion. This indebtedness to the past and to the role of religion in personal formation often carries with it the acknowledgment that the writer is less religious than the people or context recalled from the past. This raises the question of whether or not the positive qualities of the past for which appreciation is expressed can be preserved and passed on if the religious identity of the writer is fainter than that of people who had such a lasting influence. The self-account, among other things, then, becomes a way of bringing at least some of the religious qualities of the past into the present, if only to give them a measure of deserved recognition. The implication is that this religious past ought not to be forgotten, that the religious content of early life should be appreciated and the values drawn from it preserved even if, at the time of writing, the religion more fully is not.

Texts by Religious Debtors alert us to the role that religion plays in American identity more generally because as Americans we are all indebted to a past that contained formative religious components. The values incorporated within our political, legal, and even economic life can be traced, in part, to religious sources. Much of the debate concerning the role of religion in public life these days turns not so much on the question of the values themselves as on whether or not these values can be retained without retaining or reinstating their religious sources, with some people arguing that public life needs to be more explicitly religious and others that values can be retained even when purged of their religious traces.

In addition, many Americans, due to processes we already have considered, very likely have parents who were more religious than they themselves are. True, this pattern is challenged by the fact that in recent decades religion has either become a more important part of people's lives or people have become more willing to acknowledge its importance, so that we can encounter parents whose children are more religious than they are. But it also can be said that a more common awareness of Americans is that they are not as religious as their parents and grandparents were and that they are put to the task of retaining values in their own lives that are part of their identities even if their religious identities relative to earlier generations are diluted and even largely discarded.

One of the reasons why Americans, even if religiously unaffiliated, generally regard religion with respect is that they know religion was a major factor in the lives of earlier generations in their own families and for the Republic as a whole. While religion in our country has also caused problems, conflicts, and harm, it is largely viewed favorably, and it tends to be so viewed, among other reasons, because Americans see it as having contributed positively to their family histories, to the formation of the Republic, and to the enrichment of American cultural history. Continuity exits, then, between American identity more generally and the particular cases at which we now shall look.

Maya Angelou

> People whose history and future were threatened each day by extinction considered that it was only by divine intervention that they were able to live at all.
>
> —ANGELOU, *I Know Why the Caged Bird Sings*

The position from which Maya Angelou narrates her early youth in *I Know Why the Caged Bird Sings* is clearly elevated above the time of the past that she recalls. While she does not speak directly about that position, she says enough to clarify it. Approximately halfway through her narrative, she shares with her reader something to which she seems to have given a good bit of thought. After narrating a rather routine exchange between her grandmother and a man who comes into her grandmother's store, she rather abruptly tells us, "I find it interesting that the meanest life, the poorest existence, is attributed to God's will, but as human beings become more affluent, as their living standard and style begin to ascend the material scale, God descends the scale of responsibility at a commensurate speed."[1] The comment, rather than a gratuitous homily, calls attention to something that she may herself have experienced and may well think is duplicated in the lives of at least some of her readers, namely, that increased prosperity, sophistication, and security often produce amnesia concerning the religious content of where one has come from. Angelou suggests, then, that narrating her early years is designed, among other things, to avoid or redress this common fault.

Angelou's comment also has a wider significance. Writing during a time of her emerging distinction among American writers, she not only is repaying a debt to the religious quality of her past but also is asking her readers, especially those African Americans who have achieved greater financial security and social strength than their parents knew, to see the past not only as something from which to be delivered but also as a resource that should be retrieved and retained. Primarily, the resources that should not be left behind are grounded in a religious sense of what it takes to live responsibly and responsively in a complex and harsh world and to allow that world, not only in spite of or apart from but also in the face of its difficulties, to be positively transformed. We should look at the painful characteristics of the world Angelou narrates before turning to the religious understandings and practices that transform it into a realm of affirmation and hope.

I

The world of Maya Angelou's girlhood, from age three to seventeen, is complicated by the fact that she lives in at least three different places during that formative period. The first place is Stamps, Arkansas, to which she and her brother, Bailey, are sent when she is three and he is four. The adult writer looks back at that trauma tenderly, noting that she and Bailey often cried together and considered themselves to be "unwanted children." They were sent by separated parents who, as we see later, had lifestyles that could not readily accommodate young children. The vivid memory of being shipped to Stamps but then of being received and cared for there seems to account in part for the attachment to that location that Angelou affirms.

St. Louis, the second location, although marking less than a year of her life, contrasts powerfully and negatively with Stamps. Living there with her mother and extended family, she encounters the complexities of her family and of urban life. Her grandmother is German, her grandfather is not religious, and her uncles seem bound together by their struggles with opponents and adversity. Most importantly, her mother, whom she describes as glamorous, is away much of the time. This brings on a set of traumatic events in the account, particularly her sexual encounters as a girl of eight with her mother's boyfriend, contacts that end with her being raped by him. These events culminate first in a trial during which she testifies, out of fear, untruthfully; second, in the death of her assailant, undoubtedly at the hands of her uncles; and third, in her withdrawal into silence and her return to Stamps.

The third location, California, combines and complicates some of the characteristics of life in Stamps and St. Louis. She lives in Los Angles with her father and discovers that he deploys his physical attractiveness and personal charm toward leading a life of irresponsibility, particularly in his relations with women. Her time with him leads to her departure amidst the violence that results from his girlfriend's calling Maya's mother a whore. San Francisco, where she lives with her mother, is a setting more positively evaluated. She has a productive relation with one of her high school teachers, manages to be the first black employee on San Francisco's streetcars, experiences sexual awakening, becomes pregnant, and, primarily in the context of these events, develops a more mature and positive relationship with her mother. California, then, represents, by its two major cities, a combination of ingredients that have more singular, intense, and contrasting forms in Stamps and St. Louis.

Her early life, complicated by three locations, is also socially treacherous. In Stamps, her grandmother's store forms a center for the black community, and from that position she views her world as menaced by white social forces that surround and stand in opposition to it. She has a strong sense of having grown up in the "crossfire" not only of white hatred for blacks but also masculine prejudice toward women and the lack of material resources among black people to protect themselves from the intimidation and harassment of whites. It is not a surprise that as a young girl she thinks of her racial identity as the result of a curse and holds a negative assessment of her female body.

Particular experiences in Stamps epitomize the harshness of this setting. For example, she observes the difficult lives of her black neighbors when they come into her grandmother's store. They frequently turn to her grandmother for advice and economic help, and their reliance gives her grandmother stature in Maya's eyes. She records the threat to her uncle posed by white men hunting for what they think was the black perpetrator of a sexual crime, and she describes the rude exposure that a group of rough white girls inflict on her grandmother. In general, her years in Stamps are shaped by the constant realization that life is made difficult and dangerous because of the position she shares with the other black people.

When one adds to these events in Stamps what Angelou encounters in St. Louis and Los Angeles, the picture becomes even more grim and complicated. Coping with the negative characteristics of her social environment is aggravated by her relations with her parents. On the one hand, she admires their beauty, charm, and worldliness. But they also, especially her father, are unavailable to her, especially when needed, and unreliable, even questionable, in their behaviors. Forced to care for her father during her trip with him to Mexico and to protect her mother, she is cast into parental roles relative to her parents. While her parents are personally intriguing, they provide neither positive alternatives to the complex and dangerous social world nor models for coping with it.

II

Given the complexities and harshness of events and circumstances in her early years, an implied question arises, one to which the narrative gives an answer. How was it possible for a young girl reared under such conditions and undergoing such negative experiences not only to survive but also to achieve the position from which this self-account is written? The primary answer is that this harsh, confined, and deprived background also contained positive resources, and these resources, while concentrated in Stamps, are not unique to it but likely are shared in the backgrounds of other Americans, especially African Americans.

The first of these positive aspects of life in Stamps is provided by the store and its central and refuge-like position in the black community. Although Maya had no place of her own within the store or its attached dwelling that she could personalize, she organizes her personal world around this positive center. Her attitude toward the store is supported by the evaluation of it expressed by its customers. They relate to it and to her grandmother in an appreciative way. Tending the store also counters her strong tendencies to withdraw, especially into an imaginary world, as she does while living in St. Louis. While not everything that comes through the door is positive, much of what does is. And her accommodating stance, her having to adjust to whatever comes into her life, seems to be positively valued.

Particular people who are part of her life in Stamps also serve as positive resources. Her brother is one. The two children are very close, and Bailey's departure from their mother's home toward the end of the narrative is difficult for Maya. She values Bailey so highly that she thinks herself an inadequate sister to him. The reason she gives for helping to provide Bailey privacy for his sexual encounters with Joyce is that Joyce might well be for him "the sister who wasn't moody and withdrawing, and teary and tender-hearted" (150).

While none of her teachers in Stamps seem, surprisingly, to have been important cultural resources for her, Mrs. Bertha Flowers introduced her to a higher cultural and social level. Something of an aristocrat among the black inhabitants of Stamps, Mrs. Flowers's attentions to Maya deliver her from the damaged state of mind and self-imposed silence brought with her on returning from St. Louis. She records several examples of Mrs. Flowers's influence: exposing Maya to heretofore unknown levels of possible achievement and to a new sense, as she tells us, that being a Negro is something of which she could be proud, treating her as a person and not simply as

Bailey's little sister, and cultivating and extending her interests in literature.

However, it is her grandmother who stands out as the resource in Stamps most to be acknowledged and appreciated. Indeed, the text can be read as a lyrical tribute to the stature, resilience, shrewdness, and spiritual richness of this woman. While it could be said that her grandmother epitomizes potentials more generally to be found in African American communities and in their caring women, Maya's grandmother is also extraordinary. Unassuming but determined, oriented to spiritual things but reliable regarding the practicalities of life, demanding but gentle, this woman rises in the narrative not only as a figure to admire but as an example, if not an epitome, of all those women who, called on to be caregivers for the children of their own less responsible or disabled offspring, do so not only with adequacy but with genuine wisdom and love.

Maya's high estimation of her grandmother, although mostly implied, is supported by the estimation of her in the community, and it is evidenced in ways in which her grandmother responds to a variety of difficult challenges. Three examples come immediately to mind. The first is how she handles the taunting of the lower-class white girls with a calm dignity, relying on the strength given her by singing gospel songs. Another is the beautiful job she does in helping Mr. Taylor work through the spiritual and emotional impasse caused by his wife's death. A third is the persistence and the sense of justice that propel her to seek help from the white, disdainful dentist when driven to do so by Maya's toothaches.

A third major set of positive resources in Stamps is indicated by the several celebrative occasions that Angelou narrates. The narrative begins with Easter morning, her special dress, and the Easter hymns. Another is the exuberant, even chaotic church service in which Sister Monroe is carried away by the sermon, shouting "preach it" to the minister and convulsing the children in laughter. A third, more elaborated example is the revival that brings people from various churches and also, therefore, somewhat differing social/economic conditions together under one tent. The service is narrated in detail: the liturgy, the scripture, the sermon, and the transforming effects of the event on the participants. These three occasions find their culmination in a fourth, the eighth-grade graduation ceremony. The preparation for the event, the demoralizing effect on the assembly of the white administrator's speech, and the rallying of the black people to a recovered sense of joy and richness, particularly by singing "Lift Every Voice and Sing," are all described in detail. These are memorable events not only for the author but also for her readers.[2]

The resources in her past, while lodged principally in Stamps, are not limited to it. While St. Louis is primarily negative, it was a place in which her imaginative and literary life was nourished. More, she has respect for her tough uncles and is "thrilled" by their meanness. In general she learns to respect the ways in which black shrewdness can be used to outwit white, especially greedy, people, the ways, especially, by which black men turn difficult and complex circumstances to their own benefit. As also in her descriptions of her brother and father, Angelou seems aware of the particular difficulties imposed on black men in a racist society and appreciative of the ways in which they counter and compensate for such indignities.[3]

Even more, California offers positive resources. The trip to Mexico allows her to take responsibility for her own, as well as her father's, well-being. Her religiously grounded belief, brought with her from Stamps, that rules and keeping them are basic to a positive life, as is true for the community of homeless youth living in a junkyard, is confirmed. And she has an appreciation for the personality of San Francisco, a personality that she would like to have herself. The city is a place of beauty, energy, and freedom. It is there that she becomes aware of "being aware." And this new awareness leads to her sexual initiation, pregnancy, and motherhood.

III

The religious character of the past that Maya Angelou narrates is complicated by the fact that those resources are found primarily in her father's family, especially, of course, in her paternal grandmother, and not in the family of her mother, whose parents appear to be non-religious. In the course of her narrative, her growing estrangement and final rejection of her father finds its counterpart in the increased sense of rapport that develops, especially in regard to sexuality and motherhood, with her mother. This developed relation to her mother and her growing self-esteem seem also to enable her to return in her self-account to her father's family in order to reappropriate the religious resources that her mother does not provide. The principal location of the religious ingredients that become part of her identity is the life in Stamps provided her by her paternal grandmother.

Angelou constructs her life in Stamps religiously. That is, she conveys a sense of her world as housed within something that upholds and periodically restores it. For example, she views the frame of each day, both the morning and the evening, religiously. Of the day's beginning, she says, "the morning sounds and smells were touched with the supernatural" (8), and of the evening, she says, "It seemed that the peace of a day's ending was an assurance that the covenant God made with children, Negroes and the crippled was still in effect" (16). In addition, she lives in an enchanted world. She believes in "haunts" and ghosts and "thangs" (166) and finds "enchantment" in the poems and novels that Mrs. Flowers gives her to read. She admits, while writing her account, that she has tried to "search behind the sophistication of years" for the sense of enchantment that was woven into her youthful life in Stamps and that, at least to some extent, as an adult she has lost (100). Susceptibility, a sense of something more, and exposure or vulnerability to an unseen reality are basic to the religious character of her early life and are worth retrieving and retaining.

The religious quality of her past is made more explicit by the attitudes and teachings of her grandmother, whom Maya calls "super-religious." In morning prayers her grandmother gives thanks for life. She sings songs of glory when confronted by meanness. She "was so good and righteous she could command the fretful spirits, as Jesus had commanded the sea, 'Peace, be still'" (168). When Bailey queries her on the hatred that whites have for black people, she turns to the Bible, to Moses and Daniel. She combines patience, a waiting for the Lord, with personal resourcefulness, persistence, and craftiness. Rather than a compensation for weakness or a distraction from reality, her grandmother's faith forms a major part of her strength and deepens her relation to her context. This faith is confirmed by the ingrained and almost habitual way in which it functions in her grandmother's life, by the respect that she enjoys from other people in regard to it, by the strength and courage by which she encounters life, and by the genuine love and care that she gives to the daily tasks of raising two grandchildren.

But it seems that the most important religious component of Maya's early life lies in occasions when negative conditions are positively transformed. This pattern occurs in large and small ways and frames the narrative as a whole. Beginning with the Easter morning service, which celebrates the triumph of new life over suffering and death, and ending in motherhood, the narrative is a series of positive outcomes arising from negative conditions and events. This pattern seems also to warrant writing the narrative, since the position of the author is a positive outcome to the ambiguities and difficulties of the past.

The pattern of transformation and restoration is not simply a device, a convention required by narrative coherence and imposed by Angelou on her material. It is deeply rooted in the life and community she recalls. The clearest instance of it is the transformation of the graduation ceremony by singing the Black National Anthem. Negative conditions are not simply countered by a positive contrary but also transformed by the positive contrary that is invoked. She speaks directly and forcefully to this potential for positive transformations of negative conditions in *The Heart of a Woman:*

> We, the black people, the most displaced, the poorest, the most maligned and scourged, we had the glorious task of reclaiming the soul and saving the honor of the country. We, the most hated, must take hate into our hands and by the miracle of love, turn loathing into love. We the most feared and apprehensive, must take fear and by love, change it into hope. We, who die daily in large and small ways, must take the demon death and turn it into Life.[4]

The capacity for the transformation of circumstances, while not directly designated by her as religious, clearly has ties to the spiritual resources of the culture and its people.

This pattern structures the revival meeting as well. Maya is intrigued by the fact that people who had labored all day in the cotton fields sat on the edges of their seats, their faces expectant, showing "the delight of their souls" and a confidence inspired by the assurances of justice and the possibility for revenge. The revival rests on and inspires the religious belief that the present time of pain, injustice, and toil not only will be redeemed but also will yield to a truer reality in which justice has its rightful say.[5]

Events such as these are not to be taken lightly. They depend for one thing on what could be called a sense of occasion, a sense that something can and will happen, a sense of expectation. But what will happen is not simply something for which one waits. A person or a group can make something of what there is, even when what there is has little positive to offer. The outcome of such occasions reverses what was. Rather than a repression of the difficult and unsightly, it arises from a faith that, however dark things may be or become, there is something more and other to counteract them, that the negative anticipates its contrary, and that the positive can and will emerge or be called on to make its presence felt.

The cultural, moral or spiritual, and specifically Christian events, beliefs, and language of the narrative, while not reducible to a single dynamic, certainly find their residence and warrants within a unified whole. It is not so much that the Easter worship service that begins the narrative confers a religiously transforming consequence on other events, as though a specific Resurrection allows all deathlike moments to be countered and transformed. Rather, it is that Easter is one, although a major, instance of what more generally is true and experiential, namely, that "out of the gloomy past, till now we stand at last / Where the white gleam of our bright star is cast."

IV

It is understandable that some African American writers, such as Zora Neale Hurston and Richard Wright, associate religion with the time of confinement and oppression, a time gradually being left behind on the way to greater freedom and sophistication. It would be understandable that a past so difficult would be viewed as needing, along with its religious component, to be left behind because of its limits and evils. But Angelou implies that present advancements owe a great deal to the past, both in its harshly negative and in its positive, especially religious, qualities, and that it should be retrieved and retained. This affirmation may well be related to the fact that Angelou wrote the narrative on her way toward recovery from the trauma of the assassination of Martin Luther King, someone she had come to know well and in whose program, which, of course, drew heavily on African American Christianity, she had begun to work.

Writing as an act of retrieval is not simply an affirmation that we cannot be who we are if we forget where and what we have been. It is also a belief that only by facing the negative can creative and restorative potentials be recognized and released. Maya Angelou has done that. Facing the realities of her past, the difficulties of growing up as a black girl in a world dominated by whites and males, and especially facing the horror both of being sexually assaulted and of taking, however unwarranted, a degree of responsibility for that event, the narrator testifies to the reality to which faith gives access: that, in confronting evil with expectation, good can be drawn out or will follow from it. In this and her other books, Angelou is able to affirm both her own strength and resiliency and that of African American people without blunting her depictions of the adversities and cruelties that arise from being black in American society. Her narrative is an account of the working out or recognizing in the details of life patterns of transformation by which what was difficult and conflicted in personal and communal experience was and can be reconstituted and made whole.

At the end of her chapter on the transformation of the graduation ceremony, an event in which the "depths had been icy and dark, but now a bright sun spoke to our souls" and in which "I was no longer simply a member of the proud graduating class of 1940; I was a proud member of the wonderful, beautiful Negro race," she writes, "Oh, Black known and unknown poets, how often have your auctioned pains sustained us?" Angelou concludes, "we survive in exact relationship to the dedication of our poets (include preachers, musicians and blues singers)" (184). I take these deliberately crafted lines to mean that the ability to keep alive the expectation and reality that light can be drawn out of darkness and that joy will return in the morning depends on the work of black poets. Among those poets, the author rightfully, although implicitly, assumes her own place.

Finally, Angelou's narrative is a gift to her youthful victimized self, the eight-year-old girl who suffered both assault and the self-inflicted pain of misplaced blame. The trauma of self-blame is religiously reinforced; she feels rejected by Christ: "I had sold myself to the Devil and there could be no escape" (87). Not only the sexual abuse but also the resulting circumstances—the trial, the self-accusations, the murder of the perpetrator, and her self-imposed silence—are painful to recall and difficult to read. The narrative turns to and retrieves that hurt and rejected child and includes her in the life of the successful and compassionate adult.

I think it is fair to say that Angelou, in her frank inclusions of her robust sexual life in her other writings, seems also to imply that this early trauma, rather than be allowed to cast her sexuality in a negative dress, was altered by the sexual aspects of her mature identity. This accounts for the fact that the concluding episodes of the narrative describe not so much a spiritual or religious as a physical and sexual development.[6] While otherwise the question could arise as to whether, by describing the sexual events of her childhood in such detail, she goes beyond the expected limits of textual intimacy, it becomes clear that this part of the narrative is required because it forms the negative conditions that, by the end of the narrative, are transformed into positive sexual and reproductive events.

This reclaiming of her sexually traumatized childhood self, while extraordinary, is also not separate from the religious indebtedness that the narrative reveals. Along with all else that the narrative contains and accomplishes, the acknowledgment of religious indebtedness forms the inclusive context. Angelou makes clear, I think, not only how her grandmother's strength and wisdom are inseparable from her Christian faith but also how Angelou as a growing girl lived in a world largely structured and made resonant by that faith. Given the fact that Christianity can also be read as a context and warrant for white oppression of her people and male abuse of girls and women, this acknowledgment at the hand of a person with artistic and social status in contemporary America is no small thing. A direct connection is drawn between positive outcomes and that faith.

Toward the end of the narrative, Angelou affirms an additional point that has religious roots, namely, that a life grounded or framed by moral law preserves the life and light that can be found in the face of difficulty. With her mother and baby she affirms that "if you're for the right thing, then you do it without thinking" (289). This is a continuation of her belief as a young girl that if she knew and kept all the laws in Deuteronomy, her life would be protected. The religiously meaningful aspects of her early life are to be found not only in occasional transformations of the kind she narrates but also in a life of observance, a life safeguarded by law.

While it is important to give adequate place to the role of religion in Angelou's upbringing and identity, I think it is also fair to say that being black and being a woman may well be more important to her identity than religion. The specifically Christian character of her religious identity yields to a more general and integrated spirituality. She says at one point, for example, "Oh, there was no doubt that we were spiritual" and "as for spirituality, we were Christians."[7] The relations between cultural, generally spiritual, and specifically Christian aspects of her background are not directly explored by the narrative. I take this as her assumption that these resources blend into and reinforce one another. The resiliency and strength of African Americans has a cultural, spiritual, and specifically Christian content that, for her, should be recalled and retained. A personal and communal religious indebtedness is central to Angelou's identity and self-account.

Philip Roth

Growing up Jewish as I did and growing up American seemed to me indistinguishable.

—ROTH, *The Facts: A Novelist's Autobiography*

It is difficult to think of a living American writer who has worked more creatively with personal identity and self-accounts than has

Roth. His characters, narrators, and Roth himself slip into and oppose one another in what is almost a hall of mirrors, an amusing but
also deadly serious encounter with many of the questions we already
have considered concerning the challenges and ambiguities of saying
who we are. Roth's sophisticated and self-conscious involvement
in questions of identity is very clear in the text upon which I shall
focus, *The Facts.*

Roth undermines the reliability of his self-account by submitting
it to the criticism of one of his major fictional characters and narrators, Zukerman, who, after all, knows Roth as well as anybody.
However, Zukerman is no oracle; his own credibility can be challenged by the fact that he owes his existence, if that's the right word,
to Roth's fiction and can be counted on, therefore, to value fiction
more highly than Roth's attempt in this text to counter fiction with
facts. Zukerman thinks that in this attempt Roth is less truthful
regarding the past than he is in his fiction.

This is no small issue. As we have seen, reliability is crucial to intimacy, and intimacy gives rise in self-accounts to rapport between
the teller and the reader. By distinguishing reliability and truthfulness, which are ethical considerations, from aesthetic interests,
Zukerman is entering the ring of combat between Roth and his Jewish critics who lodge moral accusations against Roth's art.[8] While
Roth seeks honesty because he is tired of the masks, evasions, and
distances required by fiction, he primarily wants to defend and even
to justify himself, an aim, as earlier we saw, not uncommon in writing of this kind. He has been faulted for having treated his Jewish origins, including his family, disrespectfully, mostly by treating them
comically. Zukerman implies that Roth's two goals of being honest
or sticking to the facts and of defending or even justifying himself
are potentially, if not unavoidably, at odds with one another.

Roth also acknowledges that writing autobiography can be a form
of self-preoccupation and exhibitionism, one of the hazards in this
kind of writing. He places himself, on that score, somewhere between
the self-advertising Norman Mailer and the reclusive J. D. Salinger
among American Jewish writers. He sharpens the point about exhibitionism by including a response to the text from Zukerman's wife,
who interprets what she reads as Roth's obsessing about his Jewish
identity, subjecting everything and everyone in his life, including
himself, to material he can write about, and working hard to make
his life interesting both to himself and to others (192).

Despite the announced intention of the text to distinguish facts
from their aesthetic transformation into fiction, Roth suggests that

this cannot so easily be done. Zukerman and his wife view what Roth makes of himself in his autobiography to be no less a construction than what he makes of his life, howbeit under other names, in his fiction (164). The connections, characterizations, and self-presentations required by historical narratives are also fictional. By including Zukerman's critique, primarily that autobiography is "the most manipulative of all literary forms" (172), Roth bolsters his position regarding truth and honesty in the eye of his reader. But the question also arises whether, by leaving the critique to Zukerman, by not, that is, incorporating self-criticism more directly into his account, he also weakens the possibility of creating with the reader a rapport that requires honesty.

I

Zukerman and his wife, in their roles as Roth's counter-selves, are continuous with the dynamic of identity by contrast and opposition that appears structurally in the text; contraries and conflicts form recurring ingredients in the narrative and are presented as crucial to Roth's identity. These counters or oppositions can be placed in three arenas: social, personal, and ontological.

Roth narrates a strong sense that his social identity is formed largely by an arena whose boundaries separate Jews from non-Jews. In his youth he had to be aware of the threat to his well-being posed by the young gentile ruffians who carried out postgame "pogroms" when his school played teams away from home. He also is aware that his father worked in a firm entirely managed by gentiles. At Bucknell University and at the University of Chicago, he feels obliged to take his Jewish identity into account because these settings, especially Bucknell, were dominated by non-Jews. The outcomes of these contrary dynamics for his identity are primarily positive. The surrounding gentile world, as it does especially at the University of Chicago, gives his Jewish identity particularity without making it problematic.

In the personal arena of his life, his wife, Josie, provides the major counter-self, since her American identity is so different from his own. Much of the narrative is an accounting of how his relationship with her occurred, the complexities and frustrations it created, and why Roth's relief, when Josie dies, is justified. While the attacks on him by observant and orthodox Jewish readers at Yeshiva University are encountered in a social arena, they also have for him a personal impact. Their strongly negative response to Roth's fiction seems to strike home, suggesting that Roth is not fully at ease with his having treated his family and other Jews comically and with having used them as material for his professional and, yes, commercial designs. His almost insistently positive depiction in *The Facts* of the Jewish character of his family of origins, his community, and his own formation, while genuine, is also mustered to defend himself against the charges brought against him. Even more, he seems to validate his own way of being Jewish in contrast to that of the Jews at Yeshiva University, who are as unlike him, he tells us, as are devout Catholics (125). Indeed, he feels, during the Yeshiva session, more closely related to his fellow panelist Ralph Ellison than to these fellow Jews. The social arena of Roth's life defers, therefore, to the personal.

The ontological arena of his life is even more antagonistic. There is ample reference, for example, to sickness and death. He writes his autobiography because he had encountered a life-threatening illness and had suffered a physical and emotional "breakdown." He begins his narrative not with his birth or early years but with himself at the age of eleven, when his father suffered a life-threatening illness. At the time of writing, his mother's death is a fresh and painful memory, and his father's brother, who for forty years was estranged from the family, also is dying. Aging, sickness, and death are constants in Roth's work, and they figure largely as well in this text. While the ontological arena looms large, it is narrated more in its personal location and consequences than in its wider locations or implications. As he says, a burst appendix and the long, dicey recovery can heighten "tremendously your respect for the place of chance in an individual destiny" (138).

All of these contraries, while threatening, become stimulants to Roth's reflection on, interpretation of, and justification of his life. Rather than ignore or repress them, he turns to these counters as though toward antagonists with whom he struggles. Out of that struggle, his identity, though scarred, arises.

II

When Roth responds to his detractors by self-identifying as a Jew and by affirming his positive relationship with, admiration of, and gratitude for his Jewish family and upbringing, Roth also presents his way of being Jewish as not only inherently suitable but even as preferable to that of Jews around him, particularly those who attack him. He does this, first of all, by his emphasis on being fully American. He views himself as a Jew whose identity was formed in an American context uncompromised, as he thinks may well be the American identity of many contemporary Jews, by loyalty to the state of Israel and by sentimental depictions of Jewish life in the villages of eastern Europe. He is also an avid baseball fan, which he describes as his participation in the great American religion. He identifies with the strong post–World War II national pride and shared "belief in the boundlessness of the democracy in which we lived and to which we belonged" (123). While he admires his parents for their ability to remain unmistakably Jewish, he admires them also for their ability to advance themselves in non-Jewish America, the way his father rose to a position of responsibility in a gentile firm and the way his mother, during the interview at Bucknell, appeared "thoroughly Americanized" (44). Finally, in his literary studies he is drawn to the canon of American literature, especially to Henry James, a model whose influence on him was so strong that he later had to struggle to free himself from it. It should be noted in passing as well that the influence of James, while described more in aesthetic than in cultural terms, can also, it would seem, be attributed to the attention drawn by the fiction of James to cultural differences and conflicts.

Becoming an American writer, then, is a crucial component of Roth's emerging identity. At Bucknell a distinction arose that was in importance equal for him to the distinction between Jewish and gentile students, namely, the distinction between students interested in earning money and students with career interests in literature and the arts. Roth identifies himself positively with cultural capital in opposition to those oriented toward financial capital. This identification is secured at Bucknell by friendship with Robert Maurer, his English instructor, who, with his wife, provides a model for a life rich in cultural rather than material content but not given over to bohemian, antisocial, or politically radical views. This line of identification continues at the University of Chicago, where he associates with Jewish intellectuals. An important realization for his formation as a writer is that he could, rather than try to write like non-Jewish Americans, retrieve and depict his Jewish background by and in his art. He identifies himself with the belief that literature raises the commonplace to a higher level, and he defines this aesthetic enterprise as, if not redemptive or religious, at least "spiritual" (61). He also thinks of academia as a free location elevated above ordinary and compromising social conflicts and confinements. His writing, by raising the particularity of Jewish experience to the level of broader American life, could become thereby quintessentially American (37). Roth seems to present his compound identity as a Jewish American writer as making him not merely different from the Jews who attacked him but superior to and a possible model for them.

Roth's deliberate retrieval of his Jewish background forms a major component of his professional identity, then, because he affirms the value of Jewish life by choosing it as material for his fiction. By writing comically about it, he gives non-Jewish Americans access to that material albeit at the price of discounting the particular difficulties of being Jewish in a largely non-Jewish society. Roth defends this use of Jewish material. For one thing, being Jewish is not something he takes lightly; it is not something, for example, that an outsider, like Josie, can duplicate. Being Jewish is a deeply rooted destiny. Also, his home and background, even when treated comically, are presented as unmistakably and faithfully Jewish. Finally, being Jewish and treating being Jewish comically have much to do with one another. Healthy, mature, and authentic Judaism, which Roth by implication claims for himself, balances a serious with a comic stance, self-defense with self-disparagement. The firmness of Jewish identity in an American and mainly non-Jewish context is confirmed, Roth implies, by his willingness to treat Jewish life and himself as he does.

The accusation that by depicting Jewish Americans in ways that accommodate non-Jewish readers he has depicted Jews as crude and worthy of his readers' disdain is not easily put to rest. Added to it is the point of Zukerman's wife that Roth's use of Jewish material for his writing has become an obsession, that it controls him more than he controls it. Even more telling, perhaps, is Zukerman's point that by combining the Jewish and non-Jewish sides of his identity he has threatened that identity's unity, that the result is unstable, and that, at fifty-five, Roth may still be unclear or uncertain about who he is (162, 164).

Defending himself is one of the unifying intentions of the text because the accusations seem to have aroused uncertainty within himself regarding his entire life-project. Writing this and subsequent self-accounts, then, furthers his attempt to unify differing and even conflicting parts of himself. The question is whether the religious content of his background and of the accusations against him is more important to him than it can be made to be for his wider audience, especially his non-Jewish and non-religious Jewish readers.

III

When Roth turns to his family of origin in order, as he says, "to recover what I had lost" (5), it is a move made necessary by his

"breakdown" in 1987. It is not an easy task because he must combine a high regard for his Jewish family life and upbringing while
also both justifying his removal from it and defending, if not advocating, the hybrid form of identity that he has developed.

His first intention is to make clear that religion and his parents are
closely tied. They were children of Orthodox Jews, and his father's
father trained as a rabbi. While able to make their way in their contacts with non-Jewish people, Roth's parents do not seem to have
thought of themselves as less Jewish or less religious than their parents. The fact that Roth affirms their religious identity, despite their
need for strategies of survival in dealing positively with non-Jews,
indicates that who they were and what he owes them are inseparable
from their being religious. The religious character of his home is
taken for granted, and the lesson it seems to teach but that Roth does
not adopt is that Jews can enter and do well in the non-Jewish world
without discarding or even compromising their religious identity.

The religious identity of his home is also expressed by the fact,
as he acknowledges, that in Judaism the family of origin is itself a
religious datum: "*Hear, O Israel, the family is God, the family is
One*" (14). This parody of the *Shema* makes the point unmistakably,
although also humorously, clear. Acts of devotion and observance
center the life of the Jewish family, but the site for that centering is
itself already religiously significant. Roth's mother keeps a kosher
kitchen, lights the Sabbath candles, and observes the holy days. Of
course she does: "being a Jew among Jews was, simply, one of her
deepest pleasures" (44). Roth's father was also devout, although that
point is made more sharply in *Patrimony* than in *The Facts*. There
it is clear that his father faithfully used the tefillin of Roth's grandfather. Roth regrets that his father did not pass the tefillin on to
him, since Roth "may well have cherished them, especially after
his death."[9] I can only conclude that his father did not because he
recognized that a break had been made by Roth, that the tefillin,
having a religious and not only a personal, sentimental, or cultural
standing and significance, could not be passed on to the son without
condoning a change in their status and meaning.

The religious content of his home life became part of Roth's
identity. He had three years of Hebrew School, learned to read the
Hebrew Bible, and underwent bar mitzvah. He even suggests that his
sense of the rootedness or profundity of Jewish identity is tied to its
religious qualities. "To me," he says, "being a Jew had to do with a
real historical predicament into which you were born and not with
some identity you chose to don after reading a dozen books" (126).

And, he tells us, when he had a brush with death at the age of thirty-four, he returned to his religious youth as to a resource.

However, Roth at the same time wants to affirm that being religious is not what matters in his being Jewish. We are on firm ground by taking as accurate Zukerman's comment that Roth attempts to separate an ethnic from a religious Jewish identity, "to leave Jewish identification behind in a religious sense but retain it in an ethnic sense" (165). The question arises whether significant content will be left to Judaism if its religious character is discarded. Roth admits in *Patrimony* that, to his dismay, his nephews, who were raised in an entirely secular ethos, lacked knowledge of Judaism and were Jews in name only.[10] Roth also seems to slight the fact that, while Jews also differ from one another religiously, these differences are not as great as the differences between them in terms of their ethnic or cultural identities. To be Jewish is to identify not so much with a culture or ethos as to identify with Jewish people who may be more religiously than culturally or ethnically alike. The primacy of religion over culture is fortified by the fact that in Judaism the Jewish people themselves form a site of the sacred and are themselves to be regarded as set apart. However valid Roth's point may be that being Jewish and self-satirizing at the same time is part of Jewish identity, the comical side counts on a durability in Jewish identity that is also religiously secured. Roth's orthodox critics seem to sense that he uses his Jewish material not only for artistic but also for commercial reasons, making Jewish people available to a non-Jewish market and thereby compromising their religious integrity. While Roth insists that he is treating Jewish material as an insider, he does not seem adequately to appreciate the point that treating Jews as he does could understandably be seen by religious Jews as profanation. What may well conceal this from him is his high modernist belief in the sacrality of art. He seems to think that the sacrality of art trumps the sacrality of the people and may even impart sacrality to them, a belief in the status and force of art that he may well have drawn from his early and dominant literary model, Henry James.

While Roth insists that being religious is not what matters in his Jewish identity, his reader may begin to think that religion is more important for him than he recognizes. For example, while he wants to present his relation to his parents positively in order to counter the objection that he has treated them in his fiction disrespectfully, his homage to his parents could well be more than an act of personal gratitude and respect for them, a filial obligation. It could also be a religious act of observing the commandment to honor his father and his mother. To honor them also implicates him religiously, since by doing justice to the religious content of their identities and lives and by honoring them he also fulfills a religious obligation.

Second, Judaism tends, more than Christianity, to construe salvation as deliverance from one's enemies. While Judaism shares with Christianity an understanding that salvation is also being delivered from oneself, that is, from one's sins, in Judaism deliverance from enemies and other threats is more important. Indeed, Roth construes his life as a series of deliverances (77, 160) and constructs his account accordingly: deliverances from the gentile ruffians in his youth, from the confinements of his background, from a life-threatening illness in 1967, from his "breakdown," and from his relationship with Josie, for example. The last of these is particularly clear. He calls the driver of the car in which she was killed "my emancipator" (149), and he says of Josie's death, "I felt absolutely nothing about her dying at thirty-nine other than immeasurable relief" (153). He calls this relief a "personal resurrection" (159). Indeed, Roth took up with Josie in the first place because she struck him as a victim, someone who put him into the role of deliverer.[11] In this context also the act of autobiographical writing becomes a religious exercise, a recognition of his deliveries, especially of his having been restored to himself after the threats to his identity and integrity that Josie posed are lifted.

One could argue that these religious matters, while important to his account, pale in relation to the enormously important and more ontological matters of life and survival. Roth seems not only to contend that religion is not what matters in his Jewish identity but also that his Jewish identity is not what matters in his survival. Can it be said that, if he is not successful in separating his religious from his cultural Jewish identity, he is successful in separating his Jewish identity from the more important matter of personal survival and integrity in the face of aging, sickness, and death? Roth, by emphasizing the ontological arena, especially sickness, death, and other threats to survival, appears to be more of an existentialist than a Jew. This way of reading him is supported by Zukerman's point that Roth, by invoking Dostoevsky twice in his account, has tried to make something "Dostoevskian" out of Josie (177). Roth refers often here and in other of his writings to Franz Kafka, and he shares with Kafka threats of social and ontological alienation as well as complicated relations with women. But in my opinion, Roth's struggles to affirm his existence and integrity in the face of ontological counters like aging, illness, isolation, and death place him in a location no freer from religious significance than are other factors crucial to his account. In Judaism not only the people but also life itself is sacred. The biblical Psalms give voice to the desire to be delivered from isolation, illness, and death not in the name of life defined as biological survival but of life that is a gift from the source of life to whom the pleas are made.

My point is not so much to establish that Roth is more religious than he realizes, although I think that he is, but to establish that Roth, in his indebtedness to his past, is also indebted to its religious content. The profundity of that indebtedness may be registered by his not recognizing it. To me, he offers a clear example of an American who is a Religious Debtor. Who he is and his past have much to do with one another, as his writing and especially his autobiographical writings make clear. The most important ingredient of that past is its religious content, and much of that content persists, without his seeming fully to realize it, in the way he structures his self-account and identifies his past's continuing value and importance for him.

The question for Roth and for other Religious Debtors is whether personal values in the past retrieved and validated by their accounts can be retained and passed on while largely leaving the religious groundings and warrants of those values behind. It is a question that all share who think of religion as important for their identities because it saturated their origins. And those who share this question in terms of their particular identities and the importance of religion for their personal formation share it with nonreligious Americans, since all of us, when we self-identify as Americans, identify with and are indebted to origins formed and conditioned by religious sponsorship and content, origins that continue to carry values into the present day.

Dan Barry

Now it was time to resurrect my basketball dialogue with God.
—BARRY, *Pull Me Up: A Memoir*

In a brief prologue to *Pull Me Up*, Dan Barry crystallizes the moment in his life that gave rise to his self-account: the death of his mother at the age of sixty-one and, five months later, the diagnosis, at the age of forty-one, of his own life-threatening cancer. The implied reason for writing, then, lies in the ontological arena of his life, the effects and threat of sickness and death. Death not only prompts reflection on and appreciation for his own and his mother's life but also throws into relief the values of the past. The narrative is designed to rescue at least some of those values from being unrecorded and forgotten. This prompt to writing as rescue seems reinforced by the title, words his dying mother repeated to him: "pull me up."

The threat of losing the past to death is countered by the gift of storytelling, a gift Barry's mother possessed in abundance. He positions her for us from the very start, "her cigarettes at hand and her glass forming rings on the beaten tabletop," a position from which "she would conjure such vivid scenes that the television flickered in silence, a fire without heat."[12] His self-account, then, is also a return on the gift for narrating bequeathed by her to him, a gift on which he continues to draw not only for this account but also for his profession as a journalist. Like her, he also tries to conjure "vivid scenes."

In addition, Barry implies that his life asks to be narrated because it is odd. The eccentricities of his parents, the vagaries of nurture in Catholic schools, and the realization of his long-sought vocational goal join his encounters with death and disease to form a series of unexpected events that casts the past into lively relief.

Finally, Barry recognizes a conflict in his life that the narrative seems intended to resolve, a conflict between recording life and living it. His mother, and perhaps his father, too, did not compromise the immediacy of living by the impulse to narrate, as newspaper reporters tend to. His job as city hall bureau chief for the *New York Times* is a culminating and defining aspect of his identity, and one reason for writing the narrative is to reveal how his "mission to record moments" turned into such a wonderful reality. But journalism fosters a distinction between involvement and narration. This narrative, then, will not be only a report. As the vivid particularity of his parents was enhanced rather than overshadowed by their colorful and energetic voicings, so also this narrative will recount a life made personal by being written. Writing and living, text and reality, rather than separated, will be mutually enhancing.

I

The narrative secures the fact that Barry is very much his parents' son. His home life, which continues as a presence and refuge into his adulthood until his mother's death in 1999, is dominated by his parents. They take up space, hold strong opinions, and constantly drink, smoke, and make noise. His mother is the dominant parent, and Barry traces her strength to her Irish origins, the difficulties of her having been orphaned and sent off to America at the age of fifteen. She has the last word in the house, dances to radio music, and refuses to become an American citizen. His father, who grew up amidst poverty and alcoholism, is third-generation Irish and has strong hates and loves. He drinks heavily, smokes four packs of cigarettes a day, suffers loudly during twenty years of migraine headaches, and is a true believer in UFOs and conspiracy theories. These parents, often at odds with their world, with one another, and with themselves, dominate the home with their antics but are, as well, attentive to their children, especially to Dan, the oldest of four. The dynamics of home life, therefore, are, for Barry, strongly centripetal.

School, especially the Catholic high school, is as vivid and complex a site as is his home. There, too, admirable and offensive, disconcerting and comforting, and serious and comic elements are mixed. The hazing on school bus rides, the outrageous Christmas party, the predatory Brother Noel: such bizarre events and figures from his school life are memorable for the writer and made so for the reader. At the age of fifteen, the same point in life when his mother's fate drastically changed, Barry witnessed Brother Noel "dry-humping" one of the students: "I shed my childhood" as though it were a coat "too small to ward against the winds of winter" (117). The disturbing and captivating qualities of his school life, like those of his home, do not stand out as isolated from, but as typical of, his life as a whole.

Dan's devotion to sports also holds a secure location in his emerging identity, and he gives thirteen pages of his account to baseball. Like his father, he loves the Yankees and aspires to play the game. But he is uncoordinated and scrawny as a kid, fated to the role of spectator rather than player, a fate that parallels his sense of being more of a writer than a liver. He also turns frequently to basketball, something he can play by himself in his yard. Shooting baskets is an escape, a "ritual" or "sacred moment," to which he regularly, especially in stressful times, retreats (78). Indeed, sports have for him as much a spiritual as a physical quality, and that is clearest in the ritual by which shooting foul shots becomes a time of personal devotion, physical acts intertwined with prayers.

His years at St. Bonaventure University, in contrast to Philip Roth's years at Bucknell, are narrated far less in terms of the education he acquired or the social life he enjoyed there than as a period of emerging vocational clarity. He tells us of a "dawning sense that I was onto something at St. Bonaventure with journalism" (147). He relates this sense of vocational recognition to Thomas Merton, who taught at the university and recognized his religious vocation during walks and meditations in those very woods. Merton and the woods help Barry to "choose the writing life" (147).

While other events, such as marriage and the adoption of a child, are narrated, principal attention is given to the progress of his journalistic career. With extended descriptions of his assignments and of the stories he covers, vocational achievement is traced and celebrated by the narrative, the fact that a goal so deeply desired was, as much by good luck as by design, attained. The impact of his diagnosis and his ensuing battle with cancer are registered primarily in terms of the threat these events pose to realizing the potentials recently afforded him by his position on the staff of the *New York Times*, although the threat is also strongly felt because of his position as a husband and father.

II

Barry's identity, then, is primarily related to—indeed, is closely bound to—his vocation as a writer. Other aspects of his adult life, while important, take their place in the context of his forward and upward move toward attaining that goal. He points along the way to earlier colleagues and opportunities that prepared him for his present location, and he clearly at the time of writing is proud of his position with the *Times* and thankful for it.

His vocation is so important to him that, as he is aware, it may well absorb his sense of identity altogether. At one point he admits, "I had become my job" (196). He gets lost, he says, in his writing (199), and he finds sanctuary in the newsroom: "Often unable to think of anywhere else to go, I fled to its embrace, where the aroma of ink had displaced the smell of my mother's cooking as the scent of home" (201). He traces the emergence of his vocational goal to his origins, "my mother's vivid storytelling, my father's distrust of the powerful—and, I suppose, my understanding of the underdog's life, of being the skinny kid with braces, the one who gets beat up so often that he might as well schedule appointments" (148). It is not surprising, then, that during his illness he feels sustained by writing stories and sending them off, messages to the larger world that he is still alive.

Barry's focus on his vocation, while placing his account in a social arena, also includes the ontological. He writes in order to rescue things from escaping notice or passing out of existence. His self-account amplifies this ontological arena; his vocational development is due to good luck or, as reflected in his attention to the fact that he advances his career so successfully in a city with such an appropriate name, Providence, something more than luck. And writing

counters the threat to his identity posed by his illness. Writing
and being alive, writing and being a person with a name, and writing and having an identity are of one piece, as writing his life and
resurrecting his mother by the narrative are one. While unstated,
the realization of his vocational goal seems also accompanied by a
change in personal attitude and style, from writing marked earlier
by "sarcasm," "sneers," and "flashes of cynicism" (148) to writing
marked by appreciation and gratitude.

This tie between who Barry is and what he does sets up in the
narrative a close relation between Barry and his reader because
the reader can assume that writing this account and who Barry is
are closely bound. Although the abrupt use of "you" in chapter 15
turns out to be directed to a woman he wants to join him in Providence, the gesture toward intimacy works for a while also as a summons to the reader. In addition, the technique used later of recording
an extended conversation with his wife involves the reader in the
narrative intimately. Barry is a friendly guide into the intricacies
of his life, a life that he narrates often with comic delight, with an
eagerness to show respect for and gratitude toward others, and with
a willingness to let his reader into his thoughts and feelings. By the
time he narrates his illness, the reader is willing to be involved in it,
since the reader cares enough about him to share his worry and woe.

In fact, it may not be too much to say that Barry works harder and
is more successful in establishing a close relation with his reader
than with other persons in his account. True, moments of intimacy
with his brother and with his fellow workers during his ditch-digging
days are recorded, but these moments are brief. He seems to have
had some friends, but for the most part people are mentioned as
they are helpful to his professional development. He has girlfriends:
Carol, from whom he borrows money for tuition, and Nancy, who
causes a rift in his relation to Mary. But these relations are not narrated as close. Even courting and marrying Mary, while they imply
intimacy, are processes and events that he narrates in a somewhat
distant and summary way. His personal relations in the narrative
are less realized and substantial than the relationship he establishes
with his reader.

Barry's account of his struggle with cancer is vividly detailed and
honest. Prior to this period, the narrative is less unified and com-
pact. In the earlier parts, scenes, moments, and stages in his life
are narrated largely because they are zany and unexpected, qualities
that leave them somewhat unconnected. They are held together by
the relatively coherent world in which he moves and, later, by the

movement he sees his maturing life to embody toward his vocational aspiration. The onset of his illness begins a more continuous narrative, despite its uncertain outcome. The slow progress toward a diagnosis, the clear threat to his life that the cancer poses, and the uncertainty of how it should be treated all contribute to establishing the illness as a dangerous and elusive intruder. It is also understandable that a forty-one-year-old man with a devoted wife and young daughter, a man who is still adjusting to his new and much-sought work, should not take this assault calmly. Angry and determined, brought down by a body in which he never, it seems, felt wholly comfortable, a body that fails him again and thwarts his desires and goals, he fights back. Sickness, hospitals, treatments, and medical personnel are stripped of the interest often projected on them by popular media. This is a patient's view of things, a patient under assault and fighting back. Delay, uncertainty, mistakes, pain, the tactless words of others, and foul odors are more characteristic of the scene than are the heroics and care.

It is important to recognize how Barry avoids, in all of the attention that he gives to this extended and critical episode in his account, the effect of eliciting pity. This probably is due to the fact that even when he is recording his feelings and thoughts, he presents them as consequences of what he confronts. The focus is on living through all this and not on the one who records it. The reader is more a companion than an observer of the narrator. In addition, already in the prologue the reader has been told that this happened, so that the reader is not only prepared for it when it occurs but also realizes, if only implicitly, that the narrative is told from the other side of sickness.

III

The question of how important religion is for Barry's self-account is not easily answered because, for one thing, he integrates religion with his Irish cultural background. Indeed, there is more attention given, in his narrative, to the rehearsal of Irish culture than to the observance of Catholic rituals. His parents, while Catholic, are not highly observant, and Irish songs and memories determine more than religious language and acts the culture of his home. Indeed, his father self-identifies as an atheist or agnostic and has more interest in the mysteries of extraterrestrial life, alien encounters, and ghostly presences than in matters central to Christian faith and the church. His mother seems more observant, but here again we do not get much. For example, Catholics tend toward what has come to be called "material religion": their homes are often depositories of religious and devotional objects over which primarily mothers preside. But there is little of that here. And Catholics stress practice and observance, the context of which is primarily the church. But religious observance and participation in the liturgical life of the church, while mentioned in passing as constant, do not figure largely in his account. It is surprising, for example, that when Barry was five years old and a new church building was completed, neither its scope and textures nor the rituals celebrated in it make an impression on him deep and lasting enough to recall. The visual and aesthetic sides of Catholic life are not, as they are for his model Thomas Merton, powerful influences on him. Church, liturgy, clergy, and Catholic art and architecture occupy, at most, background locations. When the ordeal of treatments for his cancer yield positive results, Barry, in order "to celebrate a life tenuously extended," goes not to church but to Ireland (320).

Rather than church or home, school is the principal locus of Barry's Catholic nurture. He remembers the sisters who taught him in grammar school, one of them wearing a face that expressed the world's and the Virgin's suffering. He also remembers the impact made on him by one of the nuns when she told the class that they should be attentive to the calling that each of them could well receive to join the religious life (64). The religious quality thereby given to the question of vocation accounts, it seems, not only for the central role vocation plays in the formation of Barry's identity but also for the merging of his professional with his personal life. At a bar prior to enrolling in a graduate journalism program at NYU, he uses religious language to convey the gravity of the scene, "the bar's churchlike quiet, two supplicants deep in prayer" (179).

St. Anthony's High School extended and complicated his religious involvement. From his first day as a freshman, Barry is humiliated on the school bus by the older boys, but he sees hazing as a religious preparation, stripping from him whatever self-worth he may have brought with him to school. It rendered him a *"tabula rasa"* to the Franciscan brothers who would oversee his formation "as a Christian man bound for a 'profitable occupation'" (101). Barry's educational experiences, from bizarre to inspiring, seem, in addition, to carry, along with everything else, religious gravity and tension: "whether misbehavior was a sin; whether it warranted a demerit, a punch in the chest, or both; whether any of this was Christ-like—or Francis-like" (121). In the school there is a "constant struggle between the holy and the profane [that] confused me and drew me in, made me want to be a part, and apart" (124). When threatened with transfer to a public high school, he takes a job in order to help retain his place. "There was so much about the school I loved," he tells us, "that for better or worse, had become a part of who I was. I may have feared and even loathed Brother Noel [who was thought by the students to target students sexually], but I revered other Franciscans who had dedicated themselves so completely to the craft of teaching, and to our formation" (123). This is not to say that he emerges from high school with a clear religious identity. The picture is more blurry than that: "After nearly twelve years of Catholic schooling, I had neither the comforting conviction that God existed nor the certainty that He did not" (128).

Religion is primarily important for the emergence of his vocational awareness. His aspirations in journalism become firmer as his sense of direction is related to Thomas Merton's securing of a religious vocation. But while the urgency and significance of his vocational direction continue to draw on their religious base, his religious and professional identities, as he matures, do not remain explicitly tied.

Barry's wife, Mary Trinity, comes from a more devout Catholic family than he, and her involvement in various Christian ministries during and after her college years Barry seems to admire. While he jokes about the Catholic quality of her and her parents' names, it does not seem that, even if she takes her religious identity and vocation more seriously than he does his own, he is much influenced in that direction by her. Indeed, it may be that he largely turns the Catholic content of their marriage and family life over to her.

The most direct connection that Barry makes later in life to the religious content of his youth is his privately devised prayer ritual. The backyard basketball court had been his "outdoor chapel." There, he tells us, "I found that I could talk to God, if not with him, through a solitary form of basketball" (128–29). "These basketball prayer sessions of mine demanded a lot of God. I asked Him for help with girls and protection from bullies, and much, much more" (134). He retrieves his ritual of solitary basketball prayers during a December evening when he is ill. In addition, while he is undergoing treatment he mutters Hail Marys and Our Fathers. Awaiting radiation therapy, he prays to a pockmarked cross on the ceiling.

Barry does not treat his occasional and privately observed devotional acts and rituals as exceptions to or anomalies in his life. He affirms their larger connections and defends his basketball ritual theologically: "It seemed no less theologically sound than other

practices and beliefs of Roman Catholicism, from the healing pow-
ers of holy water to the purchase of indulgences to ensure one's place
in heaven" (129). His rituals also seem consistent with the rituals
of his home life, baseball, going out as a family in the hope of UFO
sightings, gatherings of the family for storytelling sessions, and eating assorted boxes of Entenmann's pastries.

Implied, as well, is a sense, derived from his Catholic culture, of
the value of detail, the significance of visual and material things.
Rescuing the life of his mother and his own life from the threat
of death and of being forgotten is a recognizably sacramental act, a
lifting up of particulars as an expression of gratitude and devotion.
Indeed, the book's title, *Pull Me Up*, not only recalls his mother's
desperate, dying plea, but also suggests raising things from obscurity
to attention.

The deepest role of religion in his self-account, though, is the early
development within Barry of a vocational awareness, one explicitly
inculcated by his teachers and implied by their own identification
with the religious life. While Barry does not think of his profession
in explicitly religious terms, the need to answer the question of what
he will do, a question closely tied, it seems, to the question of who
he is, arises from and is focused by his religious past, a past to which,
also for this reason, he feels indebted.

While during his life Barry is oriented to future success and lives
off his background, death and illness shift his attention from the
future to the past. The focus now is on his upbringing and development, a sense of gratitude for them, and a recognition that his
achievement of a life's ambition came about not merely by persistence and design, the help of others, and even good luck, important
as those things are. His position in life is primarily a gift for which
he is grateful and now hopes will continue. Facing death means returning to the sources of that gift, his parents, his own quirky life,
his religiously based sense of vocation, and his dedication to writing. Underlying these sources is something more, a personally prized
undercurrent that sustains them all, one to which he returns on a
chilly December evening when, while ill, he goes out to take foul
shots so that he can, again, pray.

It should be said, finally, that there is also within Catholic culture
an awareness that illness, handicap, and misfortune are not simply
negative or meaningless. Rather, they are potentially significant,
and people who are especially afflicted are consequently held by
Catholics in high regard.[13] While Barry does not make this point or
seem even to be aware of it, it also is not surprising that he takes

his illness and the threat of death not only as affronts and causes of anger but also as occasioning reflection on his life and recognition that his life and its value are supported by a Catholic context and content.

Despite the importance for his self-account of concrete events and physical things, Barry's identity has a more spiritual than physical ingredient. He does not seem, for example, to relate positively to his own body. He is gawky, skinny, and wears braces, and he is plagued by acne. During his illness he feels betrayed by his body; it seems a necessity for sustaining his life but not itself positively or substantially related to who he is. He also does not relate his emerging identity to a developing sexuality. Although his father owns a stack of *Playboy* magazines, he seems to have lacked the curiosity to look at them. It appears that his only date in high school was for the prom, and he engages it as a social necessity and with his mother's coaching. His lack of interest continues in college. The side of Mary Trinity to which he gives most attention is her intense Catholic religious identity. He also is in no hurry to marry, and his early married years are dominated by his work rather than by their relationship. The rare moments of physical intimacy that he includes in his narrative are somewhat homoerotic. He and his brother Brian, whom he considers to be a close friend, would take turns in bed "caressing each other's back in a gentle tickle" (38), and his relations with fellow ditchdiggers are as close as "men in this world will allow themselves to get" (169): "You sweat together, curse together, and arc your piss streams together" (170). My primary point in mentioning this is that Barry's self-account, while marked by candor, is, regarding sexuality, puzzling and reticent.

This reticence, however, also serves to emphasize Barry's spiritual side, especially his religious indebtedness. Religion is part of the familial and cultural past that must be credited as giving rise to much in the present that is of value. Barry draws on the religious aspects of his past not because they were deliberately inculcated or epitomized by his parents, as is more the case with Angelou's grandmother and Roth's parents, as because they were part of the Catholic world in and by which he was nurtured, especially the school. Vocation, ritual, the value of particular things, and illness as a time of religious significance: these are, while not exclusive to a background such as his, also specifically sponsored by his Catholic past.

Although Barry self-identifies as a religious person, as more religious than, say, Roth, he is, I think, along with Angelou and Roth, primarily a religious debtor. Barry does not retrieve the religious content of his past in order to deepen and extend it in the present. What he does is to retain isolated moments of that past, moments that, when needed, can be applied to experience (186, 273, 289, 306). As is often true of religious debtors, Barry does not face the question as to whether or not these survivals of his religious past can be sustained without the restoration as well of the religious context in which they were formed.

ANGELOU, ROTH, AND BARRY include religion in their self-accounts because religion was a positive and noticeable part of the pasts that continue to sustain them. The significance of religion for their early years is enhanced and complicated by the fact that it is interwoven with the cultural context of their origins, African American, Jewish American, and Irish American. This intertwining makes it difficult to separate cultural from religious nurture, if any of the three would want to do that. This means that they need not come to terms with religion directly, determining what of it to continue and what to leave behind. It comes along with the rest, embedded in something else. Religion is, to use a term I shall employ more fully later on, something to be assumed in the sense of taken for granted.

This is true as well of religion in our national identity. It is carried from the past as a constitutive part of the whole. It appears in our political life, in our literature, and in the personal lives and the stories of our contemporaries. It is something to be expected, assumed, or taken for granted.

Rather than say whether the religion we take for granted is a good or a bad thing, it is better, I think, simply to say that this is how it is. I happen to think that, despite the fact that religion often has caused or aggravated problems and injuries to persons and groups, it also continues, as it is in these examples, to be largely positive. Among other things, it enriches, complicates, and interrogates our personal and our shared lives. Candid recognition of its continuing presence and the various contributions it makes to who we are as a society seems to me a way of being both personally enriched and American.

5

RELIGIOUS DWELLERS

AUTOBIOGRAPHIES BY Religious Dwellers differ from those by Religious Debtors primarily by locating religion and its positive role in the present. While religion may also have been part of the past, the focus is on the way in which it helps to account for where the writer is at the time of writing. The emphasis is less on recovery than on discovery, on having found something or having reached a location, decision, or point of arrival that often is marked by a new or renewed affiliation.

Affiliation, in texts by Religious Dwellers, testifies, among other things, to the major role that joining plays in the lives of Americans. Despite their vaunted individuality, Americans associate readily and fervently. Recreational, political, fraternal, charitable, educational—the list could go on—organizations, clubs, movements, gatherings, and institutions are a major part of the lives of Americans. As Robert Putnam says, "Americans are more likely to be involved in voluntary associations than are citizens of most other nations."[1] It is not surprising, then, that Americans, when they self-identify as religious, often do so in terms of their new or renewed relations to locations, groups, and institutions.

However, religious affiliation, as Robert Wuthnow points out, has undergone changes in recent American life. The older model was one of continuing identification with a stable institution. Today's associations are more functional and tentative.[2] Correspondingly, leaders of religious institutions, aware that when Americans affiliate they often have specific reasons for doing so, diversify options by forming groups of various kinds within the institution. Religious institutions in contemporary America likely provide club-like activities for members with differing interests and of differing ages. As Religious Debtors are like their nonreligious co-patriots in sharing a sense of indebtedness to a past that was more religiously conditioned than the present, Religious Dwellers share with their nonreligious neighbors a strong desire to locate and to join. It is not surprising, then, that religious institutions create club-like groups and that when nonreligious people identify with a group, location, or institution, such as with the fan club of a university's sports teams, they often do so fervently.

I borrow the term "Dweller" from Robert Wuthnow, who uses it in contrast to what he calls religious "Seekers." A major point of difference between these two groups of Americans for Wuthnow is that the first is composed of people who are certain about their religious identities in contrast to those who are not. In my use of his term, I do not want to impute certainty to what I am calling Dwellers. A range of certainty and uncertainty can be found in all three of the orientations that I am positing. I also would make less than he does of the point that the percentage of American religious people who are Dwellers is decreasing while that of what he calls Seekers is increasing. This may well be true, but I also think that all three orientations have had long-standing, although also fluctuating, roles in American religious life. While current religious association may be more functional and more fluid than religious association in the past, it continues to be an important focus for religious identity, as does joining and location for American identity more generally.

A related form of dwelling, one that often carries religious associations in American culture, is geographical or regional. Perhaps because of its size and the variety of its physical features, America offers its citizens, despite their mobility, identification with one or another place on the landscape. Americans who are Religious Dwellers may well relate their religious identity to geographical location. The tendency to identify physical locations and landmarks with religious meaning is deeply rooted in American culture, as John Sears, among others, has pointed out.[3] Americans also associate regions with narratives, with parts or versions of American history, and these histories can support religious associations to specific locations. Geographical, cultural, and institutional locations, then, can blend to give specificity and content to American religious identities.

While many Americans have lifelong attachments to religiously important locations, unbroken constancy, as Wuthnow points out, is more characteristic of the past than of the present. Consequently, we shall find in this chapter accounts by people who, at the time they are writing, describe religious affiliation or location as a recently acquired ingredient of their identity. This marks a difference from accounts that include religion as something taken for granted. Religious identity here is more a matter of decision or choice. This shifts the meaning of "assumption" from what is taken for granted to assumption as something taken on, as, for example, a political figure takes on or assumes the responsibilities of office upon being elected.

When these accounts describe a pattern of *return* to affiliation, they also testify to a change of direction in the importance of religion for American identity noticeable during the latter decades of the twentieth century and continuing today. This pattern is from a waning of religion's importance for self-understanding to a conscious inclusion of religion in accounts of what matters to people personally. While this pattern can be seen in the other types of religious Americans, Dwellers articulate it most clearly. Such texts, then, often trace a movement away from religion and into substitutes for it, such as, to anticipate the texts we shall look at, psychotherapy, politics, or art. People leave religion in pursuit of greater personal fulfillment, new evaluations of gender identity, or freer sexual behavior, for example, but this pursuit leads to a return to or reappropriation of religious affiliation, albeit in an altered and more complex form.

However important change and movement are for these texts, place and location are as, if not more, important. The emphasis falls on where the writer is at the present time. And, while location or relocation results from a decision, it is the place itself that warrants identification with it. The clarification of self-location usually focuses on a physical place, but it also implies location as a position that has been taken concerning heretofore unresolved questions. The writer has arrived somewhere and writes from a religiously significant location, and that location often unifies an actual place and a mental or emotional decision.

Dan Wakefield

> It started that night in the class at the parish house when our
> minister asked us to draw a picture of the house we grew up in.
> —WAKEFIELD, *Returning: A Spiritual Journey*

The pattern of life that Dan Wakefield identifies with the title of his autobiography, *Returning*, points to his strong interest in places. He tells us that a sense of place was evident already in his youth. As a teenager, he was aware of the importance of place-relations for his sense of well-being: "Being in the right place, a deep inner feeling of relief and centeredness, of balance in relation to the rest of the world, is something I have experienced in most of the crucial places and times of my life."[4] This rightness of location had its sharpest negative contrary in 1980, a few years before the time he writes his account. In Los Angeles he reached an emotional and physical impasse due to health problems, an addiction to alcohol, and an urge to abandon a profitable job and the woman with whom he was living. Moving from Los Angeles to Boston, where he is located at the time of writing, he affiliates with a church, a decision he attributes to his sense of rightness in his new location: "I think the deep sense of pleasure and solace of *place* I derived from returning to the neighborhood was . . . part of the process of calming and reassembling myself that nurtured the desire to go to church" (15). His new location is even more specific; his autobiography grew out of his participation in a group within the church, a group that provided its members an opportunity not only to reflect on and record the course of the their lives but also to recall significant places.

I

The pattern of return that unifies the autobiography as a whole also unifies many of its episodes. Episodes are often described in terms of troughs and crests, of difficulties and their resolutions. Indeed, one of the reasons for writing the account is to describe a pattern of slipping into addictions, with their serious mental and physical consequences, and coming out of them. "Return," then, often can be taken as a synonym for "recovery."

In addition to a pattern of returning or recovering, Wakefield presents his life as temporally unified by significant connections. One kind is between predictions and their fulfillments. He says of his spiritualist Aunt Ollie that her glimpses into the future were "accurate enough to make me wonder if I was really in charge of my own fate" (134). Another kind of connection is between setbacks and new opportunities. His failure as an athlete, for example, turns him toward reporting. More dramatically, serious injuries in a car accident and subsequent rehabilitation provide him "plenty of time to puzzle over the meaning of life, time, God and the universe" (99), and, when his cast is removed, he finds that the curse of his life, an embarrassing case of acne, has been lifted. A third kind of connection occurs when differing interests in his life are brought together, such as his high view of literary art and his interest in newspaper journalism.

These various connections allow him to feel a kinship with the biblical Joseph, and he comments on the unlikely outcome to events in his life: "Following the spiritual thread of one's life sometimes seems like a plot of a science-fiction novel . . . in which forces are at work moving people here and there in ways they don't themselves see and for purposes they don't yet even know about" (179).

Finally, his life seems marked by a pattern of exchanges between intense moments of loneliness and strong feelings of attachment to and support of friends. The occasions of isolation are deeply rooted. He was an only and even neglected child. His parents were too preoccupied with their own difficulties, affairs, and differences to turn their attention toward him, although they interpret his withdrawal from them as rejection. He tells us that at their graves, "I could feel the anger and power of my mother and father, their sense of disappointment in what they interpreted as rejection by their only son" (216).

This strain of loneliness in his life is aggravated, he admits, by a tendency toward self-absorption. Indeed, undergoing psychoanalysis was motivated as much by his fascination with himself as by the more specific symptoms of depression and impotence that prompt it. His turn to psychoanalysis as a source not only of mental healing but of self-knowledge and fulfillment was prepared for him as an undergraduate at Columbia University. There he drew the conclusion that religion, which had been such an important part of his youth, was passé and that to be modern and educated was to agree that God was dead and that religion, rather than the solution, created or aggravated, as Freud along with Marx saw it, the problem. Wakefield accepts the belief, which was held by many with whom he came into contact, that psychotherapy had replaced God and the church as the source of transformation and wholeness in personal life (115). As he puts it in one of his other books, the analyst "became our priest, garbed in his vestments of three-piece dark flannel suit, and his orthodoxy became our religion."[5] However, his fascination for himself and for self-fulfillment did not depend solely on such cultural warrants. It was also deeply seated in him and easily followed. As he says, "How could anyone—especially a self-absorbed only child such as myself—fail to be fascinated by talking about himself for almost an hour every day?" (160).

Moments of isolation and self-absorption are countered by an equally strong pattern of association with other people and of joining groups. In his youth he is an eager joiner—Boy Scouts and churches, especially: "I wanted the immediate sense of safety and refuge implied in belonging, being a member" (20). The uniforms associated with Boy Scouts and sports give him a visible sense of belonging (53). His not being accepted by a fraternity when he enters Northwestern University is devastating for him due to this need or desire to join. This urge to relate may also be tied to the important role played in his life by friendships, many of them long-lasting, such as with his high school friend Harpie, with people he meets in his journalistic work, and with his many friends, especially women. Of friends, he says, "I have always been blessed with good friends, so richly that I've sometimes thought that perhaps to make up for my lack of brothers and sisters I was given an extra portion of friends" (186). His later church affiliation in Boston is, then, continuous with a pattern of association and affiliation and is described largely in terms of the involvement it provides with other people, especially members of the group he joins who study and practice acts of self-disclosure.

Relationships and associations seem guided, in Wakefield's account, by an expectation of and need for unconditional acceptance. One of the main lessons he learned as a boy in his Presbyterian Sunday school was "that God loved everyone regardless" (33). He cites this as something he always has believed, and he seems to carry that belief into his relations with other people. He expects unconditional acceptance from his psychoanalyst, and, when he concludes that the man does not even like him, he breaks off the relationship. He finds more complete acceptance at the Catholic Workers' house in the Bowery. He encounters a vivid and unexpected depiction of unconditional acceptance in, of all places, the New Yorker, which was publishing the short fiction of J. D. Salinger. Wakefield is struck by the way that Salinger could bring specifically religious moments of unconditional acceptance into his fiction not simply as background or embellishment but as integral to crucial recognitions. Feeling fully accepted by others seems to have been, for much of Wakefield's life, the primary ingredient in his relationships. He presents himself as the recipient of gifts that others give him, training as a journalist, sexual gifts, and care when he is desperate, for example. At the time of writing he has found such acceptance in Boston, in the church he has joined, and in the church group of which he is a member.

II

While patterns of loss and recovery, tensions resolved, and connections may grant a formal unity to the self-account, the meaning of the events receives greater emphasis. This meaning is presented as what makes life worth narrating, and it has several sources, sources identified with locations.

One location of meaning is internal. Wakefield has a strong, though often implicit, belief that if he pushes himself to extremities or exposes himself to scrutiny and even to the risk of physical harm, something of importance hidden within will be revealed. He seems eager, then, to test himself and to push boundaries. This is true in his early scouting experiences, during his fishing excursion in Israel, in his sexual life, in his abuse of alcohol and drugs, and in protracted and intense psychoanalysis.

Wakefield's major reason for entering psychoanalysis was, therefore, to enter the unexplored in his life in order to discover a more meaningful self. He thinks of his unconscious as a site of treasures. He will become a "Galahad reaching the grail—come upon it, recapture it, and in so doing dispel its power, making myself whole and free as I intoned the magic name for whatever moment had turned the screws on my developing psyche" (159). When discouragement threatens the process he reminds himself that "I mustn't settle for less than the full self-knowledge and discovery I had set out to find in the first place" (162). His belief that there is meaning buried in his deepest self that awaits discovery is not shaken by the failure of psychoanalysis, a failure he attributes to the profession and its practitioners rather than to his own, one would think excessive, expectations.

In addition to a place within himself, Wakefield turns for meaning to places he encounters around him. The meaning of places is presented as not simply projected on them by him but, rather, as residing within them. Often the meaning of a place reveals itself unexpectedly. As a boy he has a strong sense, when switching high schools, of being in the right place, a feeling of centeredness and balance. He describes his residence in "The Village" as "sharing the camaraderie of pioneers living where we did not by accident of birth or marriage or corporate or military transfer, but by our own choice and declaration, as committed to it as Brigham Young when he said, 'This is the place!'"[6] Later in his life he experiences in Boston a similar feeling, a "deep sense of pleasure and solace of *place*" (15), and he credits a feeling of calm and "reassembling" granted to him by his new location for his desire to join a church.

A third location of meaning is nature. The seasons of the year, for example, correspond to and support the cycles of loss and recovery that pattern his experiences, and one of the reasons he could not remain in Los Angeles was the lack there of seasonal changes. On his return to Indianapolis, he is helped, in his attempts to alter his relations to the place and to make peace with his past, by the sunset he witnesses, a moment that imparts to him a new sense of "glory." And when he is advised by a Catholic nun to meditate outdoors, he does so readily and with positive results.

Wakefield's attention to places and to nature seems consistent with a further location of meaning, namely, an encompassing "other" in his life. In Boy Scouts already he accepted a responsibility "to our fellow humans and to the earth, and finally and most importantly to God" (55). This outward direction is given religious resonance by a quotation from Albert Schweitzer which asserts that only those people are happy who have discovered how to serve. This orientation to something larger prompts the service in which he participates at the "hospitality house," carries over into his church affiliation in Boston, and provides motivation for his work with the homeless at the Pine Street Inn (235).

Reflecting on and narrating his life leads Wakefield to a conclusion regarding its meaning. He tells us, summing up: "Looking back from the vantage point of thirty years, it seems quite clear in a literal way that what I did to save myself nearly killed me (I have never been so close to annihilation as I was in that extended waking nightmare at the end of analysis) and what I did in the hope of helping others nourished and sustained me and maybe even saved my life" (178). The principal realization at which Wakefield arrives is found in the change from attempting to locate meaning primarily in himself to locating meaning outside of himself in places, natural events, and other people. Joining the church in Boston is an act based on this exchange. The church's pastor is a man "able to perform the enormous amount of pressurized work he did by 'emptying,'" a man who "nourished himself by constantly giving himself, and the giving out was what renewed him" (233). By becoming a member of the church he joins himself to something larger, a group of people "who share a common belief in something beyond themselves" (227).

However, this exchange from a primary orientation toward himself to a primary orientation toward realities outside of himself does not set the two in opposition. It is clear that Wakefield's church membership and participation in the autobiography group are also prompted by his desire for self-fulfillment. Rather than on one side or the other, internal or external, meaning seems to arise from reciprocity, from relatedness. The meaning of places, while not projected by him on them, does not reside in or arise solely from them. Places evoke an internal response that potentially already is there.

Dwelling, then, is not a permanent state but a sense of relatedness that regularly recurs.

III

It is worth pointing out that the location with which at the end Wakefield identifies is a Unitarian church. This form of American religion is, one can say, as close as any other to the general religious strains of American culture. It is closely related to New England and to Boston especially, and it suggests the religious identity that such canonical figures among American writers as Emerson and Melville developed. One of their traits as well as one characteristic of Unitarianism is a common emphasis on the natural context of human life and the spiritual resources of the individual, two foci important both for Americans and for Wakefield over most of his life. His religious institutional affiliation, therefore, can be seen as compatible with and focusing several aspects of his identity, a location that corresponds to and confirms the sense of who, at the time of writing, he is.

It is also important to point out that Wakefield's account is motivated by an implied argument, namely, that there are needs and potentials in persons and aspects of our world both social and ontological to which religion speaks or which it can actualize and, if religion does not play that role, persons will, and perhaps must, find substitutes for religion that can. Wakefield does not treat the failure of psychoanalysis to help him as something isolated or idiosyncratic. He takes his own expectations of its potential as shared by the culture of the sophisticated people with whom he moved. As Marxism was a substitute for religion among intellectuals in the 1930s, he tells us, so Freudianism was a substitute for religion in the 1950s (115–17, 158, 176). The argument has two parts. First, it posits that materialist critiques of and substitutes for religion, such as Marxism and Freudianism, fall short because there are human needs and potentials, call them spiritual, that require religion. Second, it concludes that if religion is rejected, substitutes for it will have to be found. This is an interesting argument, and it has apologetic force, especially when accompanied, as it is in Wakefield, by the demonstration that religious substitutes, like psychoanalysis in his own life, fail to fill the role that he assigns to them. The implied argument is somewhat weakened in his account because it is questionable that Wakefield was as thoroughly nonreligious or atheistic as he thought and presents himself to have been. But the question raised by the implied argument stands nonetheless. It is a point worth keeping in mind when viewing the amount and intensity of joining and affiliation in American society of both religious and nonreligious kinds. Wakefield seems to leave open the question of which of the two, religion or joining, is basic to and a sponsor of the other.

Letty Cottin Pogrebin

> To me, a person's identity is composed of both an "I"
> and a "we."
>
> —Pogrebin, *Deborah, Golda, and Me:*
> *Being Female and Jewish in America*

Letty Pogrebin includes religion as a major component of her identity because it supports and gives meaning to her penchant for joining. She comes by her urge to join honestly. Her mother, she tells us, was a joiner: "our Temple Sisterhood, Hadassah, the National Council of Jewish Women, Woman's American ORT, and the JWV Ladies Auxiliary."[7] Her father's many group commitments kept him out of the house almost every evening, and in many groups he played leadership roles: "the United Jewish Appeal, B'nai B'rith, the Zionist Organization of America, State of Israel Bonds, to mention just a few" (35). Pogrebin is up-front about the relation of her identity, including her religious identity, to joining. She says that, for her, "identity is composed of both an 'I' and a 'we.' The 'I' finds itself in love, work, and pleasure, but it also locates itself within some meaningful *group* identity—a tribe, a community, a 'we'" (xii). It is not that she emphasizes the importance of association or group identification because her experiences of group relations have all been positive. Instead, she describes her group participation primarily in terms of the tensions and difficulties they create and the effort they require.

The tension between her individuality and her commitments to groups finds a counterpart in the tension between the individual events and experiences of her life and an inclusive or overarching meaning. While she admits to a somewhat skeptical attitude toward coherences, her interest in constructing or evoking them suggests that she is not as skeptical about their validity as she declares herself to be. Both as a woman and as a Jew she grew up in a society in which identity constructions were imposed by others on her, and she no longer wants to be passive regarding who she is. If the life she presents is a construction, it will be, certainly, her own, but it will also be a construction that relates and is relevant to patterns and structures that are already there.

Pogrebin's self-account is an effort toward resolution and unity despite the warring factions within herself and her world. At the point of writing, at least partial or tentative resolutions have been found or formed, but the arrival is not a terminus. The formation and reformulation of her identity are also ongoing. Tensions arise for her primarily from her feminist and Jewish identities, both of which are already complex and not readily combined with one another. Political, ideological, and religious differences crisscross to create a tangle of tensions within both Pogrebin and her world. Her task is to find or construct a degree of unity in her identity and a place in the welter of opinions to which she lends her voice. Indeed, identity formation is for her primarily the negotiation or resolution of contraries and tensions in her past, within herself, and between herself and various groups and movements that are for her unexpectedly unsupportive if not opposed to who she is but movements in which she, nonetheless, constantly and actively participates. This places an unusually high importance on identity as a result of conscious intellectual effort, of coming to reasonable decisions or workable conclusions to problems that are both social or political and internal or relational.

I

While her self-account, consequently, is quite cerebral, she does not rely only on her own constructions but also employs patterns that already are there. One is temporal. Her narrative traces the linear unfolding of her life from childhood innocence or, as she describes it, ignorance, through conflict and disillusionment, to an at least tentative resolution to the quest for a unified identity despite its many, and still conflicted, parts. Also, she is sensitive to ritual, to the commemoration of special days, especially religious holidays, and this pattern also helps in her construction. She appreciates how "the demands of the Jewish calendar impose a cyclical orderliness on an otherwise fleeting, undifferentiated year" (94). Third, her life traces a dialectical pattern from an initial, high level of Jewish identity, through her neglect, even rejection, of it in favor of political interests such as the antiwar and feminist movements, and to the gradual reconfiguration of her Jewish identity in the context of institutional Jewish religious life. Most of the moments that she shares with her reader stand out not because they are isolated from these patterns but because they are closely related to them and reveal the shaping effects that patterns have on otherwise isolated events. However, while these patterns in various ways give formal shape to her life, her identity primarily is a conscious intellectual achievement, an understanding of herself as a relatively unified person because she answers some of the questions and resolves some of the tensions central to her experiences by reaching reasonable conclusions.

Pogrebin sees her efforts and conclusions, though personal, as not limited in their value to herself. An intention that unifies her self-account, along with the personal resolutions she reaches, is to free Judaism from its overt and latent antifeminism. She presents her conclusions, then, as important not only for herself but also for other Jewish women and girls and for Judaism as a whole. This goal would sound overly ambitious or even presumptuous if she did not insist that the resources for altering the nature and direction of Judaism regarding women are to be found within Judaism itself. This means that her feminist critique of Judaism can be combined with a renewed affirmation of her Jewish identity. In addition, she wants her feminism to awaken within Judaism its vision of peace and reconciliation.

However, she also sees feminism as a resource for good. Women, she thinks, are more inclined to promote peace and reconciliation than are men. In addition, women, because they share across cultural and religious divides a common burden of discrimination and even oppression, should work together to decrease the negative consequences in society created by racial, religious, and political differences. An important part of her life story, then, is taken up by her efforts to join and to form groups that facilitate dialogue between differing parties, especially between women who differ racially, politically, and religiously.

These efforts reveal an additional pattern in her narrative. Initially, she presents herself as working with political and religious issues as with something, so to speak, "out there." She moves from an earlier Jewish identity into her participation in groups and movements that are in complex and deeply felt tensions with one another. But social and political tensions and the problems "out there" seem to be irresolvable. For example, she comes to realize that a sense of mutual support between black and Jewish women based on their joint histories of discrimination and oppression can no longer be assumed or restored because black women see her first of all not as female and oppressed but as white and privileged. In addition, black women are concerned more with political and economic and Jewish women more with cultural and personal problems. More pointedly, she comes to recognize that black women identify with Palestinians and resent the aid that the United States sends to Israel and the comparatively little it sends to Africa. Slavery and the holocaust, rather than provide the background for understanding and cooperation between Blacks and Jews in America, create differences and even competition between them. Complications and reversals such as these gradually shift the center of the narrative from political engagement to religious identity formation. While Pogrebin does not abandon her drive to join and form political groups, the complexities of the issues she encounters seem sobering, and her priorities, consequently, shift. The narrative is both an account of this shift or exchange and the result of it. While retaining her involvements, Pogrebin relates her participation in movements, groups, and institutions to the question of what she should make, amidst these complexities, of her own identity as a politically aware, professional, and religious woman.

II

Pogrebin traces her impulse to identify with groups and to work toward the resolution of tensions within and between groups to her youth. Her early life was disrupted by startling revelations about her parents' pasts and distressed by the fact that her father and mother were not close but rather countered one another. She thinks of her youth as shaped by the task of having to please a rational, overbearing, and distant father and an emotional, mystical, and self-effacing mother. As a young girl she identified more closely with her father. When she is fifteen, her mother dies, and, while she mourns her mother's death, she is also grateful that she now has the freedom to grow up in her own way. But since that time she has come to recognize her mother's struggles and strengths. An immigrant from Hungary, she had low self-esteem because of her family's poverty, because her first marriage ended in divorce, and because her second marriage was not successful. At the time of writing, Pogrebin has come to a new appreciation for her mother as parent, wife, and friend to others. She especially values her mother's wisdom and fidelity in retaining the Jewish ritual life that stabilized her home.

Pogrebin has come, meanwhile, to view her father more negatively. While he lived for twenty-seven years after her mother's death, he never fully became a parent to her. She also comes to recognize the gravity of her father's having abandoned the daughter of his first marriage to her abusive mother and of having stopped making child-support payments for her. She resents that after her mother's death he allowed relatives to take all of her mother's things, leaving nothing for her. Finally, his second wife is the opposite of Pogrebin's mother and someone she intensely dislikes. However, while she says, "I don't like to write about my father" (32), her father is also a well-informed and self-conscious Jew. His participation in and support of Jewish institutions, learning, and religious practices attracted her and left an indelible and positive impression on her.

While gender is crucial to Pogrebin's construction of her identity, it is more a social, political, and religious factor than a physical one. She does not reveal a strongly affirmative relation to her own female body. She tells us, "For most of my youth, I hated my scrawny body and stick-straight legs" (83). She reports that, when she comes home from college pregnant, the significance of that event is for her the fact that her father expresses no feeling toward her when she tells him of her condition. She says nothing about the awakening of her female sexuality that led to the pregnancy, about being pregnant, or about the abortion. She mentions that she married Bert in 1967 and that they have two daughters and a son, but she tells us little about her relation to her husband and records her strongest feeling regarding her children as the guilt she feels for having raised them without religious training. Her female identity, however, while far less physical and emotional than political and social, is crucial to her. She tells us that if there were signs designating various identity categories, she would stand under the sign "woman" (149). In college and later in her positions with *Ms.* magazine, she bonds with other women and identifies strongly with the feminist movement.

What it means to her to be a Jewish woman is not something she thinks she can draw from the examples of others. While she thinks highly of such noteworthy Jewish women as Golda Meir, she finds neither in her nor in any other Jewish women an adequate model for today (157). What it means to be a woman, a Jew, and a public figure in a largely non-Jewish world has to be worked out. In her essay for *Ms.*, which she reprints in her self-account, she works at the difficulties created when she encounters anti-Semitism in the feminist movement equal to the antifeminism she has experienced in Judaism (207).

III

However important the politics of gender may be as a component of her identity, Pogrebin tends, given the difficulties of social and political problems, to draw more on religion than on gender or politics for constructing or clarifying her identity. This seems to occur because being religious can be more a matter of decision and choice than can being a white woman and, in a social and political sense, Jewish. Since the death of her mother and the departure of her father when she was still an adolescent, she has been relatively free to draw on their religious identities to the degree and in the ways she sees fit. The view of her parents as resources for the reconstitution of her Jewish identity clarifies why her family of origin seems more important for her identity than does the family she has created with her husband. What she sees of greatest worth in her parents is her mother's faithful observances and love of ritual and her father's knowledgeable leadership in Jewish institutions.

As she sees her feminist convictions as a way of being more rather than less faithfully Jewish, Pogrebin also sees the reconfiguration of her Jewish identity as a way of being more rather than less American. Religious identity, she thinks, is generally combined for people in this country with their American identity. Most think of themselves, she tells us, as Americans of a particular kind. Religion, then, both relates her to and distinguishes her from other Americans.[8]

Pogrebin grounds Jewish identity primarily in actions, in ritual and observance as enactments of value and belief (56). To become more Jewish she becomes more observant. When she contemplates the task of bringing together the tradition and the realities of the present day, especially a new affirmation of womanhood, she thinks not primarily of a new theology but of new or altered rituals.

Rituals are not for her, then, simply formal practices. She tells us, "Heartstrings and viscera connect me to a Judaism of ancestral words and melodies through which I conduct my conversations with God" (79). She testifies to a strong component of feeling along with action in the constitution of her religious identity. When she stands close to the Torah, she is enchanted. Her sense of the transcendent is strong, and she testifies to altered states of consciousness.

However, giving herself to rituals and experiencing strong religious emotions do not cloud her critical eye. Critique does not diminish Judaism in her eyes because she considers critique to be part of the tradition and not a betrayal of it. Her critical stance is established in her youth when she was not allowed, because of her gender, to be part of the *minyan* for saying her mother's *kaddish*. She assumes the role of a prophetess by affirming that God cannot want less from women than they are able to offer and that the exclusion and oppression of women contradicts Judaism, which preaches justice and mercy for all people. She cannot accept the fact that in the name of the tradition, Women of the Wall have been punched, cursed, and dragged along the ground (73). She wants to combine a soul-satisfying tradition with equality, religious conviction with feminist justice (80). She marginalizes aspects of Jewish life that oppose her female identity, and she affirms her aim to retrieve a more authentic Judaism. She implies that when anti-feminism is found in Jewish life, it is derived more from the surrounding culture than from Judaism itself.

While ritual practice is primary and feelings are prominent, beliefs and theology also have their place in her religious identity. When she becomes a cantor, Pogrebin has to come to terms with what she actually believes. The God she affirms is not so much a distant as a proximate reality, one associated primarily with ritual, with the ordinary and the everyday. Prayer, especially public prayer, is for her central to Jewish life, and prayer implies a relation with God that ritual embeds and renews. However, she also has difficulties believing in God because of her mother's early death and because of the holocaust. The principal form that her belief in God takes is her attempt finally to bring religion and politics together, working in the world to relieve suffering and to liberate the oppressed: "Thus does the theology of hope inspire the politics of social change" (310).

Since, for Pogrebin, Judaism primarily is about liberation and freedom, she finds it perfectly consistent to combine traditional Judaism with the aspirations of young Jewish women to assume their rightful place in Jewish institutions. In her bat mitzvah sermon she tries to lead Jewish women out of an Egypt of subservience. In doing so she identifies with "the prophetic tradition which esteems justice, rather than the rabbinic tradition which esteems order" (163). While there are precedents, the identity and role of the Jewish woman must be worked out now on a day-by-day basis. It is an identity with both a personal and an institutional side, and it forces difficult decisions.

One of those difficult decisions regards loyalty to Israel. She takes for granted that being Jewish means feeling a bond with Israel, and when she visits the country in 1976, she has a strong emotional response to being there. However, this loyalty is not uncritical. She realizes that the equality of women is less recognized in Israeli than in American society, and full freedom is the privilege only of Orthodox men. She goes so far as to say, "Israel has revealed itself as a false utopia in which women's equality was largely a myth" (168). In addition, she is aware that the Palestinians have not been justly treated, and she is critical of Israeli policies toward them.

The difficulties of constructing a feminist/Jewish identity are due not only to such political and social complexities but also to the construction of Judaism by the dominant, surrounding culture. She is aware of the many negative images of Jews in American culture: JAP, Exotic Jewess, Jewish Big Mouth, sexual animal, Jewish intellectual, Jewish moneymaker, etc. (217). These images enter consciousness and can produce, especially among educated Jews like her, a subtle, internal anti-Semitism. The larger society also impacts her political interests, since it is often the case that it is the more conservative figures in American political life who support Israel. Cultural and political obstacles to Jewish identity such as these lie behind Pogrebin's belief that self-identifying as a Jew in contemporary America is not an easy or simple matter. She describes the disclosure of her religious identity, then, as an act by which she "came out" (93).

When in 1970 she "comes out" as a cantor, she ties her growing personal awareness of Jewish identity firmly to institutional participation. In doing so, she relates to her parents, both to her father, who identified strongly with Jewish institutions, and to her mother, who was a keeper of ritual and an inveterate joiner. This religious institutional affiliation, which is continuous with her tendency to join other groups, organizations, and movements, reveals her to be what I call a Religious Dweller.

Jewish institutions appeal to Pogrebin because they preserve traditions. It is not as though she resists change; it is, rather, that she fears "the loss of meaning and continuity" (79). For Pogrebin, then, institutional affiliation supplies content to her Jewish identity and an arena of practice and discourse to which she can regularly turn for confirmation and focus. However, affiliating with Jewish institutions is not a simple matter. To retain her participation, Jewish institutions must include change along with continuity, and they must house variety and difference as well as commonality. This mixture of shared and differing, of required and selected, of constant and changing, and of personal and group identities forms fertile, though also thorny, ground for developing her Jewish religious and feminist identity.

While Pogrebin presents the formation of religious identity as a personal matter, it is carried out in a social and political arena. It is also a noticeably intellectual and self-conscious process. The political and intellectual qualities of her self-account raise questions about the degree of personal intimacy that the reader can achieve with her in comparison, say, to Wakefield. But it is important to point out that intimacy can be shared not only in an emotional but also in an intellectual way, in this case through knowledge of the complicated sets of tensions that Pogrebin has clarified and tried to resolve and the conclusions she has reached that are personally important to her and that she believes may be helpful to her readers. Her self-account is as social and political as Wakefield's is psychological and internal. As we turn now to Kathleen Norris, we have an account that, while it is also social and personal, gives prominent attention to the ontological arena.

Kathleen Norris

> I suspect that when modern Americans ask "what is sacred?"
> they are really asking "what place is mine? what community do
> I belong to?"
>
> —NORRIS, *Dakota: A Spiritual Geography*

Kathleen Norris, our third example of a Religious Dweller, charts her life in *Dakota: A Spiritual Geography* similarly to the way Wakefield and Pogrebin chart theirs. Her youth has a strong religious component, but for a twenty-year period she neglects or rejects her religious identity, returning to it in a way closely tied to a specific location. Her religious identity and her self-account are oriented, in the words of one of her chapter titles, by "Where I Am."

Norris, the second of four children, grew up the daughter of a Methodist father and Presbyterian mother, and her father, a church musician, tied their family life and church affiliation closely together. Participation in congregational activities was a regular part of her youth and related religious identity closely to institutional affiliation.

However, she associates her grandparents even more closely with religion than she does her parents. Her paternal grandparents were intensely religious, even fundamentalist. Her father's father was a Methodist minister and his mother a stern and judgmental matriarch. Religious identity on her mother's side, however, while also strong, was less stark and forbidding. Her maternal grandfather was the country doctor in a small, northwestern Dakota town, and, with his wife, Presbyterian. While devout, they seem to have been more accommodating toward others and less dogmatic in their beliefs and attitudes than were her grandparents on her father's side.

When Norris went off to college in 1965, she left religion behind, and there it remained for twenty years. Bennington College was not a place supportive of religious formation. On the social side, drugs and casual sex were dominant, and in the classroom, art and psychology not only set the goals and norms but were, she tells us in one of her other books, "our religion."[9] In contrast to her religious upbringing, she grew "attracted to what was forbidden, all the things the good girl had been denied."[10] An aspiring poet already in college, Norris, after graduation in 1969, took her talents and ambitions to New York City. She found her primary location within the administration of the Academy of American Poets, directed by Betty Kray, a woman Norris presents as remarkably energetic, insightful, and encouraging to her development. The organization for poetry, which Kray managed and with which Norris seems to have closely identified, not only allowed Norris to pursue her craft but also to meet other poets and to help arrange poetry readings, events that schooled her in the communal potentials of poetry. Life in the city was culturally sophisticated and fast-paced, and she immersed herself in it for five years.

In 1974, Norris moved to Lemmon, a small, remote town in the sparsely inhabited corner of northwest South Dakota. She went there with David Dwyer, a poet she had met in New York who was on the rebound from a failed marriage and a derailed academic career, and they took up residence in the home of her maternal grandparents. This radical shift in location was not a rejection of the city; Norris continued to visit New York and her friends there, and she was at Betty Kray's bedside shortly before she died. Indeed, she testifies to a pattern of moving between the city and the barren spaces of the Plains. While financial necessities may have contributed to the decision to relocate, writing, as she says, is a solitary occupation, and much in Dakota fosters the solitary life. In any event, the move seems not to have been made reluctantly, since Norris not only wills to live there but also attributes significant and positive changes in her life to her new location. Indeed, while she had some success as a published poet in New York, she also needed an alternative to the competitive, self-conscious, and often superficial culture of the city. She had become aware that she was lacking something, "and the way I had been living, pursuing an exotic nightlife and casual one-night sexual encounters with friends, no longer seemed the way to find it."[11]

While moving to Lemmon meant a radical reorientation in her life, a second occasion for change was the reappropriation, ten years after her arrival in Lemmon, of her Christian identity and church affiliation. The personal essays that make up *Dakota* describe not so much the course of the change as its consequences, her state of mind or spirit at the time of writing relative to her new location and her efforts fully to dwell there.

Relocation and dwelling, then, involve several layers, the Plains, the small town of Lemmon, and Christian institutions. One way she relates them to one another is by reinterpreting her past, what she refers to often as her inheritance, namely her family history. Her father's side of the family seems to have given her a strong argument against religion because of the high level of tension and abuse in that family epitomized for her by the suicide of her father's sister, a suicide associated, she thinks, with the judgment and shame that fell upon her aunt for becoming pregnant out of wedlock. Norris identifies with this aunt, directing her own writing in part toward redeeming her suffering life. Her maternal grandparents were made of softer religious material, and, since she lives in their house and joins their church, it is clear that they are as strongly positive for her reassociation with religion as her paternal grandparents were negative. However, she comes to see these two religious identities not only as contrary but also as complementary, since the religious intensity and seriousness of her father's parents balance the more generous and accommodating attitudes of her mother's. The religious life of her childhood home also contributes to her return, especially the importance of religious music. Gifted with perfect pitch, she could sing hymns on her own before she was able to read, and, while she does not say so, it would seem that her early memorization of hymn verses contributed at least something positive to her lifelong commitments to poetry.

The principal occasion for her reidentification as a religious person is her location. While she is also indebted to people in her past who support that reappropriation and while she does not think of her religious identity as finalized at the time of writing, she has reached a stage that allows her to reflect on her present situation as a kind of arrival. It is the outcome of what she thinks of as a struggle, one she compares to the struggle of Jacob with the angel at the Jabbok Brook.[12]

Norris is, in her self-account, clearly a Religious Dweller. Indeed, dwelling, with all the implications of location and of present time, is itself a major topic of interest in her account. She ties religious experience and identity closely to the discipline of attention to location, to where one is. Her emphasis on dwelling assumes three forms, the vast natural environment of the Plains, the small town of Lemmon, and the Christian institutions with which she affiliates and in which she becomes an active participant.

I

When Norris moved from New York City to western South Dakota, she was returning both to the landscape and to her inheritance, since her mother's family had lived there for two generations and she had spent vacations there with her grandparents. So, living in the largeness of natural exposure was something with which she was already familiar and, on returning, can more maturely address. And it is clear that living on the Plains is an important part of the identity that emerges.

In a number of ways, Norris emphasizes that the open space of Dakota, unlike cities and shopping malls that deny them, reminds its inhabitants of human limitations (2). Distances, emptiness, winds, extremes of temperature, and loneliness are a few ways in which Dakota puts the human in perspective. It is this constant presence of natural power and vastness that brings about, in response to the place, "an experience of the holy" (1). For reasons such as these, "the Plains have been essential not only for my growth as a writer, they have formed me spiritually. I would even say they have made me a human being" (11).

Norris compares the Plains to other vast spaces, the sea and, even more, the desert, and this allows her to interpret living there along lines of the early Christian desert fathers. Life in Dakota is ascetic, requires discipline, and has a spiritual dimension. She is insistent that, unlike some who assume middle-class religious fads, she does not try to relate to the land in ways owing to Native American traditions. She is acquainted with Native Americans in the region and probably has been influenced by them, but "their tradition is not mine, and in returning to the Great Plains, where two generations of my family lived before me, I had to build on my own traditions, those of the Christian West" (2–3).

Norris also avoids sentimentally Romantic depictions of the natural space she affirms. The Plains, though at times remarkable and even beautiful, primarily make life difficult. "But some have come to love living under its winds and storms. Some have come to prefer the treelessness and isolation, becoming monks of the land, knowing that loneliness is an honest reflection of the essential human loneliness" (110). The Plains, though having isolating and even depressing effects, can also create in a person a genuine regard for others, a hospitality and generosity of spirit that is not otherwise easily found. The expanses of the Plains and the harsh extremes of the climate create a sense of human limitation, even an awareness of mortality, that gives personal awareness and relationships a grounding in reality.

Dakota also plays the role of a commodious and unifying container for the otherwise scattered aspects of her life, her patchwork of jobs, her travels to speak and to read at various places, and her writing. "Dakota," she says, "is where it all comes together, and surely that is one definition of the sacred" (131). Dakota, as an ontological arena for her self-account, affords experiences that are both highly particular and humanly sharable. This is why it is important for Norris to view the location not simply as background or, even less, as something primarily with which to cope. She chooses consciously to live there and to have a relation to this place not only despite its difficulties but also because of them. The difficulties are deeply felt: "disorientation and an overwhelming sense of loneliness" (150) and "this land's essential indifference to the human" (156). But a "sense of place is unavoidable in western Dakota," and the people there "know that the spirits of a place cannot be transported or replaced" (169). That means relaxing the impulse to predict and control. "In these places you wait, and the places mold you" (170).

II

While the physical or ontological arena provided by her geographical location is a major factor in the sense of where Norris is at the time of writing, she also turns attention to the social arena, particularly the small town of Lemmon, where she resides. Like the natural setting, the town has both positive and negative qualities.

On the positive side, the people of Lemmon, due to the small population and their vulnerability to setbacks, exhibit a concern for one another and an unusual readiness to be of help. In addition, they possess a noticeable degree of integrity. False fronts and pretensions do not wear well in a town where people know who you are. People do not use language to create an impression, to conceal things, or to manipulate others. They tend to speak directly, concretely, and honestly. They also listen. In many ways the people create a society that helps you to recognize "exactly who, what, and where you are" (23).

Their orientation to the larger realities of their physical setting, their understanding of human hardships, their willingness to help, and their appreciation for honest talk make the people of the area more receptive to the language of poetry than are people in societies marked by distractions, haste, and glibness. Norris finds a response of the local people to poetry, including her own, that is encouraging.

In addition, providing public poetry readings helps to reestablish the traditional communal setting and role of poetry. People have the time and patience not only for one another and for poetry but also for telling and hearing stories. The narrative quality of conversations common there intrigues Norris, who thinks of stories as potentially more religiously important than theology. Implied by these recognitions, it seems, is that Norris had assumed in college and in New York City that literary art constituted a world separate from ordinary life and society, and the social location of Lemmon made her aware of ordinary people and their culture as potential resources for and recipients of art.

Finally, the town is unusual because the difficulty of life in such a place means that dwelling there likely rests on decision and commitment. Indeed, the dominant tendency is toward leaving and attrition. Staying, while it may be occasioned as well by habit, necessity, or fear of the unknown, carries connotations of determination and loyalty. This makes for conditions that move social location from factors of mere convenience to something with moral content. People committed to their social setting are concerned for its preservation and for the well-being of neighbors. For this reason, Norris can make several favorable comparisons between the town and the religious communities with which she comes to associate.

However, like the Plains, the social arena also has its negative side. People in the town are often resistant to change and innovation. They tend to view the outside world as threatening, and they commonly form and hold conspiracy theories. Their reluctance to expose themselves to something new also takes an anti-intellectual form. Their suspicion toward outsiders becomes a resistance to new ideas. Indeed, the desire to preserve unity often results in the gradual marginalization and expulsion of people who fail to fit the mold (64).

The combination of positive and negative factors in the social setting means that dwelling in the town, like dwelling on the Plains, requires wisdom, patience, and effort from Norris. While the benefits are real, the annoyances and lacks are real as well. "Living with people at close range over many years, as both monastics and small-town people do, is much more difficult than wearing a hair shirt," she says (120). It is, indeed, what asceticism finally is all about, namely, living with others in such a way that your own interests and tastes are not always confirmed or even tolerated.

A recurring if not constant theme in Norris's account of herself as a dweller in this place, especially in the small town of Lemmon, is that American society more generally is in danger of losing, if it has not already lost, a communal sense, and Americans are unwilling to make the effort to live in social relations with others. This retreat of Americans is noticeable, she thinks, both in their avoidance of harsh natural environments and in their strong preference for security and comfort, a retreat abetted by the effects in American culture of individuality and accumulation. While Americans exhibit a degree of longing for the sacred, they fail to find it because "all too often we're trying to do it on our own, as individuals. That *is* the tradition of middle-class America; a belief in individual accomplishment so strong it favors exploitation over stewardship, mobility over stability" (129).[13] It sets the individual at odds with society, the desire for self-protection and advancement being threatened by the prospects of communal responsibility. The contrast in her account between where she is and where American society is as a whole becomes so strong that it even carries the proposal that the locations Norris affirms hold a potential for saving American society from tendencies that, if not checked, will do serious, even irreparable, harm. However, by displaying some zeal in this direction, Norris also wants to affirm other forms of social identity in America. For example, she continues to have high regard for large urban settings, such as New York City. She treasures her returns to it, and she acknowledges the singular achievement cities exhibit of providing social environments that allow people clearly different from one another to live and work together (3).[14]

III

The third form of placement or relocation that Norris records is in and with religious groups and institutions. Twenty years after leaving the church behind and ten years after taking up residence in Lemmon, she renews her church affiliation. At first it is difficult. She must subject herself during sermons to "word bombardment" (94). She also has difficulty with "the language about Jesus Christ," its implied exclusiveness that "made me feel most left out" (94). In addition, as a feminist she is aware that the religion of a male savior has been used in the past "to keep women in their place" (94). Finally, her father's family of fundamentalist Methodists used Christological language to impart religious and moralistic certainty to Christianity. Their form of Christianity imposed limitations radically different from the limitations nurtured in persons by the Plains. Rather than being religiously beneficial, Christianity can produce objectionable confinement, and as a young woman she had come to think, along with many others in the baby-boom generation, that religion sponsored a set of restrictions and constraints "that I had overcome by dint of reason, learning, artistic creativity, [and] sexual liberation" (97).

A number of things contribute to the growth of her church affiliation. One is that she comes to recognize that her understanding of the faith was minimal, and she begins to expand her knowledge of it. Also, she develops a new appreciation for the category of "sin." She sees it no longer as a way of "being handed a load of needless guilt" but, rather, "as a useful tool for confronting the negative side of human behavior" (98). She understands sin primarily as thoughts and acts that interfere "with our ability to love God and neighbor" (98), and, consequently, as a "failure to grow" (99). In other words, she begins to see morality not as confinement and restriction but as a guide to a more fully realized life.

What Norris values in the church is not so much its theology as its liturgical language and music. These, she begins to recognize, are "essential to my identity and my survival" (133). In addition, she is asked by her church in Lemmon to preach while the church is without a pastor, and this exposes her to close readings of biblical texts. Sermon writing requires integrity, and she finds her sermons to be more revealing of who she is than her poetry. "The 'I' in a poem is never me—how could it be? But the 'I' in my sermons came closer to home, and that was risky" (171). These practices are continued when she is invited by a small church in the neighboring town of Hope to give sermons there. The people she meets in the church are surprisingly intelligent and well-read, and she responds positively to their hospitality. Indeed, she depicts the church in Hope as a kind of "ideal" Christian community (165). Sermons, like poetry readings, liturgy, and music, have a community-creating effect that is significant to her.

The understandings at which Norris arrives concerning living on the Plains and in Lemmon and her positive responses to Christian liturgy, singing, and close readings of biblical texts contribute to another form of Christian group-association, namely, her participation in the life of a local Benedictine monastery as an oblate. Norris already as a little girl was drawn to Catholicism, and she relates to the monastery not as a monastic wannabe but as a dedicated learner who will continue to be a Presbyterian Protestant.

She is drawn to the *"stability"* of the monks, their "commitment to a particular community, a particular place" (8, emphasis in original). And, as is also true for the local farmers, time for the monks is marked "by the natural rhythms of day and night, and of the seasons" (18). What the monastery adds to the ascetic quality of life on the Plains is "the affirmation of something higher that unifies people" (114). This "something higher" also creates a larger and more significant context to accommodate mortality, for in the monastery as on the Plains, death is an undeniable reality.

Silence is also a powerful part of monastic practice. It opens her to "a new power." In the monastery, silence can finally be given its due. And, like the silence of the Plains, monastic silence is not empty: "it has the power to change you" (184). Silence is integral to an atmosphere in the monastery that evokes from Norris "who I wanted to be as a writer, as a wife, even as a Presbyterian" (199).

Finally, there are three aspects of monastic life that are particularly attractive to Norris. The first is its emphasis on nature. The fundamentalist Methodism of her father's family, with its stress on deliverance from the surrounding world, had little, if any, theology of nature. Presbyterianism, with its strong emphasis on the Hebrew scriptures, in contrast, does, but Norris comes to a Christian affirmation of the natural primarily through its important role in monastic awareness and thought. This religious emphasis on the significance of the natural creates connections with and adds meaningful content to her relation to the Plains.

Second, she is impressed and affected by the *lectio divina*, the practice of monastic scripture reading. The close attention to and contemplation of biblical texts is part especially of Benedictine discipline, but it is also, one should add, crucial to Calvin's doctrine of reading scripture and to the Reformed tradition of which Presbyterianism is a part. Again, Norris, without realizing it, comes to an aspect of her own inheritance by means of monastic practice. This emphasis on reading also grants a religious endorsement to her own sense of the importance of and care for words in her vocation as a poet.

Finally, she is engaged by the "as if" of monastic life, the playfulness and role-playing. This is a strongly attractive contrary to the dogmatism that creates certainty and exclusivity not only for her paternal grandparents but also in much religious, and especially Christian, life. This "as if" does not mean contrary to fact. It means, instead, expectancy and openness. While it is an important part of the monastic life that she encounters, "as if" is also a term crucial to Calvin's doctrines of Word and Sacrament as a way to create expectation without the risks of certainty and manipulation. For Calvin, the Christian approaches Scripture and sacrament "as if" there the living Word of God can be heard and "as if" there the presence of Christ can be seen. While these are important ingredients in monastic affirmations and practices, they are also moments that, without her recognizing it, bind her to her own identity as a Presbyterian. They give a particularly religious standing to the attitude of openness and expectation that characterizes Norris's self-description. All of this gives content to her statement, although she seems not fully to recognize it while writing, that the monks helped her to be a Presbyterian.

IV

The unifying intention of Norris's self-account is to relate a variety of placements and identity factors to one another, so that they clarify and reinforce, rather than compete with one another. Her physical location on the Plains, her identification with the society of Lemmon, her active affiliation with the church, her participation in the disciplines of the neighboring monastery, and her vocation as a poet are all brought together to help her clarify where she is at the time of writing. The variety of places and of her roles in and relations to them, however continuous with one another, are also separately depicted so that she is not fully identified with any one of them but allows their particularities to grant complexity to her identity. This variety and flexibility within continuity ground her conclusion that her newly assumed religious identity, while to some degree settled, is also still in process. While stable, her religious identity is not fixed.

Norris presents where she is at the time of writing as a place of value not only for her but for her American readers more widely. She is eager to clarify why being where she is has such positive effects on her in order to commend placement to her readers. She relates identity to a location that is supportive not only for the formation of a religious identity but also as a place that counters the penchant for comfort and control that limits the lives of many Americans. In this way she combines a patriotic affirmation of an American landscape with a recommendation for redressing personal laxities that, she believes, carry moral and spiritual consequences. An orientation to American landscapes, while not set by her in opposition to other dwelling places, can and perhaps even will deepen and enrich the personal, moral, and spiritual lives of Americans. The affirmation of place relations is inseparable from her specifically religious identity.

SELF-ACCOUNTS are written in and from particular locations. Where the writer is at the time of writing, while always present, may, as we have seen, be of primary importance. It indicates, if nothing more, a location from which one views, interprets, or shares the life narrated or described, and that location may be newly achieved or recognized. Given the potential force and significance in autobiography of where the writer is at the time of writing, it is not surprising that religious self-accounts, such as those by Wakefield, Pogrebin, and Norris, emphasize the time of writing as a religiously significant position, a location that has been reached or a position or affiliation that has recently been chosen or affirmed.

In addition, we Americans, perhaps because there are so many of us and because we are so various, seem drawn to particularize our national identities. We identify ourselves with some region of the country, group, institution, movement, set of preferences, or convictions that grant us particular and recognizable locations and positions. Given the importance of placement for identity in American life more generally, it is also not surprising that when Americans, such as Wakefield, Pogrebin, and Norris, narrate or describe their religious identities, they do so by clarifying where, in many senses of that term, they "are."

Finally, religious identity as *assumed* means not only that it is something inherited, that comes along, so to speak, with the family picture album, but also that it is something deliberately acknowledged, consciously recognized. Saying where you are in terms of both a decision and location is an important aspect of being a religious person today. True, for many Americans religious location, affiliation, and participation are carried over uninterrupted and unquestioned from childhood, but this continuation also implies, however muted it may be, a decision, since Americans are, with few exceptions, exposed to many differing kinds of self-locating among their fellow citizens. Whatever form it takes, then, and despite the fact that it can be of varying importance for the way Americans include religion as a positive factor in their self-accounts, being a religious person and being able to say "where you are" at the present time can have much to do with one another, and for some it is primary.

6

RELIGIOUS DIVINERS

RATHER THAN to the past, as with Religious Debtors, or to locations and affiliations in the present, as with Religious Dwellers, texts by Religious Diviners include religion positively by directing attention toward the future. More than the others, Religious Diviners are on a personal journey or quest.

Religious Diviners noticeably seek a religious identity that confirms their particularity, and that characteristic could make this kind of religious identity seem more self-centered than the other two. In fact, I was tempted at first to refer to texts of this kind as by Religious Designers, people who fashion religion to suit their sense of who they are and what will fit. But texts of this kind need not be more self-preoccupied than texts of the other two kinds. They can be equally directed toward and open to something outside, even something that counters self-understandings and expectations, that challenges and alters previous identities. What distinguishes these kinds of texts from the others is not self-concern but the positioning of religion toward the future, as something sought. This future orientation does not mean that these texts convey more uncertainty regarding religious identity than those of the other two kinds. Like self-concern, uncertainty can be found in accounts of all three kinds. Neither self-concern nor uncertainty but a future orientation and a sense of journey or quest is what distinguishes texts of this kind from the others we have examined.

The future orientation of Religious Diviners relates them to American identity more broadly because Americans also are often characterized as oriented toward something yet to come, as on a journey or quest. While the future orientation of Americans has been largely co-opted by technological and commercial interests, Americans look toward the future not only for better cars and faster computers but also for opportunities to actualize their own and their children's potential, for a more just society, and for greater well-being not only for themselves but also for other people in the world. The language of "errand," "the territory ahead," or "the new frontier" for describing the future orientation of American identity can readily be invoked. We easily can be persuaded by political rhetoric that what we are is not what we can or ought to be, that there is much that should be remedied and much still to accomplish. And this sense of an uncompleted agenda and unreached goals is not only directed toward material goods but also to moral and spiritual possibilities. Texts of Religious Diviners, then, are related to this recurring aspect of American identity.

Texts of Religious Diviners, while here treated as the last of our three types, could chronologically be put first. The orientation to the future, to various ways in which something in the New World could be constructed that would be unprecedented especially in moral and religious terms, was a pervasive and generative spirit in the early settlements of this land. Religious Debtors, on the other hand, while treated first, have become more common in recent years as greater distance has developed between a less religious present and a more religious past.

While the texts by Religious Diviners at which we shall look are by writers who are also religiously affiliated, their affiliations are less important than is something they are trying on their own to reach or to clarify. The diminishing importance of affiliation that we shall encounter now can be extended outward to include Americans who consider themselves to be actively religious but without benefit of affiliation. There is, in other words, an affinity between Religious Diviners and Americans who define their religious identities as being noninstitutional, improvised, and personal. People of this kind often self-identify as spiritual rather than as religious, and among such people there exists a range of beliefs as to what the spiritual is, from something divine or transcendent to a human potential for wholeness or renewal. Finally, this kind of religious American holds affinities with nonreligious Americans who are also interested in and even strive actively toward kinds of personal fulfillment that they do not identify with religion. As Courtney Bender shows in her study of various spiritual groups and practices in and around Cambridge, Massachusetts, the membrane that separates religious from nonreligious participants in yoga, tai chi, and other healing and renewing group practices is highly permeable.[1] Religious Americans of the kind I am calling Diviners, then, are also continuous with their nonreligious neighbors by being, along with them although in a more recognizably religious way, in search of a more fully realized moral and spiritual personal life.

Frederick Buechner

> But one way or another the journey through time starts for us
> all, and for all of us, too, that journey is in at least one sense the
> same journey because what it is primarily, I think, is a journey
> *in search.*
>
> —BUECHNER, *Sacred Journey: A Memoir of Early Days*

Frederick Buechner strikes the defining tone of the Religious Diviner when he says, in *The Sacred Journey,* "What quickens my pulse now is the stretch ahead rather than the one behind, and it is mainly for some clue to where I am going that I search through where I have been."[2] The use of "journey" in his title, his eye on "the stretch ahead," and his emphasis on "clue" and "search" put the matter succinctly. Like others of this kind, Buechner's religious identity is future-oriented.

Buechner implicitly supports my point that this way of being a religious person and the identities of Americans more generally are related to one another because he is not hesitant to assert that everyone is engaged in a journey like his own, a search for something yet to be realized. His reference in the epigraph above to "all of us" is neither to humanity as a whole, one should think, nor to a specific group of readers but to his wider American audience.

The stretch of his journey that Buechner describes in this account is from his early years to the point, at the age of twenty-seven, when he decides to translate his sense of journey or quest into Christian language. This account of his early life is shaped primarily by that change of language.

Buechner places the description of the early portion of his journey in a deliberately theoretical context. He views his life and the lives of "all of us" as having two levels. The first or more surface level is the process of maturation, the progress through the various stages or chapters of life. People's lives at this surface level are largely shared and often similar. But beneath this shared surface there is a deeper level, one that gives particularity and significance to each person's life. This level is not so obvious or available, and finding it requires effort; "we ferret it out for ourselves," he says (4). At this deeper level, the truth not only about one's own life but about human life itself is revealed. It resembles the plot of a novel in that various incidents are taken as leading or relating to one another. Events, people, and locations are connected in such a way as to reveal an underlying, forward-oriented coherence. This deeper level is already there but needs to be surfaced and interpreted. Buechner could not value this particularizing level for personal identity more highly than he does. "If God speaks to us at all in this world," he writes, "it is into our personal lives that he speaks" (1). The particularizing level of a person's life and the Word of God are, in this way, joined. Indeed, Buechner implies that this is not simply one way but the only way that God speaks to him and to all people (95). The journey, "working out your own salvation with fear and trembling" (100), is sacred because the particular meaning of a person's life, the way moments of it are unified, and the meaningful whole called out by attentive interpretation, is divine.

At times, the two levels of life connect. This occurs when instances on the upper level stand out because by or in them the deeper level is surfaced. Such instances stand out, then, not because they are separate from the rest but because they are both unusually related to the rest and reveal, as well, that the rest is related to something more.

Buechner clarifies his point that human lives at the surface level resemble one another by describing human development as having three stages. The first stage, which for him continued until age ten, lacks a sense of time's passing. The second stage, which for him stretches from age ten to sixteen, is marked by changes in life that require conscious decisions. The primary outcome of this part of his own life is to have secured his sense of vocation as a writer. The third stage incorporates aspects of the first two, but it also differs in its being oriented primarily beyond time toward a fullness for which a person yearns or toward which a life is directed.

I

The goal of Buechner's journey is described primarily by spatial language. This spatial language is not, however, tied to his experiences of the houses of his family of origin, since, because of his father's job uncertainty during the Depression, his family moved often. True, he does relate positively and meaningfully as a boy to the home of his maternal grandparents in Pittsburgh, since their house is warmly welcoming and its attics enticing. And his paternal grandmother's apartment in New York City seems a secure place. But these do not account for the interest he has in places as havens. Rather, his spatial sense derives primarily from reading books, and he thinks of books spatially, since, "like a house in the rain, books were havens of permanence and protection from whatever it was that as a child I needed protection from" (19). Books, and one would think primarily narratives, provide significant alternatives to a world of diversity and change by supplying coherence, the coherence of an underlying or overarching plot acting as a kind of house.

A transcendent form of his goal is suggested by the words of a hymn Mrs. Taylor, who worked in his home when he was young, taught him. It's the fourth verse of "The Old Rugged Cross": "To the old rugged cross I will ever be true / Its shame and reproach gladly bear; / Then he'll call me someday to my home far away / Where his glory forever I'll share." This spatial image of an ultimate home grants specificity and future-directedness to the gradually revealed goal of his life, an emerging and significant particularity underlying the uncertainties, vagaries, and isolated moments of day-by-day existence.

His understanding of himself as continuing, coherent, and oriented toward the future provides Buechner a positive attitude toward himself and his world. An assuring forward direction in his life was from his youth a developing counter to the instability of his home. It seems clear that his parents were close neither to him nor to one another, that his father was frequently absent, and that they moved often. After his father's suicide, he does not appear to develop a close and constant relationship with his mother. Indeed, the evaluation of his parents implied by his account suggests that, at the time of writing, Buechner has come to see his father, whose suicide caused the major disruption of Buechner's early life, as a gentle and generous man and his mother as somewhat cold and even cruel. She marries a man from Bermuda when they return from there to this country, and this act suggests that their sojourn in Bermuda had some connection to this man. Indeed, the young Buechner seems to have been sent away to high school in order to facilitate the completion of that relationship. The negative factors in his parents' relations to one another and to him enhance his memory of and high regard for Mrs. Taylor, who taught him to read and to love books and who shared with him her sense of mystery. His early reading, especially the Oz books of L. Frank Baum, gave him confidence in the imagined or possible as in some way more real than daily life, and this orientation to an alternative reality is preparatory both for his vocation as an imaginative writer and for his later religious conversion. Stability, as already mentioned, is also provided by his grandparents, although his paternal grandmother seems not to have gotten on well with his mother.

The future-oriented direction of his life is also reinforced by his desire to move beyond his father's suicide. This response is facilitated by his family's move to Bermuda, a decision made in the face of his paternal grandmother's disapproval. He turns his back on his father, as apparently he felt his father had abandoned him. But between the suicide and the time of writing he seems to have come to a different evaluation of his father's act: "My father's writing on the last page of *Gone with the Wind* that he was no good, and then, because he believed that, giving his life away for what he must have thought was our good and thus in his own sad, lost way echoing with his unimaginable gift another holy gift more unimaginable still" (110). I do not doubt the sincerity of Buechner's attempt to relate his father's suicide to the positive place of Christ's sacrifice in Christian belief, but it seems occasioned by his revised view of his parents and by his general purpose, at the time of writing, to find positive meaning in negative incidents.

II

Buechner seems eager to move from very negative events to positive interpretations of them, such as comparing World War II to a rainy day when people feel unified, "rich and poor alike caught up in a sense of common purpose and destiny" (67). This does not mean that he is cavalier concerning life's difficulties and pain. He points out, for example, that people you love have two sides, with one they love you and with the other "they can sting you with like a wasp" (32). So, too, his father's death allows him to see that people carry pains in their lives, "buried griefs and hurtful memories" (56). But the reader may feel that the theoretical view at the time of writing, namely, that the underlying movement or meaning of life is positive and unifying, too readily transforms negatives into their contraries.

Buechner tends to associate painful and difficult things with a past to be left behind and positive outcomes or interpretations of them with a future that is unfolding. This tendency is supported religiously by associating important people in his past who have died with the future, since, as saints do, they go before him leading "toward whatever new shore may await them" (22). The past is left behind. As he says, "We cannot live our lives constantly looking back, listening back, lest [like Lot's wife] we be turned to pillars of longing and regret, but to live without listening at all is to live deaf to the fullness of the music" (77–78). The past is something to be left behind also because, among other things, it contains the suicides so common in his father's family, what he calls "a family curse" (83). Looking ahead resists the power of their lure and holds open the possibility of their grave force being dissolved in and by something higher and greater.

A surprising aspect of Buechner's account is that, while he is himself a narrative artist and while in his account he compares his life and the lives of his readers to a narrative, he does not narrate much of his life. He occasionally narrates incidents, the first and most memorable being his father's suicide at the outset of the second part. Rather than narrate, he describes, and often he describes things, events, and people in order to record the effects that they had on him. Descriptions lead readily to interpretive commentary, and interpretive commentary readily yields to theories about the emergence of life's wholeness and meaning.

These characteristics of the account have two consequences for the reader. The first is to focus attention largely on the writer who is describing his life in ways determined by a theory he has formed. So, incidents in the past, their effects on him, and his interpretation of them are determined by where at the time of writing they can be seen as leading.[3] The second consequence is to steer the reader's attention to the outcome of the account, his conversion. The unifying intention of the text is to record this important change in the twenty-seventh year of his life. His conversion has two stages.

The first stage is a change from what he describes as the excessive self-centeredness of his earlier years to his awareness that being a person, indeed, being alive, means and requires journeying not primarily for one's own sake but "for the world's sake" (107). He comes to this recognition, it seems, by the effect on him of his decision not to aid a man who was a colleague during Buechner's five-year tenure as a teacher in the Lawrenceville School. The gravity of this decision is deepened by the fact that his mother supported it. The turning point, then, also seems coincident with a revised evaluation of his mother and, consequently, also of his new understanding of his father and of the suicide.

The second stage is more specifically religious. During his residence in New York City he began attending church, mostly out of a lack of anything better to do. There he was exposed to the preaching of George Buttrick, which engaged him deeply. When he speaks to Buttrick about the effect, especially of one sermon, on him, he allows

Buttrick to take him uptown to Union Theological Seminary, a willingness possibly aided by the memory of a question that a clergyman
some years earlier had asked him, namely, whether Buechner had ever
considered turning his writing abilities in a religious direction. The
account ends, then, with Buechner embarking on a quest to add religion to his emerging vocational identity, and this ending reveals the
basis for describing, interpreting, and theorizing his life religiously.

His direction at the end is not sponsored by his youth. There is
not much religion in his past, and if the past is to be understood
religiously, it is so from the new position he holds at the time of
writing. His parents were not religious, something also true of his
father's mother, although his maternal grandmother took him to
church during the year that they lived in Tryon, North Carolina.
Becoming a Christian is not triggered by dissatisfaction with himself
or his world, and it does not occasion a clear change of direction.
Rather, Christianity provides a new language or perspective for interpreting his life. In retrospect he can see moments that prepared
him for the turn to Christian language. For example, he was, as an
undergraduate, intrigued by seventeenth-century English prose writers and how they made him listen for something that seemed to
reverberate beneath the surface of their words. Also, while writing
his first novel, plot became for him the principal focus in writing.
Since from his youth he had thought of the imagined or the possible
as in some ways more real than what occurs in the everyday, plot
suggests that his own life has coherence, that events "are seeking to
show us something, lead us somewhere" (95). Later he spends time
at a monastery, and, while nothing extraordinary occurs there, he
learns the discipline of silence, a discipline that leads to an expectation of "hearing someone or something speak out of the silence"
(103). He also takes seriously a monk's exhortation that Buechner
had "a long way to go" (104). Although he is positively affected by
the preaching of George Buttrick, he is not drawn to affiliation with
a church as a location he could value or as a kind of house providing
a haven during the "rain" of life. Rather, Christianity is attractive
and significant primarily by granting him a language that enables
him to talk about experiences he already has had, to recognize and
tally their value, and to anticipate an unfolding that has yet to occur.
When he says that he found or was found by Christ, he seems mostly
to mean by this a new awareness that incidents on the surface or
temporal level of his life are related to a meaning below the surface
that is lasting, that reveals personal particularity, and that someday
will be completed.

III

While Buechner's view of his identity as secured by the Word of God beneath the surface events of his life is convincingly presented, the reader may well suggest that he is also able to absorb the shocks of sharply negative experiences in his life because there are unusual economic and cultural resources available to him. His parents were sufficiently well-off to have had live-in help. His father was a Princeton alumnus, and his paternal grandmother, a devotee of Wagner, is educated and wealthy. She bankrolls their life in Bermuda and is personally rock-like, having weathered the suicides of her husband and two sons. His maternal grandmother reads French novels and is a gifted storyteller. When his father dies, the family moves to Bermuda, where he lived, he tells us, "with a sense of the magic and mystery of things greater than I had ever experienced this side of Oz" (48). Later he attends the prestigious Lawrenceville School, where he develops a vocational direction away from painting and toward literary art, and Princeton University. He was a student at Union Theological Seminary during the zenith of its academic reputation.

This does not mean that Buechner is wholly unaware of the economic and cultural privileges of his life. He recognizes that he has deeply benefitted from gifts, and he acknowledges that a gift "implies a giver" (54). Moreover, he responds to those gifts with a prayer of thanksgiving: "For all thy blessings known and unknown, remembered and forgotten, we give thee thanks" (57). Nor do I mean that being rich and enjoying the benefits of cultural capital are things that, for religious reasons, one should be ashamed of or eschew. It is only that I find it puzzling that he narrates his life as undergirded by divine presence without recognizing as well that at least some of the undergirding was provided by the economic and cultural wealth of his family, particularly of his grandparents. Divine grace and the supports of economic class and high culture, while not necessarily in opposition to one another, are also, certainly, not the same thing.

Although the undergirding or deep level of his life is also cultural and economic, Buechner turns the lacks and traumas of his past toward a positive, religiously interpreted orientation to and hopeful expectation of the future. A question to ask at the end is how specifically Christian Buechner's religious and even theological understanding of his life is. While he uses Christian language and while a theologically interpreted life is his account's unifying intention, the account seems to rely more on a religious form of identity than specifically on Christianity. Christological language is generalized by the incarnational view that surface occasions are related to the level of his life at which God's Word can be heard or read. In addition, that Word or voice at the deeper level is to be seen as the particularity of one's own life and a significance that is personally appropriated. The significance of Christianity is warranted by his own life's unfolding rather than the other way around. That is, Christianity takes on importance for and relevance to his life to the extent that it illuminates what he sees as already there, his life's basic coherence and direction.

Buechner's construal of his life and of any life as an actual or potential story organized principally by a plot, a plot constituted of particular moments and their emerging, underlying, and personalizing coherence, projects religious identity on or toward the future. Identity, then, is primarily still outstanding, and for him personal and religious identities are closely tied, since what gives meaning, coherence, and particularity to a person's life is itself sacred. Christianity is relevant to his identity in that it provides a language by which these basic beliefs or theories can be more adequately expressed and more easily recognized.

Mary Gordon

> I would have to leave the church, because to live with this new sense of lightness and clarity I would need a dwelling that let in the light.
>
> —GORDON, *Seeing through Places: Reflections on Geography and Identity*

Mary Gordon provides a striking example of an American writer with a strong religious past who distanced herself sharply from it and then, as an adult, selectively reappropriates it on her own terms. Raised in a densely, self-consciously, and even oppressively Catholic environment, Gordon incorporates Catholic material in her fiction. However, unlike Roth, Gordon displays not an indebtedness to her religious upbringing but an aversion toward it. And, while at the time of writing she participates in Catholic liturgy, she does not relate her religious identity strongly with her church affiliation, as do Religious Dwellers, but includes the church conditionally and selectively. She belongs, then, in this third group, a person who has a religious identity that, while also drawing from the past and being affiliated, primarily is future-oriented, constructed, and in process.

Her project of religious identity formation provides an answer to the question that Gordon raises toward the end of *Seeing through*

Places. "What makes me feel that I have the right to live this life I live, and then to write about it?"[4] While the two parts of the question are closely related, it is the second part that concerns the reader as much as the first part concerns the writer. What does she think there is in her life that warrants calling readers' attention to it? The answer, I think, lies in her personally determined Catholic identity and the justification of it that she implies.

Gordon's forward direction is supported by the fact that she seems not to like her early life, even not to like herself, very much. Indeed, recalling her past, especially her life with her parents, about whom she writes further in two other self-accounts, is a matter of justifying why she thinks of her formative years as bleak and distasteful. Her evaluation of her early life and its Catholic content have much to do with one another. She views them negatively from the positive position of freedom from that past.

Her separation from her past and recognition of its faults and lacks are supported by her position at the time of writing. The present marks a vocational achievement that sharply contrasts with the unpromising circumstances of her upbringing. In addition, she has come to value cities, especially New York City, highly and, by doing so, counters the prevailingly negative depictions of urban life in American literary culture. A third is that she places value on institutions and the large buildings by which they are housed and represented, and this counters the anti-institutionalism of her college years. These qualities of the present give her a newly acquired gratitude for her life. Her positive position at the time of writing owes little to her past, and if any of her Catholic identity is to be salvaged from the past, it will be she who determines what and how much. Knowing Catholicism well by her deep immersion in it and confident of her own critical and creative abilities, her position at the time of writing qualifies her to determine what kind of Catholic identity she will construct.

I

After an opening capsulation of her life-account, Gordon structures her narrative more spatially than temporally, although the chapters are in chronological order. Bracketing the account are the two places that she contrasts most sharply with one another: the home of her grandmother, which she visited often and to which she and her mother move after her father's death when she was seven, and Barnard College, where she lives, works, and is writing.

She depicts her grandmother's house as dark and constricting. An unmarried aunt, who also lives there when she arrives, is, like her grandmother, dour, judgmental, and determined that she would have "a childhood without pleasure" (38). The house in some respects is similar to the home of Mrs. Kirk, to which she was sent for day care from her first through her fifth year, since her mother worked every day as a legal secretary. Mrs. Kirk, "a slattern, with missing front teeth and witch hair" (57), disapproves of her. That disapproval is intensified by the darkness of the house and by one of the Kirk daughters, who is uncannily able to discover Mary engaged in habitual autoerotic acts and who reports them to Mrs. Kirk. "She and my mother were at war against my secret vice, the private experience of sexual pleasure, which I probably discovered out of the drowning boredom of my days with Mrs. Kirk" (60).

The narrative of her life after the death of her father turns largely to her grandmother, since her grandmother dominated the house to which she and her mother move. Her grandmother, an Irish immigrant, had had a difficult life and takes no interest in pleasure or light. When Mary is thirteen, her grandmother dies, and Mary and her mother continue to live in the house but discontinue the rigorous care that her grandmother had given it. They live in clutter, eventually unable to use some of the rooms and needing to clear spaces on the table before they could use it for eating.

Mary does not find relief from these conditions in contacts outside of her home. Her education in Catholic schools seems to have provided nothing worth recording, and her neighborhood offers little relief. The house next door is as male as her own is female, and her main recollection of its male children is of their pinning her to the ground and forcing rhubarb into her mouth. The summer camp to which she is sent after her father dies offers no alternative either, since it is a camp for boys.

From these negative conditions, largely described in relation to religion, Mary retreats. In the house where her family lived before her father's death, she had retreated to its barren attics. She also retreats into reading. She likes stories not so much of action as of places, and when she reads books she looks for "an atmosphere that I could enter" (80). "If I lost myself in the fates of virgin martyrs or fairy princesses, if I was Napoleon or one of the Salem witches, there was nothing shameful in the shiftiness of my identity" (77). At summer camp she reads constantly: "All day, my head was filled with thoughts of lovely women, virtuous, heroic, or women whose lives had neither story nor event, all of them rescued, at the last possible moment, by a man who loved them, who would save them from their dangers and their fates" (105). This "shiftiness" of her identity suggests that it is shaped less by the determinations of the past or of the circumstances in which she finds herself as by projected possibilities. These possibilities and her readiness to project or imagine them grant the bases for the confidence needed to pursue her own vocational and religious identities.

Partial relief from her darkness and confinement earlier was provided by her father during the two-year period between day care with Mrs. Kirk and his death. Habitually unemployed, he served as her principal caretaker during that period, and he played games with her, solemn games, to be sure, such as celebrating mass or impersonating famous people, but games nonetheless that allowed her to project herself into various roles. He also took her with him on his frequent jaunts into the city. These excursions and the abundance of reading that she did as a child seem most significantly related to the final location of the narrative, Columbia University, where she lives as a member of the faculty.

In contrast to the houses of her youth, New York City suggests light and freedom. It is a location to which she aspired, if only tacitly, since being an undergraduate at Columbia. And it provides the height at the end of the account from which she judges her past and traces her emerging identity. As she says toward the end of her account, "all this was required in order that I could get from where I was, the house that had been my grandmother's, to here" (241).

II

What is unusual about Gordon's narrative is not so much the importance of places, since we have seen other self-accounts similarly oriented, as the almost wholly negative view of her upbringing that she conveys, including occasional negative views of herself. For example, she describes herself as cruel and even "loathsome" (97). Her grandmother, her aunt and uncle, Mrs. Kirk and her daughters, the little playmate Ella downstairs whom Gordon hurts, the people next door, even most of the priests: all of these people and her relationships with them are recalled in a largely negative way. This depiction is supported by the fact that she narrates little or nothing about friendships in college, about her husbands, about her two children, or about her academic and professional associations as a student, writer, and teacher. At the time of writing she seems to be married but living alone. Indeed, she presents herself as solitary, a person who, as she says about her stays in the cottage she rents on Cape Cod, prefers to be alone. Her quite negative depictions of other people and of her relations to them might have led the reader to assume that she stands in critical distance above them, but this impression is prevented by the fact that she also depicts herself as at least also somewhat odd.

Her relations with her parents are also not positive. Her mother seems to identify more with her workplace than with her husband and daughter, and when Mary's father dies, her grandmother becomes the dominant figure in her life. Upon the death of her grandmother, she and her mother do not make common cause out of building or maintaining a life together. Her mother, when not at work, is less interested in Mary than in drinking sweet vermouth. Her relation with her deceased father also becomes troubled. Although he appears sometimes volatile and provocative in his conservative Catholic views, she is rather close to him, especially during the two years before he died. But she learns later that his life as an ardent Catholic convert and devoted father concealed many deceptions: he was previously married, did not attend Harvard or Oxford Universities as he had claimed but was a high school dropout, was dependent on his wife's earnings, and spent most of his time not working but trying to get relatives and friends to bankroll his many financial schemes in publishing.[5]

Gordon's self-account, then, is shaped by her view that her relations to other people, as much because of her own questionable attitudes and behaviors as of theirs, were largely unhelpful, disillusioning, or painful and that who and where she is at the time of writing are due, in large part if not exclusively, to her own aspirations, abilities, and good fortune. Her account is a tour of the unusual if not bizarre character of her childhood and of the distance between that time and place and her present position as a writer and teacher at Barnard. A question concerning autobiographical writing can be asked of a text like this, namely, whether a self-account largely devoid of positive relationships between the writer and her child-self and between the writer and other people in her life, can be a text that provides its reader the opportunity for intimacy with the writer that this kind of text normally provides.

III

The positive in her account derives from her professional location at Columbia and her identification with the city and its institutions. She points out that many writers in America have given negative images of the city, writers, she adds, who mostly were male. "The city teaches them their own loathsomeness and the loathsomeness or misfortunes of their neighbors" (252). In contrast, she wants to record her appreciation for and personal attachment to the city.

Along with the city as environment, Gordon affirms her positive evaluation of large buildings and the institutions that they house or represent. This intent is also contrary to much in literary culture and, especially during the late 1960s and early 1970s, to much of the culture in which she was a participant. During the demonstrations and riots of the anti–Vietnam War period, she was, as an undergraduate, swept up by anti-institutional rhetoric. For example, she was aware that the buildings of Columbia University were supported at least in part by Dow Chemical Corporation, manufacturers of the napalm used to burn children in Vietnam. However, since the time when her father took her into New York City as a little girl, she has also been drawn to large buildings. She is more impressed, for example, by the buildings that house museums and churches than by what exists or goes on within them. She wants now to affirm that buildings and institutions are important for the well-being of persons and for the actualization of their potentials and identities. Buildings have qualities of the sublime, intimidating as well as quickening effects. "I need the great buildings, what they provide, what they suggest, for my work," she says (252).

Gordon's affirmation of the city is not at the price of ignoring its problems. Especially as a woman, she has to be alert to the need for security, and she realizes that she lives in a particularly privileged situation. She feels, therefore, grateful for the place where she finds herself, although writing in a state of gratitude and appreciation for the city and its institutions is difficult, even dull, compared to writing out of complaint and disdain. As she says, "what I feel is gratitude, gratitude toward an institution, and how do I write that, without feeling embarrassingly jejune about that?" The simple fact is, as she admits, "I am where I am because of the benevolence of an institution" (254). The value of her life, a value that also confers on her a warrant for writing about it, is imparted by her professional position and the identity it confirms.

Her sense of gratitude and delight is amplified by the fact that she has become a member of the faculty in the institution where she matured as a student: "Thirty-two years later (almost the entire life span of Jesus Christ) I stand in front of the same mirror, a teacher now, waiting for the same elevator. And again I say to myself, Yes (but perhaps with more emphasis on the monosyllable), yes, I'm here" (228). She views this reception as a gift as much as something she has achieved. She recognizes that "I haven't earned it; or earning is not the point: it is great good luck that has allowed me to be back where I belong" (242).

It is important to notice the reasons why Gordon dissociates her sense of worth and status from material terms or social and economic success. Her lack of interest in wealth and materiality is due to religious influences in her early life: "I was brought up believing not one good thing about money," she says. "Burned into my soul were the words of Jesus, 'You cannot serve God and mammon.' 'Find for yourself treasure in heaven.' 'Consider the lilies of the field.' Of the deadly sins, I prided myself on being free of avarice" (220). The major exception to this lack of interest in possessions is the Cape Cod cottage, a former home of John Dos Passos, where she spent eight delightful summers reading and writing. When the cottage goes up for sale, she is unable to afford it and is forced to terminate her treasured relation to the place. However, she also realizes that if she had become its owner, she would know herself less clearly "by what I've written" (221). Her identity is closely tied, then, to her ongoing work as a writer.

This gesture to her religious past suggests that Gordon, at the time of writing, is not unaware that the religion of her past, however grim, also contributed positively to who and where she now is. However, the religious content of that past must be treated selectively and personally reformulated. The spiritual quality of her vocational identity and her affirmative attitude toward institutions are the clearest points of continuity with the Catholic character of her upbringing. This yield from her past is meager, given the heavy Catholic content of her parents' retreats, "visits," and daily masses, their relations with priests, and the many books she read as a girl about saints and martyrs. But however meager, Catholic content embedded itself in her language and served to shape her world: "'Sacramental,' 'Occasion of Sin,' 'Fast Days,' 'Feast Days,' 'State of Grace'" (157). However, while her Catholic upbringing contributed some positive content to who she is, it primarily formed an oppressive world of darkness and confinement from which she needed to escape. This negative depiction justifies her shedding her Catholic past upon entering college. Her rejection of religion continued, it seems, until a time not long before writing this account. At the time of writing, she has begun selectively and cautiously to reconstruct it.

A factor that may well have facilitated the shedding of her Catholic past, although she does not say much about it, is that the academic culture that she entered as a student stood in a contrary relation to religious authority. At least it can be said that she was not going against the cultural stream when she allowed the beginning of her college career to coincide with her withdrawal from the church. Another reason is that she had a falling out with the church because of the political conservatism of some of its clergy, particularly with Cardinal Spellman's support of the Vietnam War. She also severed relations with a priest her mother had devoutly followed, a man who in general disapproved of contemporary culture at a time when she had begun to "enjoy the world."

By far the most important reason for rejecting the church is Gordon's affirmation and high evaluation of physical, specifically sexual, pleasure. While she does not otherwise present herself as a physically oriented person, commenting little on her body, having no interest in playing sports, and giving no descriptions of her experiences with two pregnancies and births, for example, she does narrate her body as a site of pleasure. At a young age, as already mentioned, she habitually engaged in sexual pleasure. While she narrates some sexually charged events in early life that had negative effects on her, they seem overshadowed by positive experiences. She enjoyed being instructed by the woman next door in walking with high heels, and she develops a bond with her in relation to their shared interest in attracting men: "She knew I had, like her, a life that had something to do with pleasing men, not only with serving them. That had to do with being pleased by them as well" (135). Given, as we already have seen, the lack of significance she gives to personal relationships, we find here an orientation to relationships with men determined primarily by sexual pleasure. This orientation seems grounded by her relations with her first boyfriend, who is a college student while she is a senior in high school. When he visits her, he stays overnight at her house rather than make the trip back to school, and when he does she lies with him in her bed, engaging in "extensive activity." Afterward, she tells us, "I would lie down beside my mother, my body sweaty and lubricious from the upstairs activity that was extensive but stopped short of my virginity" (47). This relationship provided a positive reinforcement for sexual pleasure because it was secured from the knowledge both of her mother and of her schoolmates and accommodated by her own bed. This experience seems to have given her confidence to have sex frequently in college, often, she tells us, with men she did not know very well (247). She admits that she avoided church as a college student because, "If I went into a church, everyone would know I am having sex, and would order me to stop, and I knew I wouldn't because I liked it much too much" (244). The close tie between her identity and sexual pleasure is caus-ally related to the dwindling of her relation to the church.

This tension between the church and sexual pleasure and the choice of the latter over the former also seems to underlie her expe-rience of Rome, to which she makes several trips. She recognizes a contrast in Rome between the Vatican, in its massive stillness, and the vitality of Roman city life, to which she was, even as a young girl, drawn. Rome and the Vatican in their separation parallel her own sense of distance between a Catholic identity and sexual pleasure.

The process of Gordon's partial and tentative reappropriation of her Catholic identity is governed by the fact that she reenters the church to the degree that, or as long as, it meets her conditions and does not threaten her values. At the time of writing she has found a church that she can attend because it does not emphasize matters that would alienate her: "No one will shout from the pulpit here about communism and free love, or even about abortion or divorce. In this place, I feel free, once again, to pray" (251).

While she accounts for the reconstruction of her Catholic identity in terms both of the continuing role that Catholic language plays in her sense of things and of the more accommodating atmosphere of the church she presently attends, Gordon does not really say what it is about life outside the church that, in its lacks, leads her to reaffili-ate nor what there is in the church that addresses such lacks, either as she sees them in the world around her or in herself. It is clear, nonetheless, that her reassociation, although partial, is deliberate and meaningful, since the renewed role of the church in her life seems largely to determine what in the account of her early life she should emphasize and what about her Catholic upbringing warrants the in-complete and conditional nature of her present relation to the church.

One could argue, perhaps, that Gordon, by reaffiliation with the church, is a Religious Dweller somewhat in the manner of Letty Pogrebin. Gordon's objections to the political views of some Catho-lic clergy were, like the objections of Pogrebin to the male chau-vinism of some Jews, limited and not total. Indeed, there also were Catholic clergy who stood against the war. As she matured, Gordon grew more appreciative of institutions and of what it takes to estab-lish and maintain them, and her political views must have edged at least to some degree toward a somewhat more conservative position. So, as with Pogrebin, it could be argued that both she and the church changed sufficiently over the years to allow for a rapprochement between them.

However, the role of the church in contributing a religious component to her identity puts her in with other "Diviners" because of the importance of sexuality and physical pleasure in her life and self-understanding. Gordon's sense of herself and sexual pleasure have much, it seems, to do with one another. Her distance, even antagonism, toward the church on this issue was very strong: "I was furious at the Catholic Church, particularly for the sexual repression it demanded, the sexual lies it told."[6] While the church can forgive forbidden sexual pleasures, it also must condemn and call for their termination. The church stands, then, in a contrary relation to a principal component of Gordon's identity, requiring her to retain a distance from the church for the sake of vindicating an aspect of her identity that, it seems, is crucial. While as a mature woman her interest in sexual pleasure and its importance may have become less urgent, reestablishment of her relation to the church would require, at the least, agreement with the church that the past pleasures should be negatively viewed. And this, it is apparent, she is unwilling to do. Sexuality in forms countered by the church is significant for her personal identity and for her fiction, and she will not yield to any pressures that would distance her from it.

While the opinions of clergy regarding politics and war are matters of choice and while clergy need not agree on them among themselves or require agreement with their opinions on the part of laity, sexual and reproductive issues are not left to choice and varieties of opinion but are governed by church law and teaching. Moreover, Catholic stands on sexual and reproductive issues are, if not largely defining, highly visible in contemporary, especially American, culture. Gordon positions herself, then, not only as loyal to her own convictions concerning such matters but also as against the church. That position places her sense of what it is good for her to be fundamentally at odds with a highly visible and non-negotiable aspect of the church's identity.

Gordon is an example of or a participant in what José Casanova calls the third stage in the disestablishment of religion in American society, namely, the waning of religious determinations over the personal, especially the sexual, behaviors of Americans. While reaffiliating with the church, Gordon does so tentatively, on her own terms, and as part of an ongoing attempt to construct a religious identity that is faithful not first of all to the church but to who she is. Her own jurisdiction over that process is paramount.

Along with her partial and self-determined relation to the church, Gordon places the church alongside other institutions that also can be viewed, at least partially, as sacred. As she says, a sharp point of difference between her and her parents is that, for them, "the Catholic Faith was the most important thing in their lives,"[7] and this, she goes on to say, is not the case with her. Along with the church, Gordon has high regard for Barnard College and for New York City's museums and public library. One could expect the list to go on: its theaters, concert halls, and restaurants, for example. She says at one point: "I am in the Metropolitan Museum of Art, one of my places of refuge, of contemplation, a sacred place. I come here as my mother would have gone to a church."[8]

Gordon's separation from the church takes a doctrinal turn in her recent book on reading the Gospels. The Christological conclusion she draws takes exception to Catholic dogma: "What I don't think is justified in the Gospels is the notion that only Jesus is divine, the insistence that God—whoever he or she is—has or can inhabit a human life once."[9] This does not mean, however, that she wants to replace Jesus with something or someone else. She couldn't do that "without ripping out the foundations of who I am, how I have known myself and understood the world."[10] But it also means that she separates herself by her Christology from a defining doctrine of the church, a doctrine with enormous significance as well for what the church, for Catholics, is.

The conclusion to be drawn, then, is that Gordon is herself the site where the force and meanings of various locations, including Catholic ones, are, at the time of writing, brought together. She freely and selectively moves between and within institutions, but, while grateful for them, she does not fully identify with them. She is on a journey, a kind of polyphonic movement forward, relating the potentials for the sacred residing in various institutions to her own developing sense of personal religious identity.

Anne Lamott

> The truth is that your spirits don't rise until you get *way* down.
> Maybe it's because this—the mud, the bottom—is where it all
> rises from.
>
> —Lamott, *Traveling Mercies: Some Thoughts on Faith*

At the time of writing *Traveling Mercies*, the novelist Anne Lamott is forty-five, and, although continuing what she describes as her journey toward faith, she has found a church "home." She writes from a position of relative calm or strength also because she has, for the past dozen years or so, been free from the control over her life that addictions once held. Finally, she is the mother of a ten-year-old son, Sam, who appears frequently in her account as a positive constant in her life. However, this higher or firmer ground is not a terminus. She presents herself as on a journey that is marked by surprises and epiphanies, and the larger portion of her account contains brief recordings of such moments. Finding a church and her life with Sam are positive experiences in a process that is ongoing as she writes.

I

Quest, improvisation, and uncertainty, characteristics of her journey, can be related to Lamott's upbringing in the northern California culture of the late 1960s. While she thinks of her parents as self-obsessed and while she does not fully endorse their behaviors or those of their friends, she also does not look back at the formative years of her life negatively. Personal qualities that she affirms appear to be consistent with the experimentation and spontaneity that were hallmarks of the cultural context of her youth.

She relates the positive factors in her upbringing more explicitly to her girlhood friends. Indeed, she seems to have spent an unusually large amount of her time in their homes, and she attributes her quest for faith implicitly to the exposure to various religious orientations that participation in the life of other families provided her.

Yet, more than for her family of origin, the culture of which her home was fully a part, or her friends, Lamott has strongly positive feelings for her youthful self. She carries with her a picture of herself at the age of three, and she looks at it often. This attachment suggests that a positive and innocent image of herself is a constant in her life that needs to be protected, recalled, and vindicated. Indeed, the resiliency and remarkable recoveries that she records could be attributed, at least in part, to the enduring presence of, and her tacit commitment to, this childhood self.

Lamott's engagingly written account of her life is a series of recoveries, encounters, and surprises that are placed in a darkly colored context. One of the negative constants in her life is her body, to which she draws a good bit of attention, an attention that gains importance because she presents her life primarily as a spiritual journey. Already as a teenager, she thought of herself as "fat in the can," and later on she closely identifies with her body: "I *am* my skin, my hair, and worst of all, those triangles of fat that pooch at the top of my thighs."[11] She often compares her body unfavorably with the bodies of other women. But most of all, she treats her body harshly, with heavy drinking, drug use, sleep deprivation, bulimia, and un-protected sex. While at the time of writing she has largely desisted from abusing her body, she does not change her behaviors because of an altered and more positive attitude toward her body. While she recognizes that alcohol almost killed her, she affirms as much as she rejects her past addictions. Her self-identity and her consistently negative attitudes toward her body seem to be mutually entangled.

The view of her body and her addictive behaviors closely coincide with her sexual life. She became sexually active as a teenager, and, upon arriving at Goucher College in 1971, she started, as she tells us, "getting laid with some regularity" (23). Both frequency and pas-sivity regarding sexual behavior continue, it seems, to the time of writing. Sexual events seem simply to happen to her and are quite unrelated to her relationships with men. And, unlike Mary Gordon, she does not present sex as pleasure. However, on occasions, she tells us, she loved some of these men, but many of them, by being married and requiring clandestine meetings, were not reliable or viable companions. Most of all, she does not relate her sexual life to her social life more broadly described. Sexual relations form a series of more or less brief encounters that had little worth, and little of value seems to reside in or to be drawn from them. Her pregnancies are recorded without emotion, and she seems no more engaged by the decision to terminate the first of them than by the decision to bring the second to completion.

The general environment of her social life is also quite negatively depicted. The world around her seems primarily to be characterized by minor and major mishaps and problems. Most grievously, several of her friends have serious illnesses or die, such as her friend Pam, who dies at the age of thirty-seven; Ken Nelson, who dies of AIDS; Mimi, the mother of her junior tennis partner, who also dies; and the two-year-old girl who has cystic fibrosis, to name some of those she includes. She has major frights when her son, Sam, is thought to have a life-threatening condition and when she herself is found to have a mole requiring a biopsy, something frightening for her be-cause her father died at a relatively young age.

In addition, the church home that she has found, St. Andrew Pres-byterian, is not a positive contrary to these negative conditions. She seems drawn to it primarily because the congregation is constituted mostly by black and poor women, suggesting lives that are difficult and vulnerable to setback.

These negative conditions, along with other problems, crises, and uncertainties in her life, form a contrasting background to the moments of enlightenment, insight, or spiritual illumination that she records. Indeed, it is the continual contrast between these two sides of her life that structurally most determines her account. She narrates her world primarily as dark and difficult and as dotted by contrasting moments of restoration and light.

II

However, there are also some positive constants, most of them implied, in Lamott's world. One of them is nature. She places several episodes in her account near water, especially San Quentin Beach. She also describes positive outdoor experiences like snorkeling, sighting seals and porpoises, watching a lunar eclipse, and viewing the beauty of Idaho's mountains. This natural constant in her life is something that not only offers her surprising delights but also forms a refuge to which she can return. However, she does not expound on the significance of nature and her experiences of it. Her father was more deliberate in his relation to nature. She tells us that if he worshipped anything at all it was "the beauty of nature" (32). Perhaps she does not follow his example because she thinks of significant things not as physical and constant but as spiritual and momentary.

As already mentioned, friends provide another positive constant of her world. This is true from childhood on. She has a variety of friends and does not gather around her only people of a certain kind. They often, however, either participate with her in extreme behaviors or are accepting and even enabling of them.

Her family of origin, although somewhat ambiguous in terms of its positive and negative roles, is more a resource, I think, than a liability. She presents her parents as deeply integrated into the California culture of the late 1960s. While she does not endorse that culture and their participation in it unequivocally, neither does she view it negatively. Indeed, it appears that what she likes about herself, her unpredictability, extreme behaviors and states of mind, and receptivity to a variety of people, occasions, and impulses, has its roots in that culture and upbringing. She implies that what was missing in her home and that wider culture was a spirituality that matched or counterbalanced carnality and indulgence. She says of the crowd with which her parents regularly mixed that they thought "believing meant you were stupid. Ignorant people believed, uncouth people believed, and we were heavily couth" (9). This means that Lamott is one of that sizeable group of American children who grew up, in the latter decades of the twentieth century, to be more religious than their parents. However, her turn toward religion does not put her in a position of viewing either her own prereligious life or the nonreligious attitudes of her parents and friends unfavorably, as something from which she has been delivered or as something she puts behind her. Indeed, the lack of restraint and inhibition that she records in her friends and her parents seems positively related to her own sense of freedom, experimentation, and future-oriented expectations.

Her mother seems to be the member of her family who is the least positively drawn. When Lamott was in high school, her mother was studying law in San Francisco on her way to entering the legal profession and practicing in Honolulu. The only daughter of three children, she seems not to have a close relation to her mother. She says little about confidences shared between them as she was maturing, and she seems to attribute her parents' unsuccessful marriage and eventual divorce primarily to her mother. Nor does she attribute her own pursuit of a career as a writer to her mother's apparent determination to forge an identity and professional life of her own. She relates to her mother most closely when she becomes pregnant with Sam and while he grows up. However, this part of their relationship does not seem to overcome the negative strains, and, in another of her books, she describes her mother as "a terrified, furious, clinging, sucking maw of need and arrogance."[12]

Her two brothers seem not to have made her life more difficult, but she also does not seem close to them. Rather than presenting her youth as having been shared with them, she treats herself primarily as an only child. She does have contacts with her older brother, who lives not far from her, but she gives us little of their relationship. The fact that she has close relations with neither her mother nor her brothers throws extra attention and significance on her relationship with her father.

Since religion is important to her self-account, it is worth noting that her father is far more hostile to religion than is her mother, who was English and Episcopalian and took Anne as a girl to church, at least to Christmas Eve services. Her father, the son of Presbyterian missionaries to Japan, hated Christianity. Furthermore, he seems to have acted irresponsibly in his relationship with her. When she was sixteen and her mother was off studying law, she and her dad "ended up getting drunk together for the first time" (22). She implies that this was the first of many occasions. Given his irresponsibility and fondness for extremity, one wonders what else occurred, especially since Lamott includes instances of adult/child sexual interactions in her novels. Relevant to the question as well are her low opinion, later, of her body and her sexual passivity. However, Lamott counters such speculation by describing her father positively. She refers to him as her "Fort Knox," as someone who warrants the kind of confidence required to pursue the craft that is hers as successfully as she has done. Her highly positive opinion of her father may also be due to the fact that he died some twenty years earlier, and she seems, of her family members, the most to have been affected by his death. Her high opinion of him also rests on the fact that he was himself a writer who achieved some recognition with published short stories.

Another positive constant in her life is her developing career. But, while she occasionally mentions working on a project, having books published, and speaking and teaching opportunities opened by her success, she says very little about the progress of her career and how advancement occurred. This lack or restraint may be due to the fact that narrating a continuing line of development that the progress of her career would provide could counter the way she presents her life and experiences, namely, as a series of unrelated moments and cycles of collapse and reinstatement. However, the lack of inclusion deprives her reader of access to what must be a major and positive aspect of her identity.

III

The most important component of Lamott's identity for this account is religious. She ties her interest in religion to her childhood, and this relates religion to her strongly affirmative attitude toward her young self. As a girl she is exposed to Catholic as well as Protestant Christianity, Judaism, Christian Science, and Asian religions. This open attitude toward religious diversity continues into adulthood, and she has friends and acquaintances with religious identities of various kinds. While she does not detail how this is the case for her, her religious life, although located in a particular religious site, is more general than it is institutional and more eclectic than it is Christian.

The prominent Christian element in her religious identity she traces not to her childhood friends or her mother but to her exposure in college to the work of Søren Kierkegaard. On reading *Fear and Trembling,* she finds arresting Kierkegaard's dissociation of faith from reason. As she says, "since this side of the grave you could never know for sure if there was a God, you had to make a leap of faith, if you could, leaping across the abyss of doubt with fear and trembling" (27). She goes on to say that Abraham's willingness to do the one thing in the world that he could not do just because God told him to do it makes no rational sense. This dissociation, in the story of Abraham, of faith or belief from reason and morality accounts for the fact that Lamott understands the relation of people and God to one another neither doctrinally nor morally. What she seems to find most arresting in the church she joins is the combination of people's difficult circumstances and their ability to be joyful, accepting of others, and generous. Consequently, while she joins a Christian church, her religious identity remains vague, eclectic, and occasional. And while, during a particularly low point in her life, she felt the presence of Jesus, she conveys little interest in Christian teachings regarding the person and work of Christ. Nor does she come into the church with any noticeable degree of conversion. Indeed, she seems to associate specific Christian beliefs and Christian morality with what she does not like about religion.

The principal content and norm of her religious life is the ability to be nonjudgmental, to be unconditional and indiscriminate in love and forgiveness. This attitude seems at least somewhat consistent with the "anything goes," nonjudgmental quality of the California culture in which she grew up. She attributes this attitude and ability to God, contending that God loves Susan Smith, who killed her children, as much as God loves Desmond Tutu. She admires unconditional acceptance wherever she encounters it, as in her friend Pam, and she tries to practice it in response to extreme circumstances, such as with a man who is cruel to his dog.

IV

What emerges, it seems to me, are four constitutive factors of Lamott's religious identity. The first is the dualism that structures her world, her separation of spiritual and physical, momentary and constant, and internal and external realities from one another. She holds the physical and external at a distance, since they seem mostly to be threatening, although she also treats them in a lighthearted way. The positive exceptions to the dark background occur in moments of exposure to natural beauty and to the physical and personal beauty of friends. But she does not seem to draw from these exceptions any conclusions about real or possible relations more generally between the spiritual and physical, the momentary and the constant, and the internal and external. She carries this dualism into the center of her account by the distance that she creates between her observed and her writing selves. She presents herself and her behaviors often as from a distance, not a distance of disapproval and regret so much as a distance of nonrelation. Indeed, at times she seems to create a closer relation to her reader than to her observed self, even to compromise her observed self as a price worth paying for a close relation to her reader.

A second component of her religious identity is her need and ability to receive from others. Indeed, this defines most of her relationships with people. While she is herself a caring person in her relationships, she primarily is a recipient. It becomes difficult to trace this strain of receptivity to her relationships with men, since she receives or records receiving very little from them. This need and ability to receive from others largely describes, as well, her relation to and thoughts about God. She calls on God when she needs something, and thinks of God as an unconditional and reliable giver. Her little spontaneous prayers of asking for help and then saying "Thank you" are expressions of this basic need and ability to be given things. Also, while she seems to give to other members of the church, she primarily receives from them, including packets of dimes from a woman poorly positioned to afford them.

The third component is her religious, moral norm of nonjudgmental forgiveness. It is God's defining, if not sole, attribute. She admires this capacity when she sees it in other people, and she tries to cultivate it in herself. However, forgiveness does not carry much content. It seems to be more an attitude than an act, an attitude that resembles acceptance more than forgiveness and love. Indeed, she comes to accept a great deal about herself and her world. She accepts her family of origin, her body, her addictions, the losses in her life, and the crises she creates for herself through extreme behaviors. Acceptance is more passive, more lacking in content, and more inconsequential than forgiveness and love. In fact, acceptance in the forms that she narrates it looks a good bit like resignation. She resigns herself to things generally, and, in contrast to all that she resigns herself to, she posits moments of meaning and delight. It should be said, however, that acceptance and, even more, resignation are less Christian than Stoic. She narrates her identity as determined by a world described primarily in a negative way, by her having resigned herself to that world, and by occasional, edifying, or revealing moments that stand apart from those general conditions.

Finally, she is religiously forward-looking. She draws few conclusions or values from the past. She lives expectantly. She takes Sam to church because, she says, "I want to give him what I found in the world, which is to say a path and a light to see by" (100). She is oriented to the future, to what comes next, and to isolated and surprising gifts yet to be received. It is not accidental or incidental that there is no conclusion to her work. It is open-ended. She will continue to receive and will continue to write about what occurs to her. She is a good example of the kind of person I have in mind when I distinguish Religious Diviners from Debtors and Dwellers.

ORIENTED AS they are to something still outstanding, Religious Diviners are less specific about the nature and content of their religious identities than are representatives of the other two kinds. All three of our examples turn attention primarily to what is still outstanding or what has yet to be realized. There is an openness, a susceptibility, and an exploring that marks religious identities of this kind, and it reminds us of the fact that the future is important both for religious identity and for autobiography.

A future orientation is also important for religious identity because aspects of a religious identity depend on something that is looked for and, it is hoped, will be received. Assumption, according to another definition of the word, means being received. And religious receiving is most fully the gift of being received. Part of assumption as reception is to be found in the text itself, in the at least partial fullness and finality of one's life having been narrated or described. Texts not only surface and unify what is elusive and disjointed but also have a future, can and possibly will be read. The expectation embodied in a text is of being received, so that writing one's life, accounting for one's religious identity in terms primarily of the future, and the potentials and possibilities of textuality are mutually supportive.

Mutually supportive, as well, are religious identities of this kind and American identities more generally. Both contain an ingredient of expectation for and high evaluation of what lies ahead or is yet to occur. Personal future-orientation and the national aspiration to be something we are not as yet, while by no means the same thing, also interact with and at points support one another. Religious Americans, then, and their nonreligious neighbors resemble one another by being intrigued by what is yet to come.

III

PERSONAL

7

MOVING OUT
GROUNDING A RELIGIOUS IDENTITY

I WOULDN'T have thought of attempting a self-account of my own if it were not for the fact that, having attended to those of others, it would be unseemly simply to walk away. These nine people have proffered generous and intimate acts of self-disclosure, and, having heard them out and having commented on them, it seems a bit like the room has grown quiet and at least some eyes now turn toward me, as though, going around the circle, it is my turn. Isn't it unseemly to receive the confidences of others without responding in kind?

I could, of course, plead that, lacking the narrative skills they display, I should be excused from the otherwise obvious courtesy of responding to their candid self-disclosures with my own. Also, since in the first part of this study I singled out style as the primary point of engagement between the implied writer and reader of autobiography, my lack of stature as an engaging and entertaining writer would exempt me from what feels like a social obligation. People whose lives are in themselves unusual or newsworthy may well bypass the requirement of an engaging or delightful style, but I cannot choose that route, since I do not count my own life as extraordinary either in oddness or accomplishment.

However, since I have commented on the religious self-disclosures of nine of my contemporaries, it may seem somewhat natural or even expected that I disclose my own. Since I spend a good bit of my time studying religion, it may seem fair or at least not irrelevant to say something along these lines about myself.

I also justify doing this by the fact that it gives me an opportunity to extend or more fully to clarify the theory of religious identity implied and occasionally referred to in the previous sections. Primarily by placing the writers in one of three groups, I implied that religious identity can be thought of as constituted by three orientations or facets. The first is toward the past and emphasizes matters that have come to be taken for granted, that were part of formative conditions. The second, which is oriented primarily to the present, is constituted by matters that, primarily in response to intellectual or experiential challenges, have been consciously selected, crafted, and affirmed. The third facet is constituted by matters that are projected toward a future completion, especially in the form of being accepted or received. The theoretical framework of the second part of this study will be carried over into my own account. However, because my own account is more internally based, it will also alter somewhat the terms previously deployed.

I hold religious identity personally viewed, then, as having three facets that can be brought together by a single word, namely, "assumption." Among the several meanings of "assumption," three stand out. First, assumption points to what is taken for granted, what I carry with me from the past, at times without being fully aware that I do. Second, assumption means taking something on as a conscious act especially in response to a challenge, as when I assume the responsibilities of parenthood by fathering a child. Third, an important but less widely used meaning of the word is assumption as future-oriented, and it suggests being received. This is the meaning of the word when used to refer to the assumption of the Virgin. When I distinguish the three facets of identity from one another, however, I do not mean that they are temporally discrete; they can at any time all be present and can affect one another. However, they are also distinguishable, and to distinguish them begins to do justice to the contribution each makes to the construction or content of a religious identity.

I begin, then, with attention to my origins and the assumptions regarding religion that I continue to hold or have difficulty doing without. Obviously, this part of my identity cannot be fully disclosed since I am not aware of all that I assume. The best I can do is to describe my upbringing and infer from it some of the things I grew to, and am aware that I continue to, assume.

Hoboken

I, the last of four children, was born in my parents' bedroom on the fourth floor of a Hoboken brownstone, 310 Hudson Street. I was conceived in Lebanon, Iowa, and carried to New Jersey in December 1934 because my father had accepted a call to serve as the pastor of a small church in Hoboken and as chaplain for the seamen of the Holland-American line. Although it was never discussed, my father's position at the church in Lebanon had been terminated. I think my parents were also glad to leave. My mother hated it there, and my father, who had been called to fill a pulpit vacated by a rising star in the church, apparently was unsatisfactory to its membership. It was also the middle of the Depression, and tension had arisen, I gather, regarding inadequate or irregular pay. Glad as my parents were to leave Lebanon, Hoboken, while in every other sense its opposite, was, like it, no easy assignment.

Hoboken was alien to my parents because their experience of America was confined to the Middle West, where their families lived. Also, both had been born in the Netherlands, children of migrant farmworkers, and they emigrated to this country as young adults, my father just before and my mother just after World War I. They met in Grand Rapids, Michigan, where my father attended Calvin College and Seminary and where my mother was working as a practical nurse in training at the denominational hospital for the mentally ill.

How my father had gotten it into his head not, like his brothers, to follow the family tradition into farming but to study instead for the ministry I shall never know. But doing that certainly took initiative, and all the effort rewarded him with two very difficult positions. Nothing in his background prepared him for urban life, and handling his work in Hoboken and helping to raise four children in a port city of factories, ships, drunks, and Irish and Italian Catholic neighbors was a struggle. His tenure there was abbreviated because in the fall of 1943 he was discovered to have inoperable stomach cancer and died from it the following March.

The home we lived in was directly above the church sanctuary, which was on the second floor and had large stained-glass windows. Below the sanctuary were the meeting rooms, and our home was on the top two floors. Home and church, then, could not have been more closely joined. The location also formed a center for me because people came to our house, so to speak, in order to go to church, and we invariably had Sunday visitors in our living room, often bulky seamen smoking cigars who brought little gifts for my mother from Surinam and had animated conversations in Dutch with my father. Sundays were full, with morning and evening services and frequent guests for lunch, including, during the war, sailors from

denominational churches in other parts of the country who came
from bases in New York City to worship with us. Sundays, then,
were eventful days, and weeks were oriented to and affected by
them. They were days when normal activities, such as shopping,
outdoor play, and entertainments, were suspended. And Sundays
required special dress. As a consequence, Sundays stood out for me
as more particular and meaningful than the rest of the week. It is
not that Sundays were made special by going to church; rather, going
to church was part of observing Sunday. This status of Sundays has
stayed with me. Now additional rituals mark my Sunday behavior,
like a glass of sherry before my tuna fish sandwich lunch, and I go to
church on Sunday primarily because the day suggests that I should.

We were Dutch Reformed; more than that, we were Christian
Reformed, which we thought was superior in every way to the more
Americanized Reformed Church of America. Not only were we very
Reformed; we were also very Dutch. The morning and evening services in the church alternated between Dutch and English, and I
remember well standing as a boy in the Seamen's Home on River
Street amidst the seamen as they sang with gusto the Dutch Psalms
that I still love to hear. This identity put us at a distance from our
neighbors, who were largely Irish and Italian Catholics. My closest
friends, however, were Chinese. Ganzi and Fui Woo lived around the
corner behind the laundry and came unusually dressed to stand with
their parents in front of my father's casket in our living room. Most
of our neighbors, though, were associated with the large edifice of
religious power and prestige half a block away, Sts. Peter and Paul
Catholic Church and school.

I was thereby led to assume that the religious identity of my parents and the churchly location of our residence put us in a minority,
even odd, position. My religion is something, I assumed and continue to, that puts me interestingly at odds with my surroundings.
When I moved out of my family circle into the surrounding world, I
found myself in unfamiliar territory, territory in which other people
felt more at ease than I did. Getting on there took attention and
instilled awareness that I lacked what full acceptance and participation required. Acceptance, since it could not be expected, was
deferred to the future.

My home life, not surprisingly, had substantial religious content.
Dutch Reformed Christianity is very textual and heady. The Bible,
the Heidelberg Catechism and Canons of Dort, theological books, and
the *Psalter-Hymnal* were, among other texts, always there, deserving

attention and carrying weight. My father's study was on the fourth floor, and, when my mother was busy with other things, I played there while he worked. The room was lined with books. A huge dictionary on its own stand occupied one corner, and a large, windup record player stood against the wall. I liked it there and could, my mother told me later, either in my father's study or in our living room, play for hours with my collection of toy figures. Despite the family feeling of discontinuity with the rest of Hoboken, we carried intellectual as well as emotional assumptions about the value of who we were. It is difficult to communicate the gravity and substance granted by a Dutch Reformed identity and the large, resonant, and elevated world it supported.

A difficult factor of my early life, in addition to religious difference, was poverty. My parents came from Iowa with almost nothing, and pay in the small church was inadequate even for the spare needs of a frugal family. When my father died he left his widow and four children with a thousand dollars in insurance, which mostly went for his funeral and burial in Grand Rapids, and with little if anything in savings. Visible signs of poverty mortified me, especially the cardboard I wore in my shoes to cover the holes and my mother's extensive darning in my socks that showed above the heels. We seldom went anywhere, and treats were rare. Lean financial resources and frugality were a part of life, and they were confirmed and balanced by the religious austerity of our home. My siblings responded to poverty by becoming, in various ways, preoccupied, perhaps competitively so, with financial aspirations, but I assumed I would always have less than plenty. I am a bit disoriented by having to abandon that assumption, since, compared to my youth, I am now financially rather well-off.

The effects of these conditions on me were, I suspect, complex. I did not feel at ease with kids on the block, although I played with them. Since we differed but did not feel inferior to our neighbors, we did not strive for acceptance, although my brother Hank, three years older and more venturing than I, adopted local customs like riding, while clinging to the spare tire, on the backs of the buses on Washington Street, swimming in the Hudson River with its treacherous currents, and playing hooky from school. We were sent to public schools, but that exposure also did not question who I was. My father's position elevated us above our context, but most of all a religiously based sense of life's seriousness and richness gave us participation in something large and important that related us to something more. Since we were as much Dutch as American, we also had a sense of connection with Europe. Religion, then, rather than confining, gave our life weight and range and related us to something broader, higher, and more important than the world immediately around us. These deep assumptions linger.

This largeness of life allowed us, I would think, to take not only the difficulties but also the splendors of our location in stride. We lived in full view of the New York skyline, and we often took walks as a family to the campus of Stevens Tech in order to view the city, the river, and the George Washington Bridge. I sat with other boys on the wall of the Fourth Street Park to watch great ships being towed in, and occasionally I went aboard them with my father to greet the captains and crews. The dock area was always abuzz with machines, longshoremen, and the movement of various kinds of goods. And we regularly worked the drunks on River Street, asking them for money which we spent on candy.

Given the difficulties of our life there, it is not surprising that we read my father's death in 1944 as a release. It was a second-best release, since the opportunity to leave had been offered to us shortly before when he accepted an appointment to serve as chaplain in the merchant marine. Plans to move to Clifton were tentatively in place, but his cancer was discovered when he went for his qualifying physical. Reading his death as a release was especially true for my oldest sibling, Calvin, whom my father had been pressuring to enter the ministry. Cal had no interest in such a future, and, after my father's death, he took an exam that gave him a full ride at Stevens Tech. We stayed in Hoboken until December, when we moved to Glen Rock.

Difficult though in many ways it was, I would not readily exchange my youth in Hoboken for something else. There was an intensity there, a sense of difference from but not indifference toward others, a compactness of place in the midst of immensity. Although only nine at the time and glad to leave, I also carried out of Hoboken a mostly positive sense of the urban. Cement was more natural to me than grass, and the religious/ethnic diversity in the world around me was something I took for granted. I remember an incident when I must have been only five or six years old that occurred in the car while we were stopped by traffic in the Holland Tunnel. Someone in the car, not a member of my family, said something about the "colored" people in the car next to us. I looked out of the window thinking I would see people of color, blue or green, say, but I was disappointed to see only people of a kind that I had often seen before.

Glen Rock

When we moved to Glen Rock, one of us kids began singing what became a kind of family song, a variation on a hymn:

> He brought me up and out of a horrible pit
> And from the miry clay;
> He set my feet upon Glen Rock
> And established my way!

We liked the change. My mother bought a suitable house, which was a lucky break. It was owned by two elderly sisters who had no heirs and were persuaded by the clergy who intervened for us to sell the house below value. Also the marketability of the house was in question because African American people lived in houses behind it and on the street where ours ended. This was not a problem for us. We were used to living in proximity to people who were different from us, people we did not reject but whose world simply was unlike our own.

It was fateful that my mother did not move back to the Middle West but chose to stay in New Jersey. I grew up without relatives, therefore. I'm not sure why she acted as she did. One reason, of course, was that my brother was going to school in Hoboken, and moving would have left him behind. But I also think that it was based on the elevation above her own family that my mother felt. Her family, located in and around Chicago, had a vaguer Christian identity, and my mother, by marrying a minister, felt, I think, not only distant from but also superior to her siblings. Nor did we, because of the affordable house, settle in one of the several Dutch Reformed communities in northern New Jersey. Our situation in Glen Rock, then, while radically different, turned out also to be somewhat continuous with what we had known in Hoboken. We were the only people of our kind in the neighborhood. Not only that, we were also sent to schools run by churches in the denomination that were several miles away. Plus, my mother decided that we should not join a church near one of those schools but rather a small church in Ridgewood, since it needed, she thought, the added membership we could provide. Consequently, my neighborhood, school, and church were discontinuous with one another.

The process of becoming part of my new location was an uncertain one. I entered the fifth grade of my new school midyear and had to develop contacts slowly. When we ate our lunches, which we took from our homes, I threw most of mine away because I didn't think, for some reason, that it was right. But I began to make friends, building up to the most important of them in the eighth grade, my first girlfriend, Jeanette, whom I kissed in the school basement before leaving each day.

But my closest friends were in the neighborhood: Kenny Welch across the street; Wes Adams, whom, without intending to be cruel, we called "Fats" and who was the first among us to own a television set; and Teddy Schreier. Teddy was a year older, and he was enterprising. In the lot next to his house he built a basketball court that was blessed with spotlights so that we could play after dark. We had leagues of two-guy teams and held tournaments. We did that with Ping-Pong, too. He also owned a volleyball net that we stretched across the street. The sources of these goods were dubious, since Teddy stole things, especially from Drapkin's Variety Store in Ridgewood. My first baseball mitt, which I still have today, came to me from Drapkin's by way of Teddy's stealth.

My world was constituted, then, by two realms, one organized by a Dutch Reformed ethos and the other not. I slowly adjusted to and moved freely within both, and I did not treat one as superior to the other. Each held valuable content and provided opportunities, although both had recognizable limits. This two-ness was structurally continuous with Hoboken, although the two realms now were larger, less contrasting, and personally more confirming than their earlier counterparts. I assumed as natural, then, living in differing but equally important arenas, and that assumption continues to the present day.

While I had many contacts in both parts of my divided world, I also was alone a good bit of the time. My mother, soon after my father's death, went to work as a receptionist and secretary for a man in the Hoboken church who had a flower bulb business in New York City. My older brother commuted to Stevens, and my sister, Jo, who largely ran the house, was busy with her own life, as was Hank with his. I had been accustomed to being alone and entertaining myself in Hoboken, and I didn't take it as abnormal. Once, when I had the mumps, I was home alone every day for a week, and I didn't mind it. I read and listened to the radio, following suit when told by Don McNeil on *The Breakfast Club* to bow my head and to pray for a world united in peace. The radio was a constant companion in my youth and gave access to a larger world. While I listened to many programs, on Monday, Wednesday, and Friday at seven thirty I was glued to the radio when out of the past I would hear "the thundering hoof beats of the great horse Silver."

Baseball was big, too. We had no teams at my grammar school, but I pitched and played second base in the Glen Rock leagues. I was also a huge Giants fan and knew the averages of all the batters and the records of the pitchers. When walking down a street by myself, I imagined the announcer introducing me to the cheering crowd as coming in to pitch for the Giants. When the team later left New York for San Francisco, I terminated in my grief and dismay all loyalty to major league baseball, but I valued highly my play in town leagues, high school, and, for one year, in college.

High school was not the Ridgewood school the kids in the neighborhood attended but Eastern Academy in Prospect Park, a school in the same system as the Midland Park Christian School. Although the school was distantly located, I had a good time and a good education there. Many of my teachers were men: Mr. Bontekoe in history and social studies, Mr. Bangma in science, Mr. Van Til in English, and Mr. Van Tielen in math. It was good for me, fatherless, to be exposed to these intelligent and dedicated male mentors. Socially I also thrived. I took part in many clubs, sang, actively engaged in sports, and had many friends, including girls. My first real love was as a senior. Gerry Hagedorn had recently broken up with her boyfriend, who was not in our school, and I began to date her. Slowly, in the spring, she took up with him again and edged me out. I spent graduation evening alone vowing never to let anyone have an effect like that on me again.

While in Hoboken the world outside my home was huge and mainly impervious, Glen Rock was, while also challenging, less forbidding. I had no doubt about the gravity and richness of my religious life and identity, even though it was not shared by my neighborhood friends. I encountered teachers, pastors, and laymen whose intelligence, dedication, and knowledge of biblical texts and Reformed theology warranted the sense I had of my religion's rich content. Not infrequently, I heard sermons that struck me as profound and illuminating, and music in the church, home, and school was constant and uplifting. But I also was aware of a large world beyond both arenas, a world I viewed as enticing, unexplored, and richly deserving of my desire.

While religion affected me in various ways, I especially looked forward to and appreciated good sermons. These were not uncommon, since the clergy were trained in respect for and knowledge of biblical texts, including Old Testament texts. Sermons struck me often as insightful and profound and gave me great respect for texts and for taking them seriously, something I carried over into my education and to the present day. I have never chosen, contrary to what now seems increasingly to be current academic practice, to work on texts that I felt were inferior to me. I always have tried in my work to be worthy of the texts to which I gave critical and interpretive attention.

I also associated religion with music, and music continues to play a large role in my life. My parents were musically untrained, but we moved in a world of Dutch psalms, Protestant hymns, and major choral works of which they had recordings. I took singing for granted and never realized that I had a voice with which I could, perhaps, have done something vocationally. Music became a fuller part of my life by way of Johnny Beversluis, a high school friend who knew a great deal about classical music because his father taught piano. Often on Sunday afternoons I would go to his house, where he would play recordings of symphonies and concerti from his large collection, telling me what to listen for. More importantly, he conveyed his reverential attitudes toward composers, performers, and orchestras. Music became a substantial part of my life, and, while music and religion were also separate spheres, they formed, when joined, a potent combination for me, as did also religion and reading texts. Music and texts, along with Christianity, directed my attention and expectations, then, to something edifying beyond the ordinary, and that continues to be true.

My mother often commented on how happy a child I was, particularly during those years in Glen Rock. Perhaps it was important for her to see that I was in good cheer when she had to leave for work every day, but I do recall those times happily. While my world was disunited, I had positive relations to and within its several parts. I was kept busy by them, and I added to my activities part-time and summer jobs that I also enjoyed: waiting on customers at the Pee Wee Superette in Prospect Park, checking out at the Acme Supermarket in Ridgewood, and working on a truck that made deliveries of soft drinks to stores and bars in the small towns of northern Jersey. I threw myself into my activities and contacts and did not think much about myself or fret for my future. I did well in school, although always less so than Stu Kingma, whose father was a doctor and likely gave academic encouragement if not help at home. Nobody in my home had time or inclination to urge or help me to do better in school or in anything else. My life was simply absorbed by my many contacts and a variety of things to do that filled my days. Grave and frivolous, solitary and convivial, ordinary and exceptional moments and interests were parts of an emerging identity in a location and with resources that accommodated them all. While not in every respect easy and supportive, Glen Rock was good.

Grand Rapids

I probably did well enough in high school to have explored more challenging educational opportunities than our denominational college, but there was no room for choice. College meant Calvin College. In addition, Calvin admitted my sister and me tuition free because of my father's position in the church and our family's financial state. Hank did not go to college, and Cal was well out of Stevens Tech and married by the time I left. Both Hank and Jo married that summer, and it was decided that my mother should sell her house and move with me to Grand Rapids so that I could live with her.

Since going to Calvin College was not a matter of choice, I really didn't think very much about the institution and what I would find there. I expected and needed college to offer me new, challenging, and expanding levels of intellectual and cultural development. To a degree it did, likely because my needs and expectations drove me to explore almost all of the opportunities it offered. But from the outset it was also disappointing. I had had good teachers in high school, and instruction at Calvin often felt like a step down. There were exceptions, but overall my classes were not stimulating. Perhaps my experience was affected by the fact that for the first time I lived entirely within a Dutch Reformed culture, and that may well have contributed to my feeling less than fully challenged by the place. I also expected my teachers to provide access to a world beyond the ordinary, a world that held elusive but real possibilities for me. But campus life was culturally more secured than challenging. In some respects the cultural and religious homogeneity was freeing, since I basically resembled my peers and did not have to struggle to make my way. And, since it was a denominational college, many of the students were, like me, sent there even though they could have been accepted by stronger institutions. So, I had intelligent and gifted friends. They, some of my classes, and my many extracurricular activities and experiments made staying there, though also restricted, enjoyable and rewarding.

I was drawn to the English Department because my freshman English instructor was the best among those I had that year. More importantly, in those classes we read primary sources, and, because of good English classes in high school, I was able to take advantage of the opportunities. One member of the English faculty, Henry Zylstra, was by far the most impressive and effective teacher I had in college, and I took all the courses he offered. Most importantly, English classes and the texts studied in them related me substantially to a larger world, including a larger religious world. As with music in relation to religion, then, I found the combination of religion and literature to be potent. It was not as though teachers talked about those relations directly or assigned only texts that incorporated religious interests. It was more that reading and interpreting works of literature, as was also true of sermons on biblical texts, made me aware of things beyond my immediate cultural and intellectual context. Literature, I saw, granted access to an expansive and abundant world, and I never lost that view of it. But the courses I took did not turn me into a budding scholar. Little emphasis was placed on methods of literary study, and literary theory was largely undeveloped. Perhaps that was a good thing. Rather than subject literature to critique or theory, we simply enjoyed and talked about it, and that led me to new views of things. English and American literature, then, opened a world that, I began to see, supported my desires and aspirations.

The courses that I took in other areas should also have been helpful in these ways, especially philosophy, history, and languages, but they did not equally engage me and generally were not well taught. Saying that will spark protest among distinguished alumni who, as students, made the Philosophy Department their home. But the half dozen courses in philosophy that I took never put before me a philosophical text. We read textbooks, summaries of the work of philosophers and of movements, memorized dates and positions, but never grappled with philosophical texts or analyzed arguments. History was the same. We read textbooks. And languages, although I took several, were poorly taught and, of course, lacked the help that sophisticated pedagogical tools for language study now afford.

Strangely, perhaps, my religious identity was not extended, deepened, or complicated there. Courses in religion were narrowly focused and lacked a spirit of inquiry and appreciation especially regarding other branches of Christianity and, even more, other religions. I began to sense that the religious core of the enterprise at Calvin, in terms of its educational mission, was primarily to shelter students from outside influences and to protect its religious and theological base from scrutiny. Up to that point, religion had granted me a distinctive and resonant identity and had opened up horizons broader than I thought would otherwise have been available to me. Religiously based caution and defensiveness, detectable at Calvin, puzzled me and put me off.

The college also made little if any attempt to acquaint students with larger social issues and problems. It was socially and politically a very conservative place. The primary moral questions were personal, especially sexual. This morality was less proclaimed than assumed. If there was sex on campus, I was unaware of it. However, my restlessness and eventual dissatisfaction with life at Calvin College had nothing to do with its sexual mores. I did not feel repressed by them, although perhaps I was. I enjoyed dating and dated heavily, sometimes more than one girl a week, something acceptable because we didn't really do all that much. I learned later that I had a reputation for being "fast," something unjustified because I was a virgin when I married at age twenty-five. However, I was affectionate and, I suppose, still am. So we made out, but the limits were clear. I accepted these limits not as arbitrary or imposed but as reasonable and even natural. For one thing, I assumed that girls did not have sexual motivations similar to my own, and I simply assumed as a fact of life that my interests in such matters outstripped their availability. Also, having always been a year younger than others in my class, being a skinny kid, and sharing the fair complexion of my mother, I lacked the physical self-confidence that would have supported more extended adventures. Finally, I was not ready for a serious relationship because my vocational plans were not as yet secured and because of my vow subsequent to the pain of rejection in high school. The sexual mores at Calvin were, for these reasons, more aligned with than contrary to my personal inclinations. And by not being complicated by heavy sexual content, dating was delightful.

Although Calvin was not a place that challenged my assumptions or expanded my horizons dramatically, I was a happy undergraduate. I had several good teachers and courses, engaged in a wide range of activities, and had intelligent and talented friends. I enjoyed college life. In addition, the ethos was affected by a high evaluation of education and learning, and, as long as it did not threaten institutional identity, intellectual inquiry was taken seriously. Also, undergraduate life was not dominated, as seems so much to be the case on campuses today, by preprofessional obsessions and academic competition. And in a small college there were opportunities to test or develop my interests and talents in a variety of areas, such as acting, journalism, student government, baseball, and music, especially singing. However, while inquiry was valued, it ultimately deferred to the institution's welfare and that of the denomination that supported it with money and its student population.

One consequence of my not being fully challenged by my academic exposures was that I took time to work in a variety of jobs off campus. While my outside contacts in Hoboken and Glen Rock were with my own age group, here I became acquainted with adults of backgrounds and goals very different from my own. These experiences increased my regard for people working in jobs they disliked in order to support their families. They also convinced me that vocationally I had to avoid commitments or complications that would hamper my aspirations for something higher.

An important assumption I carried with me that has not as yet been mentioned, one that affected my sense of who I was and would be, concerned ministry in the Christian Reformed Church. This assumption took hold of me at an early stage. When I was eight years old and my father was in the hospital with cancer, I stood outside the church door to greet the parishioners as they left the sanctuary. Perhaps because my siblings did not, I assumed that I would follow my father into the denominational clergy.

Assuming that I would become a minister served to free me from anxiety about my vocational future, since I knew that I had the requisite abilities and that the position would not elude me. So, I could enjoy my studies, activities, and social life as a student without the worry and competitive tensions that students experience today. However, this assumption began somewhat to erode in college. For one thing, my interests in literature were expanding, and I began to feel, as I realized more later than I did at the time, that the church would have a confining effect on me. I did consider, during my senior year, applying for graduate work in English literature. However, assuming that I would have a life in the ministry was too deeply embedded, and I did not, at the end, question it. So, upon graduation I dutifully, though also somewhat reluctantly, followed the narrow path to the little building at the corner of the small, square-block campus, Calvin Theological Seminary.

It is difficult to convey how awful Calvin Seminary was and why. For one thing, there had been a house cleaning a few years prior to my arrival when several faculty members were relieved of their posts because of questionable orthodoxy. The vacancies were filled mostly by retired and inept people. Our New Testament professor, who, poor man, had had a stroke, could hardly make himself heard, not to speak of understood. Ralph Stob, we thought, was senile, and our Old Testament professor was too obsessed with battles from his past, particularly over the dating of the Exodus, to worry about communicating with us. Martin Monsma, who made practical theology a joke, was so intolerable that we played pranks in class, reaching over to destroy the notes that a neighboring classmate was taking or gradually edging our movable chairs out of the door while he lectured.

There were younger faculty. Our man in theology suffered not from age but from lack of an inquiring mind, since theology for him was wholly contained in our textbook on Reformed dogmatics. Our church history teacher was also president of the seminary and had little time for or interest in teaching us. Our professor in homiletics was better, but there's not a lot of content to courses like that. Harold Decker in missions was energetic, but his best ideas focused on pedagogical tactics that facilitated discussion, and there was not that much to discuss.

Henry Stob needs a separate paragraph. He was a well-trained scholar, principally in ethics. Here was a thoughtful and sophisticated man who deserved our attention, and he was for the seminary what Henry Zylstra was for me during my college years, an exception. I also joined a group of students who met with him outside of class to discuss texts, primarily Calvin's *Institutes*. However, while he formed a bright spot in the dimness, I must also say, although reluctantly, that Stob did not take us into the process of what he was doing. He lectured to us from manuscripts that were relatively finished, but the nitty-gritty processes of working through problems and weighing options or of exposing moral questions to various arguments for reaching decisions were not taught. This lack of access to the process was intensified by his personal reserve. In addition, the purge a few years earlier was probably a fresh memory for him, and, by virtue of his intellect, he very likely was suspect. This may also have contributed to his caution and reserve. So, while I listened eagerly to him, Stob was not all I needed and desired. I don't think I was alone in this; none of us was or could have become in a real sense one of his students.

While I was generally miserable in the seminary, there were some good things. One was writing and giving sermons, aspiring as I did so to meet a standard of preaching to which I had at times in my life been exposed. In my second and third years I began to supply in churches, often traveling on weekends to rather distant places. I became intrigued by what happened when I gave close attention to a biblical text. Although familiar with biblical texts by lifelong exposure, I began to read them closely on my own, and I was often surprised by their resonances and angularity. What developed, then, was a realization that has stayed with me to the present day, namely, that theology, for the sake of coherence, was formulated at the expense of the complexities and particulars of biblical texts and the tensions within and between them. Without realizing it, although reading Calvin with Stob may subtly have prepared me for this growing realization, I became, by means of this shift of attention from theology to reading scripture, more Reformed than the institution around me. This sense of the primacy of the biblical texts and of reading them was also nurtured by my conversion to literary studies in college.

Writing and giving sermons also contributed to the positive summer experiences that I had. My first summer assignment was a small church in Champaign, Illinois, with Hugh Koops, who later joined the faculty of New Brunswick Theological Seminary. We had good talks, and I appreciated highly the quality of his work. Also, there were educated members of the church who took an interest in what I had to say, and all of that gave a liveliness to ministry that contrasted with the deadness of the seminary. On the strength of that summer experience, I returned to the seminary for my second year.

The summer after my second year I went to Alaska for ten weeks and worked in two churches there. I did not benefit very much from associations with the pastor or members of the Fairbanks church, but the church in Anchorage and its pastor were very positive influences. Most people in the church were not Dutch, and the separation between ethnicity and religious identity was important to experience. The scenery was also inspiring, and, for someone who had had few opportunities for travel, the exposure was exhilarating. I should add that my cousin and I drove to Alaska from Chicago on the Alcan Highway, which was a dirt road from Calgary, Alberta, to the Alaskan border. We sold the car up there and flew back to Oregon, and, visiting sites along the West Coast and Rockies by train, made our way home. The whole adventure was wonderful.

The second good thing was that I bonded with several of my classmates. Every Thursday evening five or six of us gathered in one of our homes to talk about our classes, about the whole enterprise, and about the world in general. We did this over large quantities of beer. Drinking was new for me and had not been part of my college life. Beer and discontent fueled our conversations, and they were lively and intense. Only one member of that group stayed in the denomination. I continue to have contact with these people and am thankful for the support and release they provided.

The third good thing was that in my first year at the seminary I began to date the girl I would, four years later, marry. Our relationship developed slowly. I knew her older brother, who was ahead of me in college and also sang. She was a freshman, and I was drawn to her not only because she was pretty but also, I think, because I saw her as too young to be thinking of marriage. Not to take anything away from her, I very likely was also drawn into a relationship because I needed something pleasantly distracting to offset the negative qualities of the seminary. We shared interests, too. She sang, and she liked literature and conversation. Also, the friends in my class either were married or had steady girlfriends, and I needed someone to play a comparable role for me. I say all of this because the process of overcoming my vow against emotional attachment and my fear of commitments prior to vocational clarity and security were major matters, but the ground was also fertile for the growth, although gradual, of a serious relationship.

A fourth good thing was writing "The Open Prison." Calvin College sponsored a contest for a play to be presented in the spring of 1959 to commemorate several important events in the life of John Calvin. I had done a bit of acting in college and knew the drama director and her artist husband quite well. They urged me, although I'm not sure why, to try my hand at writing a play. I had done some reading on Calvin's life and on the Servetus affair. I also determined that Calvin may well have been working at his commentary on the Gospel of John during the time, so I projected a play that would deal with his domestic life, the challenges posed by Servetus, and the theme of freedom in John's Gospel. While having an actual base, the play itself was fictional. I did not write an outline and did not sketch in the acts beforehand. I simply began dictating to Phyllis, my girlfriend, and it just went along. While I do not remember realizing it at the time, the theme of limits and freedom was also very much a part of my experience within the denomination's institutions. My relation to the material, then, was focused by a real question, one that I thought had also been important for Calvin, since he removed himself from much ecclesiastical authority but also feared ideas and actions that revealed what he thought of as a misuse or excess of freedom. The play I submitted was pretty much what was taken down in dictation, and it was performed successfully. I enjoyed doing it because it gave me a different way of thinking about things with which in less interesting ways I was engaged. It did not occur to me, however, that the ability to dictate a three-act play whole hog probably indicated some talent for that kind of thing.

Whether justified or not, I took the seminary not as unrelated to the denominationally circumscribed world but as its epitome or heart. While there were some students and even a few faculty whose attitudes and interests extended beyond its borders, the seminary and its ethos were, I thought, defining. However, turning my back on the denomination was not a simple thing to do. There were able people—students and faculty—who continued to work within it. It had actual and potential content to commend it, and, most of all, leaving that culture behind meant losing a coherent world and the commonality it provided. I became, after leaving it, a more reserved and solitary person than I was while within it, and I am quite a bit that way today. Once you experience the values, assumptions, and humor that a homogeneous culture can provide, relationships outside of it require more effort and have, in comparison, less content, resonance, and vitality.

During my final year in the seminary, I supplied one Sunday for the church in Wheaton, Illinois. I tested my own answer to the question by asking its pastor, George Stob, if, in his opinion, there was a place for me somewhere in the Christian Reformed Church. I am grateful that he was honest and caring enough to tell me that he didn't think that there was. This explicitly released me from the filial obligation that had sustained me during much of my life and throughout my mostly painful and frustrating years at Calvin Seminary. In addition, on graduating I was single, had just turned twenty-four, and was hardly ready, as we put it, to stand for call. George Stob's response, the predominantly negative experience of the seminary, and my position in life freed me from the claims that my background made on me. Most importantly, my desire and need for something broader or higher were undiminished. The question was what to do or where to go.

I don't remember how, although it may have been from Nelvin Vos, but I heard of a graduate program at the University of Chicago where a person could study religion and literature together. This seemed to me a good solution. For one thing, I had no doubt that my theological education was deficient and that I needed to continue along those lines. But also, this program would allow me to retrieve or continue my literary interests. I did not think that further study would radically change my vocational options; after further education I could switch to another denomination, say Presbyterian, and still become a minister.

Not knowing of anything else and not getting any advice, Chicago was the only institution to which I applied. I also had no money, so I was in need of help. I don't know what would have happened to me if Chicago had turned me down. I was admitted and given a fellowship. So, in September 1959, I lit out for the territory ahead.

While the three locations of the first part of my life, Hoboken, Glen Rock, and Grand Rapids, were very different from one another, I lived for my first twenty-four years in a world shaped by a specific and strong ethnic and religious base that gave me an identity that survives, however attenuated, complicated, and altered, today. I operate at least partially from my Dutch Reformed grounding. This is not only because of conditioning or habits but also because I took it and continue to view it as having valuable content, much of which I could draw on and redeploy. When I set off for Chicago, then, I did not go eager to exchange what I had been for something new. Although I had too many questions to allow my religious identity to close me to what lay ahead, I also did not think that there were alternative views out there that were necessarily richer in their potentials to my own. I thought of my religious identity, then, as broader and more resilient than the world I left behind, especially the seminary, but also as needing substantial clarification, augmentation, and complication. This assumption or grounding made me less susceptible than I otherwise would have been to the many intellectual currents and, at times, fads I encountered in my subsequent life. I was uneasy with my background but also not at all confident that alternatives out there offered enticing substitutes for what I had received and at least in part retained. Perhaps this was because I thought that the institutions that I left behind were less interesting than the heritage they claimed as their own. This assumption, namely, that institutions, while valuable, are partial and self-preserving, continues with me to the present day. When I left that world behind, then, I felt less conflict than continuity between my religious identity and my strong desire to expand my horizons and deepen or complicate my understanding and appreciation of the larger world.

Calvin College and Seminary are institutions of a denomination that was formed in the Netherlands during the nineteenth century from two movements, one pietistic and the other, led by Abraham Kuyper, academically and culturally sophisticated. These two currents, potentially and often actually contrary to one another, continue to vex the denomination by their contrary status. But the pietistic stream, merging with general American evangelicalism, has gained the dominant position in the denomination and in the college and seminary. This distances me even more from them since I am chilled rather than warmed by evangelicalism. This is very likely rooted in the fact that my father, who in some respects probably would qualify as pietistic, deliberately distinguished himself from evangelicalism, which he thought of as personified in Dwight L. Moody. Moody on the one side held in his mind a position balanced on the other side by Henry Emerson Fosdick. His self-positioning likely resembles my own awareness of the sharp differences between Reformed Christianity and both American evangelicalism on the one side and American religious liberalism on the other, especially their differing but equally firm sense of clarity and certainty.

I don't think that the waning of ecclesiastical authority was matched in me by an equally waxing self-confidence. I was too Reformed, I guess, to look to my own convictions or experiences as sufficient warrants for the world that opened itself before me. There was, I believed, continuity and mutuality between my religious orientation and the invitingly expanding world before me, and I looked for confirmations to my identity in what lay outside and ahead. And I can say, I hope with some accuracy, that this sense of a larger and enticing world drawing me outward was never confused by me with material gain or public recognition. I had in my past, I think, too much sense of a richness in life independent of wealth and fame. This may also ground my continuing belief that cultural capital need not defer to questions of economic or political power. What gave purpose to my life and beckoned me to more were cultural and religious, not material, realities.

The assumptions that I formed and carried from my formative years, primarily that my religious beliefs and my view of the world as expansive and engaging were related to one another, did not seem arbitrary or forced because it was and continues to be confirmed by many experiences by which either the one or the other pole or realm of my world testifies to that relation. The two, religion and an intriguing world, were and continue to be mutually challenging and supportive, and a sense of one triggers a sense of the other. Together they produce or sustain an awareness that I live in the presence of something, actually or potentially, that precedes and outlasts me and that is more important than I am. I acknowledge that confirmations of the relations of the two arise also from encounters with the resources of institutions, but when encounters have that effect it is because institutions, as they sometimes do, point beyond themselves to the broader, though not always recognizable, mutuality of religious expectation and world.

8

ON MY OWN

TAKING ON A RELIGIOUS IDENTITY

RELIGIOUS IDENTITY'S second facet is assumption as in consciously taking something on, like assuming the responsibilities of office upon being sworn in. Usually the second facet is a response to challenges that question or present alternatives to a religious identity that, heretofore, had simply been assumed. These challenges need not result in radical change, although, as we saw earlier in some of the self-accounts, they can. More often they produce a process of distancing, uncertainty, and reformulation.

Some people who teach religion hold as their principal pedagogical aim to prod students into questioning their religious beliefs so that if beliefs remain they will have been tested and consciously adopted. But I am not certain that this facet or stage of religious identity holds primacy over the first. While I think that something of this second kind of assumption is a good thing to undergo and may well in our society be difficult to avoid, a religious identity that is not consciously interrogated and reconstructed need not, thereby, be mindless and shallow. And challenges to beliefs should not be lightly posited. Furthermore, it is not necessary or even possible to question everything, and religious beliefs do not strike me as the most obvious candidates for testing and purging. Being a religious person and taking things for granted, assuming things that it would be difficult to do without, have a great deal to do with one another. However, in my own life I also have been forced by my locations to ask who I am religiously and whether the challenges confronted required changes.

The second facet of my religious identity developed in the context of academic institutions where I was required to face alternatives to my own religious identity. While my locations within these institutions raised questions, they did not offer answers to those questions or orientations with which I could identify myself. But their contrary relation to who I was occasioned assumption in this second sense. However, these institutions in many ways also positively related to this second stage because, among other things, it was not out of place for me to think about my own religious identity. Consequently, I owe a great deal to these institutions for who I am, while I also was and am not closely identified with any of them or with anyone in them.

The University of Chicago

Little in my background prepared me for what I would encounter in Chicago. Perhaps, in some ways, my early experiences in Hoboken and Glen Rock helped me to enter this urban place and alien culture. Had I grown up entirely within a Dutch Reformed community, I very likely would not have had the courage to steer myself toward and then within this unknown terrain.

It was helpful that I did not need to make a sudden and total break with my past. There were Christian Reformed churches in and around Chicago, and I preached in some of them during my four years there. The transition to Chicago was also eased by my relationship with Phyllis, whom I had been dating for almost three years. She was entering her final year at Calvin, but, since her family lived in Cicero, I would join her there on her visits during the year.

I knew very little about the University of Chicago or about the program I was entering. Nor did the people there know anything about me. Calvin did not send graduates to Chicago the way its graduates were sent to the University of Michigan, which actually had a house for Calvin students. In addition, the program I entered was a departure from the distinction between religion and literary studies in my past. Had I entered a graduate program in English or a recognizable field in religion, such as the history of Christianity, there would have been continuity with my past and some of the people I left behind. But I would be working in Religion and Literature, and, although I thought that people there knew what that was, the nature or rationale for the program turned out not to be clear. The program and my work within it, then, needed itself to be interpreted, and I already had the task of interpreting the relation between my

religious identity and the alternatives and challenges to it, especially
theological, that I would encounter in this new place. So, little, if
anything, was obvious or could be taken for granted.

The transition would have been easier if I had met, on entering
the university, an open field of inquiry about religion. What I encountered instead was a theological certainty that matched if it did
not surpass in intensity what I had left behind in Grand Rapids.
The reigning orthodoxy was process theology. Indeed, it was thought
that anyone adhering to another theological position, especially one
tied to traditional Christianity, had either not come to grips with
its deficiencies or had not thought with sufficient rigor about the
advances made available to theology by the work of A. N. Whitehead
and Charles Hartshorne. Bernard Loomer was the principal advocate of process theology, and, when I talked with him about taking
courses in theology, he told me in no uncertain terms that I needed
to leave what I had been taught behind and to begin afresh. This I
was unwilling to do. While I was open to questions and complications, I did not rise to the invitation to exchange what I had or was
for something that was fundamentally quite different. I also sensed
that a metaphysically grounded theological position could not
accommodate the kind of magnitude and mystery that I carried with
me from my Reformed upbringing, especially the august God that
process theology, by joining God to material processes, reduced in
stature and freedom. Loomer's implied point, that Reformed Christianity and process theology differed and forced an either/or decision,
confirmed my impression that here was an alternative at odds with
what I brought with me. Rather than trying to reconcile the two
or rejecting one for the other, I decided to hold both as unrelated
options.

It was not that I could simply ignore process theology. I did my
Religion and Literature work primarily with Preston Roberts, who
had been one of Bernard Loomer's students. Initially, I was drawn to
Nathan Scott, and what was most compelling about him was that
he had a very expansive and exhilarating sense of things, of a larger
world. A big man of enormous confidence who brought a wide range
of matters into view, Scott inspired a sense of the grandeur of things
that I retain to this day. He also lectured in distant places and knew
prominent people, like Ralph Ellison, whom he brought to his home
for us to meet. I took all of his courses, and I was edified by them. But
like other teachers who inspired me in the past, he did not give me
ready access to how I could do what he was doing. His methods were,
to put it briefly, Longinian. That is, he was drawn to what he saw

as a certain quality in a text, something related to style that, when combined with moments in other texts, enabled him to sketch very broad descriptions or interpretations of modernity and its defining styles. Theologically he blended an Anglican natural theology with selected bits from the ontological views of Paul Tillich and Martin Heidegger, but he was, religiously, less theological than churchly. I could not turn to him, then, as a theological alternative to Roberts and Loomer. In addition, while I did well in his courses, it was not clear what the norms or expectations were by which he judged the quality of my work. He was expecting, I concluded, a certain style or largeness from his students that I was not confident I could supply.

Preston Roberts was very different from Scott. He was deliberate about method, about how he thought things should be done and why. The side of him attached to Loomer I could not employ, but on the literary side he was related to the neo-Aristotelians in the English Department with whom I also did course work. So, I understood and found wider applications for what he was doing. Also, he was very patient with my written work, giving me point-by-point suggestions for improving my arguments and style, and was more focused in the selection of texts to which he gave attention. Unlike Scott, who roamed freely and eclectically not only through modern literature and criticism but also through visual art and architecture, Roberts worked primarily with Greek and Renaissance tragedies. He also worked with contemporary, especially American, texts, placing them in comparative and contrasting relations to earlier literature.

My sense of being on my own was not relieved by the presence of other students with traditional religious backgrounds, such as the several Lutheran students there. They had mentors on the faculty like Jeroslav Pelikan and Martin Marty who shared their background so that they were not left to themselves to sort things out. I had nobody like that. There was Coert Rylaarsdam in Old Testament, and I did audit his course in the Psalms. But my Hebrew was not strong enough for me to think of doing substantial work with him. However, the presence of Lutherans was somewhat reassuring to me, since I knew that they would also not easily identify with the process option.

Courage to champion my point of view was lacking because I also recognized that my educational background was relatively weak. It would not have been surprising if I had associated my religious identity with that weakness, but I did not because of the partial separation I already had made between my own religious identity and that of the denomination's institutions. The other students and, of course, the faculty at Chicago, were more widely read and intellectually sophisticated than I was. What sustained me was a basic attitude whereby, rather than look within myself for the needed resources, I deferred to something outside of myself, something that I did not identify with a particular form, whether institution, theological position, or cultural ethos. So, while I was intimidated, I also felt sustained and could maintain a critical distance from my environment that kept me from being overwhelmed by it.

What I began slowly to realize was that both Scott and Roberts were doing something not unlike what I had grown to resist at Calvin College and Seminary, namely, allowing theological interests and conclusions to determine approaches to texts. Scott did this, although also in a more general way, more fully than Roberts, since Roberts grounded his literary approaches in Aristotelian literary theory. I had concluded long ago and with profit that texts needed, as much as possible, to determine how they should be read, to be subjected as little as possible to theory, and to be allowed to challenge or to alter theory. What I had come to see as a Reformed principle concerning the relation of biblical texts to theology and doctrine also, I concluded, pertained to the relation of literary texts to theoretical and critical interests and methods. What I found most useful in Roberts's work was that he located the force and significance of a dramatic text not in something separable from but in something basic to it. What was limiting in his method was his theologically fortified assumption that the primary source of a text's force and meaning was always its plot.

Midpoint in my four years at Chicago I derived encouragement in my reluctance regarding process theology. The first was from a conversation that was arranged between Charles Hartshorne and Paul Holmer of Yale. I was impressed by how deftly Holmer handled Hartshorne. It became clear to me that Hartshorne, whose work I grew more to appreciate when, later, I had gotten some distance from it, was, though interesting, not oracular. The second occasion was the arrival of Joseph Haroutunian, who primarily taught Calvin and Barth. I enjoyed his classes very much, and he deepened my understanding of Calvin, although it was difficult in his classes to distinguish Calvin, Barth, and Haroutunian from one another. Nonetheless, the alternative that he provided to the prevailing orthodoxy was encouraging. Finally, Karl Barth visited the university, and he presented a series of public lectures and talked to us at the Divinity School. He was, as a human being, enormously impressive, and I was sufficiently acquainted with his emphases and method to be able to understand what he was doing. He presented a sharp alternative to process theology, but I also was aware of the differences between Barth and my own version of Reformed themes and aware of what I viewed as a Barthian epidemic in American theology. Indeed, I have not altered my conclusion that Barth is much more Lutheran than Reformed.

Although the dominance of process theology prevented me from benefitting fully from the resources at Chicago, the faculty and curricular offerings were challenging and rich. In addition to faculty in the Divinity School, there were prominent scholars in the English Department, and I took memorable courses there. One was Ernest Surlock's Milton course, and I was encouraged in his class when, after I had responded to a question, he struck his desk and said, "Kort, you are on your way to Yale!" I was not sure what he meant, but I took it as complimentary. I lacked confidence, however, to take full advantage of my encounters in English, and I hastily retreated to the more familiar ground of the Divinity School.

In the middle of my second year at Chicago, Phyllis and I were married in the Oak Park Christian Reformed Church. The distance between that world and my new life can be measured by the fact that nobody at Chicago knew I was going to get married, and Preston Roberts was, I think, a bit hurt or at least surprised that he and his wife had not been invited. It would not have been possible for me to join these increasingly separate arenas. Although I could not identify with the dominant theology at Chicago, I was engaged by my work both in literature and in religion, and that arena of my life was clearly becoming the more important one.

Phyllis was, by then, a full companion in an outward direction. Although upon graduating she took a position teaching in a denominational school south of Chicago, we were joined in the quest for a life beyond those boundaries. Indeed, our marriage, although it was also much more, constituted a joint venture, and we formed a team, if that's the right word, that provided, among other things, a stable center to my life, which was so complex and uncertain. From that center I could move out, and to it I could return. And this center was, rather than static, itself evolving, although slowly. Together we were outwardly oriented. As much as our limited resources allowed, we explored the downtown, which Phyllis, having grown up just outside of the city, knew rather well, and we grew fond of Hyde Park, which was an exciting place to live in the early 1960s. The civil rights movement, demonstrations by the Fair Play for Cuba movement, and other politically charged ingredients of the setting made the world beyond the classroom as challenging and engaging as that within it.

We also, when Anne was born in 1962, adjusted readily to parenthood, and I liked being a father more than I could have imagined. But assuming the responsibilities of parenthood also made me anxious about the future and focused my attention on completing my program. This was joined to the fact that I had become increasingly engaged by my studies and by the prospect of an academic career. This produced a sense of urgency that put pressure on my work. Due to my eagerness to complete the program, I did not do as well as otherwise I would have, but after four years of study and the completion of my exams, I was able to begin my dissertation. That same spring, Preston Roberts told me that he had submitted my name to the Department of Religion at Princeton University to fill a temporary position there. So, having begun my dissertation that summer, we set off in September 1963 for New Jersey.

Before turning from my years at Chicago, I should say that my discomfort while there was as much a consequence of my lack of confidence as of the dominance of process theology. It's curious to think, in retrospect, that part of the sense of difference I felt with the place was due to the fact that I was myself in process while the process theology at Chicago held a fixed finality. The challenges to my religious identity that it posed I would have faced more directly than I did if they had been presented as only a possible and interesting option rather than as something to be accepted. I regret that I lacked the confidence in my own abilities fully to take on the challenge, since it is rare to encounter an entrenched position that is both so interesting and so vulnerable. Indeed, process theology had at least some positive influence on me, making me more attentive to human temporality, especially in what I later called its polyphonic quality, and more affirmative of creativity and change. Conversely, I came to be, even more than I was earlier, distrustful of finality and certainty. In general, as well, Chicago confirmed and extended my orientation to a larger world, my sense of something more. People there were learned and helpful, and I was given fellowships for all four of my years. I am grateful.

Princeton University

Although we liked Chicago, it was good, especially with a child, to be out of the city and in a more pastoral setting. We rented a lovely apartment in junior faculty housing that overlooked Carnegie Lake and was free of the huge water bugs that frequented our apartments in Chicago. Relocation was also eased by the fact that my mother and three siblings lived only fifty miles away.

My position in Princeton was radically different from that at Chicago because I was, although on a temporary appointment, a member of the faculty and not a student needing to satisfy the requirements of a program and the expectations of the faculty. However, I had only begun my dissertation, and knowing that my position at Princeton was temporary, I was fully aware that I had to finish it in order to be a more qualified candidate for a position elsewhere. So, I could not fully throw myself into my work at Princeton or benefit from being there as much as I otherwise would have.

Fortunately, writing the dissertation was relatively unproblematic. Perhaps like the Calvin play that I conceived as a whole before I began it, I was able to project the whole of the dissertation from the outset and was never stuck along the way. What I did was to shift the method Preston Roberts used from narrative plot to the narrators of fiction by three writers. I did this because I recognized that narratives are built not only on plots but also on other components any one of which could be dominant. The confessional fictions I selected for the dissertation clearly were dominated by their narrators, and their narrators were clearly engaged by problems raised for them by the contrary relation of their religious upbringing, assumptions, or beliefs to a larger, more complex, and increasingly secular American culture, problems that I, of course, shared.

Two things were helpful for completing my program at Chicago. First, it did not require an oral defense of the dissertation. The prospect of that would likely have unnerved me. Second, Preston Roberts read and approved the dissertation before his breakdown occurred. His breakdown was a surprise to me, and I do not know firsthand what occasioned it. He was a fragile man, slight in build, sensitive in character, and, as a heavy smoker and drinker, not robust. He was, in all of these characteristics, Nathan Scott's opposite. Roberts also exhibited an availability, even vulnerability, that students could exploit, and it is my understanding that one of them did so. The circumstances that arose produced a sad result, and the loss of Roberts for the field, the institution, and for me personally was unfortunate. If I'm not mistaken, my dissertation was the last completed under his guidance.

Rather than resolve the question of the relation between religious faith and the larger American context in my dissertation, I posited, as I thought the writers I treated also did, basic tensions between kinds of religious beliefs and between religious beliefs and the larger cultural context. This allowed me to accept difference not only as a problem to be resolved but also as a condition to be accepted. My understanding of the complex character of narrative discourse and of the social or polyphonic quality of human temporality granted me a basis for this affirmation, although I was not able at the time fully to expand on these theoretical supports.

We adjusted quickly to our new setting and made friends with engaging neighbors in our university housing. Bob and Barbara Nozick, who later moved to Harvard, lived next door and brought us into contact with other faculty in philosophy. Especially memorable was a dinner that included Walter Kaufman, who was fascinated by my location in religion and had been antagonistic toward the founding of the Religion Department a decade or so earlier. His objections lay not primarily with the addition of religion to the curriculum but with the kind of department that was founded, one shaped by the curriculum of a Protestant seminary. That evening with Kaufman opened up for me the question of providing a base other than theology for the study of religion in such as setting as this. Attention also was drawn that evening to my own identity as a religious person when Bob, equally intrigued by my location in religion, asked me, quite out of the blue, if I prayed. "Well," I said, "I do, although probably not as well or often as I should." "What do you think you are doing when you do that?" he shot back. I replied that I supposed I was trying to be grateful. The answer seemed adequate, because he sat back in his chair to consider it.

That's the way it was there. Only junior faculty lived in our building, many with children. I had substantial interactions with them, and Phyllis could sit in the playground, watch Anne, and talk with other intelligent and talented mothers. In the fall, many of us would walk over to attend the Saturday-afternoon football games, and during our two years there Bill Bradley completed his career on the basketball team. There were many other events within walking distance—concerts, plays, lectures— more by far than we could take in.

Another rewarding relationship was with Bart Giamatti, who read and commented helpfully on an essay I wrote out of the introduction to my dissertation. It appeared in the *Journal of Comparative Literature* and was my first substantial publication. But my most rewarding contacts were with the younger faculty in the department, who had offices, along with mine, in an old house on University Place, people like John Wilson, Malcolm Diamond, and Victor Preller.

John Wilson showed a particularly strong interest in my work because of his uneasiness, to put it mildly, with the way courses in Religion and Literature were taught by Paul Jones in the department. I was there to fill in for Jones, who was on leave, and Wilson thought that Jones, although he drew large enrollments for his courses, did not have a detectable or defensible method for the work he was doing. In addition, since I had chosen American writers for my dissertation, John, who was an American religious historian, saw the relevance of what I was doing to the broader study of religion and American cultural history. Finally, John, even more than the other younger faculty, stood at a distance from the older faculty, who were housed, during that first year, up in McCosh Hall and near the chapel. John viewed most of them as apologists for Protestant Christianity, and his opinion of the department was not all that different from Walter Kaufman's. John's opposition to religious or theological bases for the study and teaching of religion in and by an arts and sciences faculty had political ramifications. Paul Jones was a favorite of the department's founder, George Thomas, and a fellow Methodist theologian. Also, on his return during my second year, Jones was up for tenure.

I was aware that during the review that led to denying Jones tenure the question of continuing me as his replacement came up. The issue was resolved by not doing that, by not hiring me in place of George Thomas's prodigy. I must say, however, that I had been, during my time there, also preoccupied with writing my dissertation, and I did not give to my relations, especially with senior faculty, the kind of attention that might have supported my candidacy. I think that I made the right decision by setting my priorities that way, but I regret not having been able to make more of the opportunities there and not staying a bit longer.

My involvement in the issues raised by John Wilson, especially his reaction to the only partially concealed theological interests of many of the department's faculty, was complex. I agreed with him that theology should not shape the curriculum of academic religion or determine the study of religion in such a setting. Nor should religious identity determine the methods or goals of teaching. John was particularly disdainful of what he called the "zoo" concept of a religion department, one constituted by faculty of various religious identities, by specimens, in other words, of religious types. This, however, raised the question of whether, by freeing it from theological and religious determinations, the study of religion would then be subjected to non- or even antireligious interests. One answer to this question would have been to expand rather than to shrink the application of "religious" so that reading and interpreting literature would become religious acts, a move that others in Religion and Literature, often citing T. S. Eliot as a warrant, had made. This was an option at that time because literature in academic culture still comprised an elevated canon requiring its own modes of edifying interpretation. Also, John himself did some of that, seeing nonreligious aspects of American society, such as Memorial Day celebrations and athletic events, as religious because they had characteristics that could be so identified. Literature or reading and interpreting it could also be thought of that way. This extension and neutralization of the category "religious" continues in religious studies today, especially among Americanists. Although I saw similarities and overlaps between religious and nonreligious phenomena in American life, I preferred, also, to distinguish religious and nonreligious from one another. It seemed to me that the picture was blurred more than clarified by the loss of distinction. However, this meant the question was not, now, created, as it had been for me at Chicago, by tensions between differing theologies but, rather, by tensions between religious and nonreligious interests directing the study of religion. Protecting the study of religion both from theology and from methods and assumptions that arose from non- and even antireligious interests became the new project.

It is noteworthy that materialist analyses and interpretations of both literature and of religion, especially Marxist and Freudian, while marginally a part of the agenda at Chicago, got little attention at Princeton. This absence of radical critiques of literature, culture, and religion created a more supportive context for both religion and literature traditionally understood than would otherwise have been the case. However, this lack meant that severing the study of religion from a religious base did not occasion a clear shift to an antireligious base. That shift came more centrally into view later on.

What prevailed at Princeton was an assumed humanism, a high estimation of the human. The study of religion in such a context was, then, a study of human needs, potentials, and constructions. While I took this view as, to a large degree, valid and useful, it was not, as totally explanatory, as fully satisfying for me as it seemed to be for others. I had a dimmer view of the human not so much because of my Calvinist upbringing, although that may have been an enabling factor, as because of my exposure to high modernist culture and theory. I was very influenced by negative appraisals of the human both in literature after the First World War and in the theologies of Barth, Niebuhr, and Tillich. Although at Princeton this issue was visible, it was not pursued by the faculty and certainly not resolved. I left there, consequently, with a strong feeling both that the basis for the study and teaching of religion in an arts and sciences faculty was not firm and that what the basis should be was not evident.

Leaving Princeton was difficult for reasons in addition to the fact that I liked being there very much. For one thing, I had by that time pulled the safety net of ministry out from under myself. All along it had played a vague but reassuring role—something, if needed, to fall back on. As both my dissertation and my teaching went well at Princeton, as I developed my own methods, and as I felt a personal attachment to this kind of work, ministry as a viable backup faded. The matter came to a head when a church in northern New Jersey asked me if I would consider being their pastor. I had no hesitancy in turning their invitation down. However, I was also aware that by doing so I was throwing myself on the mercy of the academic job market.

In addition, when I began, quite late in my second year at Princeton, to cast about for openings, I found that, for some reason, there were very few. To my relief, I was offered a position in the English Department at Westminster College in New Wilmington, Pennsylvania. However, I didn't want to go there. I was put off during my interview by the college president, Will Orr. I vividly remember the scene in his office, which included the chairman of English, whose last name was Beasley. Orr leaned back in his chair, enumerated the things he had done for the college, and, pounding his fists on the arms of his chair for emphasis, turned to the chairman of English and asked, "Right, Beasley?" To which Beasley replied, "Yes, sir!" Meanwhile, I heard that Duke University had a possible opening, and I withheld my decision from Westminster in the hope that I could get word from Duke. I've forgotten how much time elapsed between my having to decline Westminster and hearing from Duke, but I took the chance. This was nerve-wracking since I had the well-being of my family to consider. When it arrived, I gratefully accepted the invitation to join the faculty at Duke.

Leaving Princeton was difficult, too, because the department made the mistake of hiring neither Giles Gunn, whom they interviewed for the job, nor me but the very student from Chicago who, as I had been told, was the principal cause or occasion for the collapse of Preston Roberts. I had, then, quite unhappy feelings about his arrival to campus for the interview and his subsequent appointment. I also felt hamstrung about expressing my views since I could not involve myself uninvited in a process that, I knew, already was complicated by the termination of Paul Jones. When their hire later turned out to be a disaster, I must admit to experiencing a bit of *Schadenfreude*, but most of all I felt sadness for the loss, which turned out to be permanent, of potential connection between two institutions that I admired and of which I had, briefly but intensely, been a part.

I should say, before leaving my discussion of Princeton, how grateful I was and continue to be for my two years there. I learned much from my colleagues and from teaching. I especially enjoyed advising senior theses in Religion and Literature, and I learned a great deal precepting in other courses. Preceptors were expected to attend lectures for the courses in which they worked, and I listened appreciatively to able lecturers like John Wilson and Malcolm Diamond. Indeed, Princeton more than Chicago put me on my feet intellectually and vocationally. Free from the anxieties of graduate student life, I thrived in the presence of gifted, kindly colleagues and intelligent undergraduates. All of this was supported by a rich and attractive cultural and natural context. It was wonderful, and I would like to have stayed.

Instead, on Labor Day Weekend in 1965 we packed our stuff, with John Wilson's help, into a rented truck and, expecting our second child, headed for the unknown South. While at Chicago and Princeton I had thought of many possible locations where we might end up, I never considered the South among them. The image of the South at that time, especially in the minds of northern academic Americans, is difficult to reproduce. It's not too much to say that we were even concerned, on going there, for our physical safety. We had never been farther south than Washington, D.C., and, as we drove beyond that point, we felt that we were, as we expressed it, being lowered into a pit.

Duke University

The Department of Religion and the whole of Duke were in culture and quality distant from what I had known at Chicago and Princeton. Duke was a regional institution with a student body drawn heavily from the Southeast. Indeed, after a couple of years I served on the university admission and financial aid committee and saw that there were quotas for the numbers of students accepted from other parts of the country. Special caution seemed to be taken in regard to students from the Northeast.

The Religion Department had emerged as a project sponsored by the Divinity School, and it had close ties with Divinity and with the chapel. It was wholly Protestant in identity. Even Pat Sullivan, who taught Asian religions and was my principal conversation partner until he left for Vassar five years later, was an Episcopal priest. The department was, to be even more precise, largely Methodist, and departmental meetings were opened with prayer. Tommy Langford, the chair who hired me, was a prominent Methodist clergyman who later became dean of the Divinity School and, later yet, provost of the university. He like others, especially Barney Jones, conveyed an unmistakable air of ownership by virtue of being southern and Methodist. Duke was really a big house with self-designated custodians, and the rest of us were guests, welcomed to be sure, but there as indications of our hosts' hospitality. Nor was the department academically strong. Several of its members, I quickly could see, lacked the credentials, abilities, or productivity to qualify as members of a university faculty. And the department, given the religious identity of the institution, was not called on to clarify or to justify its role. Two religion courses were required of all undergraduates, and one of those courses had to be in Bible. Only a few of the faculty participated in a graduate program that, a few years before my arrival, had been constituted by faculty drawn from both the department and the Divinity School. To raise questions about the nature and role of a department of religion in a faculty of arts and sciences or about the consequences of the department's close ties to the Divinity School and the chapel would have been impolite. I had difficulty relating to a department so defined, and I simply set about doing my own work.

My work assignment was mainly to teach courses on the Bible, since all undergraduates at that time were required to take at least one such course. I did not mind this task because I had a strong interest in biblical texts and at least some scholarly background from work at Chicago and, more, from precepting in Frank Young's New Testament course at Princeton. I developed ways of treating the texts as literary as well as religious documents, and viewing them in that way enhanced my sense more generally of the relation of religious and literary factors to one another, especially in regard to narrative. I was also allowed to teach one and later two courses on Religion and Literature, and it was a challenge for me to construct them. Drawing on my dissertation and influenced as I was by John Wilson and by my interactions with Giles Gunn, I concentrated, although not exclusively, on religion and American fiction of the twentieth century. I also built into my courses a growing interest in narrative theory, so that early on I combined American cultural history, literary texts and theory, and religious studies.

From the outset, I gave much of my time and attention to research and writing. For one thing, I did not feel at home at Duke, and I thought I should try to publish in order to increase my chances of finding an alternative location. Also, I needed to develop my own position concerning a basis and method for the study of religion, since raising the question within the department would not be productive or even possible. Also, my field of study was inadequately defined and understood, and publishing would have clarifying results at least in terms of how I went about relating religious and literary studies to one another. Finally, ideas for projects came readily to me, and I was drawn to pursue them. So, the principal form of my intellectual development during the ensuing decades at Duke was working on my projects.

In addition to my research and writing, I gave attention to my classes, and I was pleased that my efforts were well-received. I did not think all that much of it at the time, but I was given an Outstanding Professor award by the student government three years after my arrival. That recognition was confirmed forty years later by an award for distinguished teaching given in 2008 by the university administration. I did not think of teaching as a burden or bother. I found the students to be intelligent, conscientious, and appreciative. I had considered the all-male undergraduate population of Princeton to be odd, and I thought of the gender mix in my classes at Duke, in contrast, as healthy. In addition, since Duke admitted only one woman for every three or four men, the women were generally brighter than the men. The presence of gifted female students prepared me, along with my wife's professional development a few years later, for readily supporting the inclusion and advancement of women in the department and the university.

I became a member of the Graduate Faculty of Religion soon after my arrival at Duke, and initially I gave attention to this dimension of my work. However, although I continue to participate in the graduate program, that participation gradually became less important to me. One cause was my engagement in undergraduate teaching. Another was the lack of colleagues on whom I could depend for support and cooperation in developing a Religion and Literature area. For a few years early on, Giles Gunn was on the faculty at the University of North Carolina at Chapel Hill, and, while he was there, my involvement in the graduate program was more pronounced. But when he left for California, there was really no one else, since the possible candidates were not collegial. Prospects improved later with the arrival of Bill Hart and, a bit later, Nelson Maldanado Torres, but both, unfortunately, left Duke for more supportive academic environments. In addition, the culture of the graduate program put me off. It seemed primarily determined by the entrepreneurial efforts of individual members of the faculty and by the formation of ideologically defined cliques. The spirit of the program was more competitive than cooperative, and I was not drawn to enter the fray.

I also lacked certainty about the definitions of my field and about how marketable graduate students in it would be. As I said, Religion and Literature was done at Chicago, as it continues to be done in many places, basically from a theological position, and I did not identify with that basis. The alternative was to move in the other direction, to translate religion into something cultural or even political. I did not want to do that either, although Religion and Literature was also done by some along those lines. I wanted to retain the distinction between religious on the one hand and literary and cultural on the other while also attending to and accounting for their interrelations. But I was not sure either that this way of doing things could be made sufficiently clear to graduate students or that it would secure places for them in the academic marketplace. Indeed, the field as an independent enterprise began to suffer diminished institutional standing, due to the increased interest of religious scholars in literary studies and the increased interest of literary scholars in cultural and religious matters, and it is, as a separate enterprise, hardly visible today. For these several reasons I allowed my role in graduate teaching gradually to diminish.

While my relation to some of the faculty members in the Divinity School was facilitated by the cooperation between the two faculties in the Graduate Program in Religion, we also, initially, had social relations with several of them. Since I had done my Ph.D. in the Divinity School at Chicago and my primary teachers there worked from a theological base, I thought of Divinity faculty as different from but not as foreign to me. However, beginning in the mid-1980s, the Divinity School faculty became intentionally more Methodist and churchly, and I increasingly withdrew. I am not certain from what my distaste for Methodism arises. Perhaps it's that Methodists can be anything. Quite a few of the more fervent graduate students in process theology at Chicago were Methodists, but Methodists can also be evangelicals. In addition, John Wilson's uneasiness with Paul Jones, George Thomas, and Paul Ramsey, all Methodists at Princeton, was something that, given my own feelings, I immediately could understand. But it's also—and this may be the main reason—that Methodists have a sense of rightness, normality, and entitlement, and the Divinity School at Duke, it seemed to me, manifested such attitudes. I have always thought that being religious was, at least to some degree, odd. It was not that I was jealous of their sense of normality, rightness, and ownership of the university. I simply thought that identifying with people like that confirmed the questionable sense of themselves that I took them to have.

Due to increased numbers of new faculty with differing religious interests and identities, the homogeneity of the department began to break down. But a new identity for the department did not, as a consequence, emerge. Prayers to begin departmental meetings ended, but faculty members did not take the opportunity of a shift from a Protestant to a more diverse identity as an opportunity to redefine the nature and role of the enterprise. The opportunity was allowed to pass for several reasons. First, change in the makeup of the department occurred slowly, and some of those identified with the earlier mission sought to retain it with a bulldog-like tenacity. Second, some of the new appointees were themselves taken to be religious people, so that the question of teaching religion seemed better left to personal approaches than organized by shared principles. The department fell, at least partially, into the form of what John Wilson called the "zoo" model. A third reason was that, early on, faculty members were added who were not trained in graduate religion programs. This meant that they were not eager or accustomed to engage questions about the nature of religion and the role of religious studies in a complex academic environment. A fourth reason is that the primary goal of several members of the department increasingly appeared to be developing their own interests and establishing contacts outside the department with like-minded people. But the final reason is, I think, the gradual conformity within the department to the pervasive assumption in the university that shared discourse must be based on and limited to material accounts and causes. Materialism took clear form in the dominant critical approaches that arose toward the study of culture and literature, and this led to viewing religion, too, as less important than material factors within it, that gave rise to it, or that were concealed by it. While I do not think that the members of the department all became philosophical materialists, although some are, all seemed obliged to study religion in deference to materialism. The question of the department's identity, integrity, and role in arts and sciences, therefore, was not directly addressed and still is not today.

I was not distressed by these conditions. I was more fully engaged by questions about religion raised in my own work than by questions lying unattended within the life of the department. I took religious diversity for granted, having grown up with it and having encountered it socially at Chicago and Princeton, and I was aware of what earlier I called the increasing normalization, if not the normativization, of the nonreligious person. I worked with texts that engaged religion variously and to varying extents, and I developed ways of emphasizing religious differences as much as constants. Religion was early on for me many things, and I was aware that there were not only kinds of religious people but also that differing kinds created major tensions within religions, so that the use of the singular in any of these cases was questionable. Among other things, this meant that there would be a variety of answers in any religion about its relation to other religions and to the nonreligious.

Materialist-based critical stances within the university that influenced the department bothered me more by their being merely assumed and inadequately theorized. It was, then, not made clear in the name of what, finally, the critique of religion was carried on. This undertheorization gave to these approaches or stances a kind of certainty that was derived not from materialism itself but from the general assumption that a thoroughgoing critique of religion was realistic and intellectually rigorous. At the risk, if not the price, of appearing, in contrast, soft and "confessional," I was also intent on developing ways of viewing and comparing the similarities or continuities as well as what makes for sharp and even volatile differences in ways of being religious, so that the critique of religion could be seen also as internal to it. More, I could not conclude that theoretical materialism held fewer difficulties and objectionable consequences than did religious beliefs and practices, and I was put off by the certainty detectable in materialist-based critiques of religion. So, while I do not think it is healthy for a department to leave to its individual members decisions regarding the nature and role of religious studies in an arts and sciences faculty, I also do not think that the members of the department shared assumptions that would sponsor discussions of religion and the study and teaching of it that would balance critique and suspicion of religion with appreciative understanding.

What determines the situation, then, is a separation between secular or materialist and religious or theological understandings of religion and of studying it. This falling out is not isolated; it is widespread in contemporary American society in the present division between aggressively religious and equally outspoken nonreligious positions, a division that often takes political form. It is readily visible at Duke. On the one side is a Divinity School faculty largely defined by a centripetal, church-based exclusivity, and on the other a department largely affected by a willingness primarily to locate the study of religion within a materialist, that is, a social, economic, and political, framework. My own location, interests, and work assume and confirm multiple relations and interdependencies that appear between religion and secularity, particularly in literary culture and texts. I understand this view not as theoretically dependent but as justified by the texts. As is generally the case, however, when clear options stand in contrast and even in conflict with one another, a position like mine between them is seen as not a position at all but as a vague or tepid compromise, a refusal to take sides.

During my decades at Duke, the university has undergone dramatic changes. Once a white, Protestant, southern, and male-dominated institution, it is now richly diverse. Diversification and higher standards of selection produced a student population of striking quality. The administration is to be commended for this achievement. The institution became more like contexts I had known in the past and even surpassed them. Consequently, I feel far more at home in the institution now than I did in the past.

However, while changes in the university and department were mostly positive and while it can be said that Duke and the department are now more dynamic, complex, and engaging than they once were, I continue to be unable closely to identify with them. There is in all of this improvement a detectable ambition to compete with other institutions, and this produces the formation of identity by means of opposition. The ambition is not so much for excellence as for status, visibility, and marketability. There is a market mentality pervasive in the institution, and a business model has become dominant—administrative managers, faculty employees, and student customers. Also, a competitive spirit has been injected into faculty and departmental life. While there is no doubt that financial resources are limited, especially in recent years, a culture of scarcity is sponsored by the administration so that departments and faculty within departments will compete with one another in a zero-sum game. Self-promotion and visibility become determining factors, and they set faculty and departments at odds with one another. Given the loss of other dynamics in university life that would encourage a sense of common cause, the culture of the university produces a centrifugal and at times isolating effect.

In addition, students come to Duke largely because it is a good place from which to move on to professional schools. This means that many of them take courses not because they are interested in them but because they are required. These courses set up sharply competitive relations between students who are vying for high grades, and students are required to work hard in order to excel. Consequently, a sharp division appears between the work required of them by their courses and what they do in their free time, a division that was not present during my early years at Duke. While these characteristics and dynamics are likely pervasive throughout higher education in America, Duke embodies them, it seems to me, in an intense form because of the ways in which the university's life and identity have developed. When I meet faculty from Chicago or Princeton, I pick up from them more institutional loyalty and more appreciation for the shared academic enterprise of their institutions than I do from my colleagues here at Duke or see in myself. However, having said this, I also would not exchange Duke as it is today for what it was when I arrived, and, despite my reservations about the culture of the place, I would not exchange my position in it for most of those held by members of faculties at other institutions whom I talk with about such matters.

An opportunity arose rather early in my time at Duke for changing vocational direction toward a career in administration. During the early 1970s, I served as associate dean of the college and, also for one year, in the administration of the Graduate School. John McKinney, a sociologist and dean of the Graduate School, told me I had a bright future in administration and offered me a continuing position as associate dean. The offer had its appeal, and a higher salary was a part of that appeal. For many years after my arrival at Duke, I did not earn a salary that enabled us to live without hardship even though we were by habit frugal, and we were unable to do with and for our children what we would have liked to have done. Second, I would be brought by this position into administrative circles, and the atmosphere of such circles encouraged their members to consider themselves, relative to most of the faculty, as in a superior position. I was strongly tempted by this group feeling. Third, I did not feel at home in the department, and this would have provided an escape from it. While I considered the change of direction McKinney's offer opened to me, I was by then sufficiently engaged by my scholarship and teaching to resist the temptations that an administrative career posed.

I put my administrative interests and abilities to work over the years chairing several university committees, and, beginning in 2002, I served a four-year term as chair of the department. I became chair following a rather stressful period in the department's life created by differences among its members concerning the allocation of resources either toward maintaining and even increasing its "traditional strengths" or toward developing several "newer fields." So, my administrative efforts were aimed primarily at creating a more cohesive department and avoiding the interference in its life that the administration not only threatened but had initiated. Fortunately, I was able to ease the conditions that prevailed, and the department, while continuing to have its tensions and difficulties, began to function more smoothly. However, these conditions militated against the possibilities, if there were any, of using the time while chairing to turn the faculty's attention to the task of clarifying the department's identity and its role in an arts and sciences faculty.

Cultural and social changes over the decades also affected our private life. Phyllis, after we began to have children, was primarily a homemaker, although she kept up her interests in music by playing the organ in churches and in English by working at Duke on the Thomas and Jane Carlyle correspondence. But in the early 1970s, while playing the organ for a chapel service in the hospital, she met a hospital chaplain and took an interest, while talking with him about his work, in doing something of that kind herself. When she came to my office fresh from that conversation, I said that she should get an application to the Divinity School and submit it. It was accepted, and, because our third child, Alexander, was in school, she began her program, including extensive work in clinical pastoral care, and received her master's of divinity degree in 1979. She was ordained a Presbyterian pastor and subsequently held several pastoral positions. Her career, while clearly distinct from mine, was also interesting to me, given my earlier direction toward ministry, and her work increased our sense of constituting a team.

Affiliation with the Presbyterian Church, which began a few months after our arrival in Durham, has been constant, and Phyllis, in her work and by means of the denominational offices that she has held, strengthened those ties. Her work involved us more closely in the church, and we were made aware of factors that limit and even counter what would give the church integrity and inspire loyalty. Perhaps because of my father's less than positive experiences in churches and because of the growing distance between my own development and the church in which I was raised, I did not find the weaknesses in churches and clergy surprising. But the liturgy of the church we attend is sound and edifying, especially the music. I am not anti-institutional in regard either to the church or to the university. However, while I respect and appreciate them, I also cannot identify closely with them.

Although at the outset I planned to stay at Duke only for a limited period because of its location and ethos, Duke and the South began dramatically to change. At the same time, the availability of attractive academic opportunities outside declined. Duke also became not only more diverse but also developed a much higher academic standing, due to aggressive marketing. The academic quality of the department followed that trend, as weaker members were replaced by more able scholars. During my decades here, Duke and the department moved from a regional identity and comfortable homogeneity to a recognized national and even international standing.

I have professionally participated intensely in the life of three remarkable universities. In each of them the construction of my religious identity, what I mean by "assumption" in the second sense, was carried on more in exception to than in rapport with the institutions. However, in all three I also benefited enormously from so much that was made available in and through them. One of the gifts granted to me by all three was the freedom to spend a good bit of time doing my own work and thinking about my own views of things, including my religious identity.

I want to affirm my gratitude for the opportunities that these institutions—especially, because of the long duration of my tenure there, Duke University—have afforded me. The distance or dissonance between my own and the identity of the institutions in each case and in differing ways forced on me the task of consciously taking on a religious identity rather than simply accepting an identity that conformed to or was conferred by my institutional affiliations.

9

LOOKING AHEAD

RELIGIOUS IDENTITY AS
BEING RECEIVED

THE THIRD facet of religious identity is assumption in the sense of being received or accepted, what we mean when we refer to the assumption of the Virgin. While the need or desire for acceptance or inclusion may seem to signal weakness or low self-confidence, I think of it as a sign of health and as part of daily life. Even more, however, it is part of religious belief and behavior. Indeed, the religious desire for inclusion or acceptance, among other things, accounts, it seems to me, for the expectation of a positive outcome beyond death, which can arise less from a desire that an individual's identity should survive than from a desire to be received, incorporated, or completed. This religious desire and need for reception and inclusion is related to, while also distinguished from, the desire or need to be recognized and valued. While the conditions of a person's life may frustrate the desire for reception and while people differ as to how much and what kind of inclusion or reception they need and desire, this form of assumption is an important part of what it means to have an identity generally, and, as to a religious identity, it is basic.

In the previous chapter, I discussed my relations to institutions, and I emphasized conditions that account for my not having felt closely identified with or fully received by them. This sets me apart from people who may find the need for inclusion answered by their associations with movements, groups, or institutions. By not feeling fully identified with institutions, I am thrown back on the task of clarifying some other way by which reception or completion could occur.

This is not to slight my having been accepted in various ways in addition to institutional locations, especially in personal relationships. I was received by my parents, affirmed by many friends, encouraged by teachers, and loved by my family. Indeed, although I do not group myself with those who have many intimate friends, I have friendly relationships with colleagues and with people in general. But the need and desire outstrip these otherwise highly valued affections and relationships.

These affiliations and relationships are complemented by work I have done that has been accepted, published, and read by others. This may be an odd thing to suggest, but John Updike puts it nicely when he says: "My early yearnings merged the notion of print, Heaven, and Manhattan. . . . To be in print was to be saved."[1] I know what he means.

The third facet of my religious identity, then, is partially provided by the housing that writing and being published serve to create and adumbrate. Since texts belong more to the future than to the past, given that they carry the potential of being read, they do not cease to carry the potential as well of my being received. However, what I have not done in the past is to cull from my work the principal beliefs implied in or supported by them. Nor have I, because they were scattered among separate projects, gathered and ordered them so that they would be given at least some coherence. I propose to do that now, howbeit in a brief and even skeletal form. In addition, I shall do it as a kind of gambit in what I hope will be a continuing conversation, so that the gesture will prompt neither full rejection nor acceptance but religious self-disclosures in response.

Before beginning, I should say that I think of myself as a religious person. I also do not balk at being called a Christian or refuse so to self-identify, although I am uncomfortable by being grouped with many people whose identities confirmed by that designation put me off. Also, I would not resist being called a Protestant, although, again, I would be uneasy about being associated with many others who so identify themselves. Finally, I do not shirk the label of Reformed, although I would place myself under that sign for reasons different from those that prompt others to stand there, too. But I also am uneasy with such identifying labels, and this is less because I question the principles that define any of them as because they both conceal differences that may be as important as the similarities between people in the labeled groups and are applied top-down. Although I do not reject such labels, appreciate the willingness of people to stand under them, and am willing, if they admit me, to stand there, too,

I much prefer working from the bottom up. That means clarifying basic matters first. I shall proceed that way now, starting with belief itself, its status, function, and legitimacy. After considering belief, I will move forward toward religious beliefs and finally to beliefs that are Christian.

Identity and Belief

The question of belief, its role and legitimacy, became part of academic culture shortly after the time when I was working on it, and that change in academic culture confirmed conclusions I already had drawn. The cultural change, in a word, was toward a greater acceptance of the premise that scholarship is not as free from beliefs and values as previously it was thought it could or should be. While disinterestedness and objectivity have their understandable and in many circumstances indispensable roles to play, they have been too easily assumed and in general overvalued. People do not encounter things, even when they try to, in a wholly raw or free way but in the context of a culture, especially a language, by which what they encounter already has been affected. Although we may try to suspend presuppositions and though there are situations in which it is very important for us to try doing so, we cannot be fully free from them. As a result of this change in academic culture, scholars are often more forthright about their own locations, how they have arrived at what they are putting forward, and what view of it they hold. Belief, then, has become part of academic culture, and when scholars step forward as persons, what they frequently admit to are the assumptions and norms that guide them, in short, their beliefs.

When this cultural change occurred in academic work, I already had identified a basic role or place for beliefs, a place or role that I concluded was not only unavoidable but also productive. As I pointed out earlier, an assumption in my life has been a sense of something more that beckons me to pursue it, something beyond me that is more expansive, primary, and valuable than I am. My orientation and relations in and to my world are affected by this belief, and not only my work but also my identity would be very different were I not to believe this.

Already at Chicago I was led to recognize that beliefs of this kind occur, persist, and determine personal outcomes. This recognition was extended by attention to Aristotelian poetics and to the work of myth and ritual literary critics. Their interest in narrative and human time, it became clear, was entangled with beliefs, and I began to see that discourse, especially narrative discourse, because of the importance for it of human time, was inseparable from belief. I also became aware that the narrativization of characters, that is, understandings and images of other people, are likewise entangled with beliefs, such as whether people are trustworthy or not and what makes them commendable and what makes them objectionable. In my first book, I moved in another direction, toward the teller. The beliefs included by the teller concern what is deemed worthy of attention and how things are evaluated, and it becomes clear, on analysis, that the language of tellers in narrative also carries beliefs. Finally, I realized that the language of location and situation in narrative discourse carries beliefs as to the value and force of the conditions with and under which people live, whether those conditions and their effects are supportive of or contrary to their well-being. My own orientation to something else as to something large and more important than what is present or even than who I am, I saw, was a belief integral or applicable to this fourth aspect of narrative. Since such beliefs do not simply occur in narrative discourse but are constitutive of it, narrative discourse and beliefs are inevitably entangled with one another.

This led to a new appreciation for the questions to which beliefs stand as answers, questions that, while requiring answers, resist being finally and fully put to rest. In order to keep these questions at bay, people are not easily dissuaded, even by evidence, from their beliefs corresponding to these four sets of questions. Furthermore, we read and listen to narratives because, among other reasons, by so doing our own beliefs and responses to these four sets of questions are confirmed and/or challenged. Finally, it became clear to me that these beliefs, while constitutive of narrative discourse, are not limited to it. Rather, all four beliefs are necessary for a person or people to have a world. I need to have answers to questions of all four kinds before I can go about my daily life. A world, then, is structured by responses to questions, and these responses are beliefs. Who I am, the world in which I find or place myself, and the beliefs I hold (or, as Stanley Fish somewhere said, the beliefs that hold me), are closely bound. Identity and beliefs, then, while not the same thing, are also not separable.

A further recognition followed. From graduate work on, especially in regard to biblical texts, the role of myth engaged me. The relation of literature and religion to one another could, at least in part, be addressed by their common dependence on myths, rituals, and symbols. Taking myth in its simplest sense, now, as narrative in which gods and other more-than-human characters appear, I recognized that myths, rather than forming a specific kind of narrative, are narratives in their most fully developed form because the four sets of questions, which resist being fully and finally answered but require to be answered nonetheless, are pursued in myth until the discourse reaches answers that are, in varying degrees, transcendent. In other words, I moved in regard to narrative in a direction contrary to that of Mikhail Bakhtin, who finds narrative most fully actualized in its ontological liberation from myth. Rather than separate modern narratives from myth, I was struck with how often they bend toward myth as toward that by which the questions still smoldering within them can find fuller force.

I pursued the status and role of questions in my work on Maurice Blanchot and Julia Kristeva, concluding that questions are primary to and generative of beliefs and the world they form and that discourse, including narrative, can and often is a protection against the force of world- and identity-threatening questions or mysteries. This recognition allowed me to place persons in an unavoidable position relative to questions that need to be answered before they have or can inhabit a world, questions that cannot adequately or finally be answered. And this is true both for a person's world and for that person's identity.

This set of recognitions shaped a good bit of my research and writing. I wrote a book on each of the languages of narrative, on the questions that underlie them, and on the beliefs to which those questions give rise. These efforts demonstrated and, I hoped, confirmed my theory that narrative discourse arises from questions that require beliefs for answers and that narratives, especially fictional narratives, are culturally and often religiously important because they incorporate beliefs that challenge and/or confirm the beliefs of the culture and of readers. This work also gave basis to the notion that narrative discourse and having a world can have a mutually reinforcing relation to one another. Finally, it delivered belief from marginalization, from the lingering assumption that beliefs are optional, arbitrary, dispensable, or disabling.

Beliefs, then, are not confined to some people, as though a distinction can be made between believers and nonbelievers. All believe. It would be good if that were acknowledged and if there were more open discussions of beliefs, of beliefs that we do and do not share, of how to surface the beliefs operative in our culture, and of what it is to which various beliefs lead.

My own beliefs of these four kinds I am more than willing to share with others, and I openly espouse them. In response to the question raised by my encounters with other people and by the requirement that I have beliefs as to what others are like, I say, for example, that I take other people to be both similar to and unlike me. And I mean by that all other people. This is an alternative to the observable tendency of people to distinguish between people who are like them from people who are unlike them.

As to beliefs about human temporality that I think would be good to share is that we are, in our temporality, related and not alienated. And this relatedness is threefold. First, we are related by natural rounds, by cycles that are oriented primarily to the past. Also, our temporality finds us in present time operating within the dynamics of relations with other people, groups, and movements in our society. Finally, we move temporally in relation to a future toward which we are oriented as the locus of the fulfillment of our potentials or of our being the persons we should be. Temporality, then, is the means by which rhythmically we are part of something in the past, polyphonically related to others in the present, and melodically related to a future that invites us to be more or other than we are.

Finally, I think it would be good to affirm the value of place-relations that make us appreciative of and caring for the places not only that we call our own and have personalized but also for social and natural places. This is an alternative to the tendency observable in our society to distinguish private places that I or others own from public places. We have real or potential place-relations of many kinds, relations with natural sites, with social locations, and with future placements and conditions in which human potentials can be more fully realized.

Beliefs and Religion

While my efforts to clarify the basic and unavoidable roles of beliefs in worldviews preceded and was confirmed by the change in academic culture toward more personal investments in scholarship, my next step was preceded by such changes. This step, related to the first but also distinguishable from it, concerns the status and role of texts for our beliefs, identities, and the worlds we inhabit. This was an important development for me because my work, both in literary and religious studies, depended on texts. Preoccupation with texts could, otherwise, be thought of as secondary or removed, relative to what stands outside them.

I began to wrestle with this problem by dealing with the interest recent literary critics and theorists had taken in biblical narratives.[2]

While most of the theory in this direction challenged the assumption that we could divest ourselves completely of cultural conditions and deal with what is there unimpeded by assumptions and beliefs, I challenged the notion that beliefs are unmediated and self-generated. Drawing on the work of Jacques Derrida, on literary and religious theorists influenced by him, and on the hermeneutics of Gadamer and Ricoeur, I argued not only that no position is free from presuppositions and beliefs but also that the beliefs by which people find themselves shaped are textually located. The work I had done earlier on human temporality made me appreciative of Derrida's skepticism about the availability of present time, since, as St. Augustine already made clear, it cannot be grasped or even referred to. We always encounter the present in relation to a past and future that are texts constituted, among other things, by memories or assumptions and by expectations or goals.

I continued these developments by looking at the practices of reading texts, especially reading integral to texts as scripture.[3] I pointed out that Bacon read nature as a text and that his principal justification for doing so came from the Reformed adoption of the medieval trope of nature as a second scripture. Bacon's theory of reading nature was one by which a person as much as possible suspended expectations and previous knowledge in the hope of encountering something new. It was interesting to me that the notion of raw facts and their accessibility, a notion that people tend to support by appeal to scholarly rigor generally and to scientific observation specifically, arose not from theories of observing natural things as objective facts but from reading nature as though it were a book, indeed, as though it were scripture. I traced this way of reading texts as scripture from Bacon on nature to eighteenth-century ways of reading history as a second scripture and then to reading literature or poetry as scripture in the nineteenth century. I ended by finding similar emphases in the reading theories of Maurice Blanchot, who was oriented to texts in the Hebrew Bible, and Julia Kristeva, who was oriented to texts in the New Testament.

I drew two conclusions from all of this. First, our worlds are principally textual, and when we are studying our world we are doing so in ways conditioned by texts. Although we are not wholly imprisoned by texts but also enabled by them, we encounter whatever there is that lies beyond texts in ways related to them. The second conclusion, one that stands in opposition to Derrida and many who follow him, is that we cannot be and are not simply anywhere we choose to be on the textual field. We are all already located on it somewhere, although our locations may be complex and unsteady. Another way of saying this is that persons, groups, and institutions have identity because of texts, texts that locate them somewhere on the textual field. I call these textual locations "scriptures." What "scriptures" indicates, then, are texts that stand somewhere between what is meant by "canon," namely, texts that are separate from the wider textual field, and "writing," which suggests the textual field in its entirety and without a center. Scripture, unlike "canon," is related to the field of texts, but scripture is also distinguishable from "writing" because it suggests the center where any person, group, institution, and, perhaps, even culture already are. Everybody, then, already has a scripture, a location on the textual field. Identity in general and religious identity in particular cannot be separated from textual location and determination. Derrida, influenced as he seems to have been on this point by Sartre, denies that people already are located somewhere on the textual field, and this implies a theory of personal identity based on will and agency, on the ability to transcend the textual field and to select what on it will constitute a center. Derrida's unsupported elevation of freedom above textual determinants is shared, it seems to me, by many other theorists who otherwise are materialists.

The primacy of textuality is an emphasis important for literary and religious studies because both of them deal not only with texts but also with canons and scriptures. While the literary canon in recent years has been dismantled in order to include otherwise ostracized texts, a new set of central texts—I would say inevitably—has arisen, a new scripture, and the question needs always to be raised as to why these texts have that centrality and whether what now is taken as scripture ought to be supplanted or augmented. Religious people and those who study religion need as well to ask both what actually are the central texts of religious persons or peoples and from what central texts the scholar is viewing and interpreting those people.

Beliefs in general are related to religions, therefore, because beliefs are not spontaneous or internally generated but are textually embedded and mediated, particularly beliefs concerning what it is important to remember and what we anticipate or hope for. Since, as I suggest, all people have a "scripture" by virtue of their being textually located or identifiable, it is not surprising that people who are aware that their beliefs are crucial to who they are have an awareness as well of texts, even if those texts, as is sometimes the case, are not written down but are recorded in the memories of people who rehearse them. There are similarities between religious and nonreligious people, therefore, in that both not only have beliefs but also have scriptures. Religious people may well, however, give more attention to their beliefs and scriptures than their nonreligious contemporaries do to theirs.

The problem with texts, as I already have suggested, is that they are constituted primarily by answers, answers to the questions that I have clarified as both unavoidable for constructing a world and as not finally subject to resolution. This problem is aggravated by the fact that we favor texts that give us answers because we do not like living in a world based on questions, since this causes irresolution and uncertainty. This is why we are so vulnerable, for example, to advertising, propaganda, and ideological advocacy, since rhetoric of these kinds offers answers to our questions and quandaries. We are so easily shaped into consumers, are so easily subjected to fads and fashions, whether of clothing or of ideas, and so easily seduced by ideologies because of our eagerness to turn from the primacy and unavoidability of questions to the comforts and power of answers.

Religious people err as much in this respect as do others. They tend to give their answers to the unsettling questions addressed by their scriptures primacy over the questions. This, I would be willing to say, is the threat to any religion posed by religious idolatry, dogmatism, and authority. The most important contribution that religious people can make to their culture, relative to its tendency toward arrogance and imperialism, is to urge recognition that the uncertainties and mysteries of life and world to which answers are given keep those answers from being final and certain. This important function of religion relative to its culture is blunted or lost by acts and attitudes of religious certainty, since certainty, rather than subvert cultural imperialism and personal arrogance, warrants them.

Religious texts, I conclude from all of this, and texts that encourage religious readings have the primary role or effect of bringing us to an awareness of questions and of our uncertain positions relative to them. The principal disservice that can be done to a religion and religious texts is to treat them as, or to transform them into, sets of answers and placing them in competition with answers of other kinds. This is often done, especially when, in place of texts of complexity and diversity, texts of assumed coherence and certainty, such as theological formulations, doctrines, and institutional authority, are made primary and control texts and reading. While institutional and theological establishments need not be avoided, and are, indeed, understandable consequences of reading, they should always stand as needing to be challenged by reading that returns to the questions to which they are responses.

Another way by which beliefs in general and religious beliefs are related to one another has to do with the more or other that lies ahead or beyond and to which I have from time to time alluded concerning my own world orientation. I find it important if not necessary to take this as something significant not only for me but also for our culture, if we are to have a viable world. That is, we should take this something more as in some sense real. It does not do for me to think that only materiality and physical events are real and to think that what challenges who we are and beckons us to something higher is only a projection or conjecture.

A crisis for religion today, one that can be felt across religious differences, is created by the dominance in modern culture not so much of relativism, as is often thought, but of materialism. I think that the crisis for religion created by the dominance of materialism, that is, by the belief that the source and explanation of everything is finally material, is created for the culture as well. While I affirm that there are many materialists who have values, morals, and ideals that are more admirable than those of many religious persons, I am not sure how nonreligious people can convincingly secure the standing of those values, morals, and ideals by relying on materialist views as exhaustive and wholly explanatory.

To put it another way, the crisis of the culture is created by the inability of idealist modes of thought to stand up to or to complement the widespread acceptance that presently is enjoyed by their materialist contraries. In the past, religions were supported by idealist assumptions about the reality of spirits or immutable ideas, for example. The assurance that there is more to life and to our worlds than what meets the eye, so to speak, and the support for both culture and religion that such assurance provided have been threatened, if not jettisoned, by the pervasive and powerful materialist assumptions that are prominent, if not dominant, in the culture.

Our culture lacks, either because they are inherently untenable or because those who hold them are inept in advancing them, forms of idealism that challenge or at least complement cultural materialism. We do not balance analyses and interpretations that move downward or behind to material factors with analyses and interpretations that move upward or ahead to their spiritual counterparts. This means that religion must stand without cultural support and is asked now to carry by itself the burden that in the past was partially borne by cultural assumptions concerning the spiritual and moral.

I am or try to be a religious person, then, primarily for three reasons. First, I find it necessary to be up-front about what texts I take or read as "scriptures" and to distinguish them from and relate them to "second scriptures," such as nature, history, and literature. Second, I think it is important to retain or recover an orientation to something beyond and more important than I am or that we are. I have an understanding of and respect for people of other religions because I take them, in their own ways, to be doing something similar. Third, while I think that there are materialists who live by values and moral norms that make them more fully realized and valuable people than I am, I do not think that materialism provides adequate resources to account for what is very important and productive for our being persons. In the absence of convincing and adequate forms of idealism, religion stands as the principal complement or alternative to materialist views, and I am a religious person in part for that reason.

Religion and Christianity

Turning now to my being a Christian, I should say that who I am and being Christian are, of course, not wholly the same thing. I do not pretend, in outlining the principal marks of my being Christian, either to exhaust the resources within the faith or to imply that what is meaningful to me is all that can or should be salvaged from Christianity and the rest of it discarded. Rather, I think of Christianity primarily as a repertoire of principles that are only partially understood and operative at any one time. Anybody's or any institution's Christianity, especially when consciously deployed, is a partial rendering of that repertoire.

To put it the other way, I acknowledge that the Christianity summarized by confessional principles is not all relevant or applicable to my Christian identity or to my attempts to deploy and understand my world. I would feel more uneasy about saying this and at the same time thinking of myself as a Christian were it not for two considerations. First, I do not think that these principles are immutable, or, to put it more directly, more important than reading the biblical texts from which they are derived and by which their merit or status is warranted. Second, I take these principles as similar to the role of moral principles in Christianity. I do not pretend to be fully aligned, in my life, with Christian moral principles, and, I would think, no Christian would claim to be. Likewise, I am neither aligned with nor put into practice all of the principles guiding Christian belief.

Furthermore, while we take it for granted that Christians will differ as to how they interpret and apply to their own lives the principles of moral behavior, one detects far less flexibility and tolerance for differences when it comes to the principles of Christian belief. What is central and what is peripheral in moral principles and how what is central is applied in and to particular conditions by Christians in particular cultural situations is as true for the principles of belief as it is for the principles of moral behavior. Finally, having said this and implying by it that all Christians are more or less partial in their identities, partial in both senses of that word, I am eager to add that, while no Christian is or can be fully realized either in belief or in practice, there certainly are Christians who are far more faithful and fully realized in belief and practice than I am.

In other words, my Christian identity puts me in a complex situation of similarity and difference with other Christians, as it also puts me in relations of similarity and difference with religious people of other kinds. This is not to say that, because I feel more similarity religiously with some people of other religions than I do with some Christians, all religions are somehow the same. Nor do they, however, differ in every respect from one another. They are, like persons and cultures, both similar and different from one another.

While I don't wear being a Christian on my sleeve, I am glad and thankful to be one. I find biblical texts and interpretations, reflections, and applications of them, Christian culture, especially the rich tradition of Christian music, and devotional literature rich, compelling, and edifying. I can only assume that Christians who differ from me and people of other religions would say the same thing about being who and where they are.

I am also glad and thankful for being Reformed. In fact, I am only half joking when I say, as I sometimes do, that I am more Reformed than Christian. I would be bewildered if somehow it were to occur that I would have to try being Christian without at the same time being Reformed. And the reason for this has already been given, namely, that being Reformed focuses attention on one's textual location and on the mysteries or questions that are always primary to and generative of the representations and answers with which we respond to them.

I take Calvin's theory of scripture, then, which is a theory not of the text or of its origins but of reading the text, as a basic and reliable description of how I am and want to be located textually in my world and to the mysteries upon which it and I are dependent. I do not assert, though, that only the Bible can be read as scripture, since

I affirm, along with Calvinists, the importance of "second scriptures."[4] I do assert three things. First, reading scripture primarily
means questioning the answers that we have a tendency to use as
a means to repress or occlude questions. Second, biblical texts do
that; they subvert and at times even counter the expectations of
readers who carry into their readings conclusions, including theological and doctrinal conclusions, formulated in abstraction. Indeed,
I would say that biblical texts are primarily about how they should
be read, namely, by acts that can be called humility, confession, self-
emptying, and the like. Third, I suspect I would or could feel more
kinship with non-Christians who read this way than with Christians
who substitute for it a kind of reading determined by and subjected
to institutional and theological certainty.

This understanding of reading, I should add, connects with the assumption that, as I said early on, I retained from my youth, namely,
the desire or anticipation of something new and more ahead or above
me that calls for a releasing of my hold on what is or its hold on me
in order to be open to something new. That expectation or desire
and the world opened by this kind of reading are mutually reinforcing. What I think of as crucial to my religious identity, this sense
of expectancy and desire for something more and new, which I take
to be basic to and necessary for what is meant by belief in God, are
related by the interplay between answers achieved and their being
destabilized by questions. At times I have a sense of what all three—
God, world in all four of its aspects, and I—are, and at times I am
perplexed and mystified by them.

This understanding of the location of biblical texts and of the act
of reading them is not as isolating as it may appear to be because
in my work I have recognized that biblical texts and Western culture are more deeply entwined than I previously had thought. For
example, I have argued that biblical wisdom literature is crucial to
the formation of modern culture in general and of American culture
in particular. The sapiential religious elements in our culture are as
biblically warranted as are other manifestations of biblically based
Christianity, priestly and prophetic. A corollary of this point is not
only that biblical texts sponsor a variety of theological and religious
orientations but also that these orientations stand inherently and
unavoidably in contrast, if not conflict, with one another. Consequently, the adequacy and finality of any one of them is internally
challenged.[5]

Returning to Calvin, we can say that for him reading scripture is
the central and defining Christian practice. The church arises from

it, and the church is constituted primarily by readers of scripture. What can be said of Calvin's Ecclesiology can also be said of his Christology.

When considering Calvin's Christology, it must first be said that he is highly attentive to and appreciative of the Hebrew Bible, more, I would say, than most Christians. Calvin did not think that the New Testament added all that much to the Old, although it did make what was in the Old Testament clearer, broader, and higher, meaning, by that last word, more spiritual. In other words, Calvin had a Christology not at the expense of but in relation to the biblical texts more generally. And, since Calvin was himself also a proponent of reading nature as a second scripture, he had a Christology that was continuous not only with the range of biblical texts but also with one's encounters with the larger textual world.

The second thing to say about Calvin's Christology is that for him Christians can have no dealings with Christ apart from reading scripture. "If we would know Christ, we must seek him in the Scripture. Anyone who imagines Christ as he will gets nothing but a mere blur. So, we must first hold that Christ is known rightly nowhere but in Scripture."[6] This is a remarkable statement, and nowhere does it become clearer than in their Christology that Christians generally, if not inveterately, substitute doctrinal and creedal formulations for or place them in a determining position relative to reading the texts.

Let me give an example of what it would mean to take Calvin's point as basic and to move from it to Christology. Looking, for the sake of economy, only at the gospels, it is fair to say that the figure of Jesus, increasingly so from the earliest of the gospels, Mark, to the last of them, John, combines historical with ascended or transcendent factors. To put it directly, whatever else it is, Christology generally and the doctrine of the incarnation particularly are drawn from this textual or narrative occurrence. There was for the early church a relation between the two, between the historical Jesus who was remembered and the ascended Lord who was both present to the church and anticipated by it. The two were affirmed as continuous with one another. It was not as though the early church conspired to concoct this combination of two, dissimilar and otherwise separated elements. However, it is also the case that Christians do not know a Christ apart from this textual or narrative occurrence. What the pre- and post-textual Christ are remains conjectural. Saying that does not necessarily or completely oppose the creeds, however, because they, especially the Chalcedonian formulation, set out to protect Christology from easy solutions and to retain its mystery.

If we adhere to text, narrative, and reading for a Christology, it should be stressed that the principal structure of the gospels, especially the synoptic gospels as established by Mark, is the journey from Galilee to Jerusalem, and the principal injunction is to follow Jesus on that journey. Whatever else it is or means, the journey to Jerusalem and the divestments that occur there are crucial to the act or process of reading the narrative as scripture, namely, divesting oneself of claims, certainties, and protections, especially the answers that stand as idols in lieu of the mystery, especially the idolatrous answer of the self-sustaining and certain self, dogma, or institution.

Soteriology, then, along with whatever else it is, has as its essential element the act of reading scripture as a disciple, of taking up one's cross, an act of self-surrender and abnegation. While it may mean more, soteriology refers first of all to the act of reading, the act of divesting and being reconstituted, or, to put it in such graphic terms as those used by Maurice Blanchot and Julia Kristeva, dying and being reconstituted.[7]

The doctrinal preference of answer to question is contrary to the primary direction of the languages of biblical narratives—character, plot, atmosphere, and teller—from answers to questions, from assumptions to challenges, from certainty to mystery. I do not think that creedal and theological formulations are to be eschewed. We need them to construct and articulate a coherent response. But they are derivative, approximate, and vulnerable.

A second principle in Calvin, which also is central for me, is his use at absolutely crucial moments in his work of the word *sicut*, "as if." For Calvin, one reads scripture "'as if' there the living words of God can be heard."[8] This is not a casual thing. Basic to Calvin's understanding of Christian practice is reading scripture, and the defining aspect of reading scripture is reading "as if." With what can only be taken as intentional consistency, Calvin also uses *sicut* when he talks about the presence of Christ in the sacrament, so that it is received "as if" there the real presence of Christ can be discerned. I would think that one could extend his use of *sicut* to reading second scriptures as well.

When we ask what Calvin could possibly have had in mind by using this word at these crucial moments in his discussion of defining Christian practices, I think we can immediately cancel the possibility that what he meant was an act of pretending that something is the case when actually it is not. "*Sicut*" in Calvin does not mean, as it does for Hans Vaihinger, contrary to fact or fictional.[9] Nor, in my opinion, does it mean something like what is carried by the legal situation in which someone or something stands in for something else, as a lawyer represents me in court or a down payment stands for my commitment to complete a transaction. It is not as though reading and taking the sacrament are related to but also substitutes for the Word of God and the presence of Christ, tokens or symbols. Rather, Calvin is describing a certain and particular expectation of reader or recipient, namely, a readiness and eagerness to hear and receive. In other words, "as if" does not have the skeptical force of undermining or minimizing something but the force of opening something up.

I substitute a hermeneutics of "as if" or of expectation for a hermeneutics of suspicion. It is a hermeneutics of looking toward and hoping for something more, something new. And one comes from reading and receiving enabled by them to bring similar expectations and desires to one's other encounters. The hermeneutics of "as if" directs attention not to something less that lies behind or below but to something more that looks ahead and above. It is an orientation that prizes edification over reduction, the hyperbolic over the ironic, gift over control. A critical task of the hermeneutics of "as if" is to counter or dismantle the assumption, one that, unfortunately, I also retain and am attached to, that there are people, texts, and occurrences in my world that cannot be, or do not deserve to be, read in that expectant way.

In other words, the third facet or assumption of my religious identity includes something that is not already accomplished, a place where I do not as yet reside. It is a possibility that invites me to live within it and promises to receive me. I feel invited by it to be at home in the habitation or orientation it provides. So, the third facet of my religious identity is not only constituted by the acceptances that I have experienced because of the graciousness of others, of my inclusion in institutions, especially universities and Reformed churches, and of my writings having been published and read but also by the understandings that these inclusions have led me to project as a continuing way of being in the world.

However, since we are, by reason of this topic, looking ahead and at the same time reaching the end of this book, thoughts move in an eschatological direction. Furthermore, I have far less of my life left to live than has already transpired. Finally, I am aware that questions regarding personal identity have traditionally been tied to the continuation of personal life in the face of and even subsequent to death.

The thing that makes Christian eschatology so interesting is that it fully eludes understanding. Perhaps this is why the creedal principle of the resurrection of the body, which raises more questions than it possibly can answer, is easily brushed aside by Christians in favor of some doctrine of a soul that survives death and goes to heaven, a doctrine that seems easier to understand. But in the creed I am asked to affirm not the immortality of the soul but that I look for or expect the resurrection of the body and the life of the world to come. What in heaven's name that possibly could mean, I cannot say. My response is twofold. First, I am invited by this affirmation to allow what I have somehow been given since early youth, namely, the expectation and desire for something else or more, not to be intimidated or terminated by the reality of death. Second, I can invoke Calvin's *"sicut"* again, moving toward my ending, both of book and life, in a way that is similar to the move constitutive of reading Scripture and my encounters with the sacrament, that is, expectantly.

One thing is certain, it seems to me: if there is something more, a world to come, it will be radically different from what presently is. The relation between what is and what then will be is separated by a distance similar to but even wider than other gaps that, when one reflects on the world in which we find ourselves, come to mind: the gap between there being nothing at all and there being something, the gap between there being only chaos and there being relative but sustaining order, the gap between inorganic material and life, and the gap between living organisms and self-conscious persons. No matter how unlikely and remarkable the crossings of those gaps may strike us, the gap between this life and what is called the life of the world to come is ever so much greater. Therefore, if that gap is crossed, as I "expect" it will be, that crossing will be infinitely more incredible.

NOTES

Introduction

1. Janet Varner Gunn, *Autobiography: Toward a Poetics of Experience* (Philadelphia: University of Pennsylvania Press, 1982).
2. Janet Mason Ellerby, *Intimate Reading: The Contemporary Women's Memoir* (Syracuse: Syracuse University Press, 2001).
3. See *Critical Inquiry* 24, no. 2 (Winter 1998).
4. Sau-ling Cynthia Wong, "Autobiography as Guided Chinatown Tour? Maxine Hong Kingston's *The Woman Warrior* and the Chinese-American Autobiographical Controversy," in *Multicultural Autobiography: American Lives*, ed. James Robert Payne (Knoxville: University of Tennessee Press, 1992), 263.

1. Telling You Who I Am

1. For a strong defense of including personal ingredients in scholarship, see the essays collected in *The Intimate Critique: Autobiographical Literary Criticism*, ed. Diane P. Freedman, Olivia Frey, and Francis Murphy Zauhar (Durham, N.C.: Duke University Press, 1993), especially the essay by Jane Tompkins, "Me and My Shadow, 23–40.
2. Jonathan Glover, *The Philosophy and Psychology of Personal Identity* (London: Allen Lane, 1988), 132.
3. Michael Keith and Steve Pile, "Introduction Part 2," in *Place and the Politics of Identity*, ed. Keith and Pile (London and New York: Routledge, 1993), 30.
4. David A. Jopling, *Self-Knowledge and the Self* (New York and London: Routledge, 2000), 2.
5. Roger J. Porter, *Self-Same Songs: Autobiographical Performances and Reflections* (Lincoln: University of Nebraska Press, 2002).
6. Arnold H. Modell, *The Private Self* (Cambridge: Harvard University Press, 1993), 24.
7. David Parker, *The Self in Moral Space: Life Narrative and the Good* (Ithaca: Cornell University Press, 2007), 170.
8. Judith Butler, *Giving an Account of Oneself* (New York: Fordham University Press, 2005), 23.

9. Charles Taylor, *Sources of the Self: The Making of the Modern Identity* (Cambridge: Harvard University Press, 1989), 211–47, 418–93.

10. Adriana Cavarero, *Relating Narratives: Storytelling and Selfhood*, trans. Paul A. Kottman (London and New York: Routledge, 2000), 14.

11. See C. R. Snyder and Howard L. Franklin, *Uniqueness, The Human Pursuit of Difference* (New York: Plenum Press, 1980). This sociological study is particularly valuable in establishing that people tend to assume or to construct for themselves a degree of uniqueness but tend as well to need or to assume a degree of similarity with other people. "Emotionally, therefore, our pursuit of difference may be best conceptualized as a pursuit of *some* degree of dissimilarity relative to other people" (36).

12. Taylor, *Sources of the Self*; Jerrold Seigel, *The Idea of the Self: Thought and Experience in Western Europe since the Seventeenth Century* (Cambridge: Cambridge University Press, 2005); Raymond Martin and John Barresi, *The Rise and Fall of Soul and Self: An Intellectual History of Personal Identity* (New York: Columbia University Press, 2006).

13. Raymond Martin and John Barresi, *Naturalization of the Soul: Self and Personal Identity in the Eighteenth Century* (London and New York: Routledge, 2000), 11.

14. James A. Holstein and Jaber F. Gubrium, *The Self We Live By: Narrative Identity in a Postmodern World* (New York and Oxford: Oxford University Press, 2000), 168.

15. Ibid., 14.

16. Stuart Hall, "Who Needs 'Identity'?" in *Identity: A Reader*, ed. Paul du Gay et al. (London: Sage, 2000), 19.

17. Kenneth J. Gergen, "Warranting Voice and the Elaboration of the Self," in *Texts of Identity*, ed. John Shotter and Kenneth J. Gergen (London: Sage, 1989), 71–75.

18. Raymond Martin and John Barresi, "Introduction: Personal Identity and What Matters in Survival: An Historical Overview," in *Personal Identity*, ed. Martin and Barresi (Oxford: Blackwell, 2003), 45.

19. Jopling, *Self-Knowledge and the Self*, 18.

20. Modell, *The Private Self*, 10.

21. Lawrence E. Cahoone, "Limits of the Social and Relational Self," in *Selves, People, and Persons: What Does It Mean to Be a Self?*, ed. Leroy Rouner (Notre Dame, Ind.: University of Notre Dame Press, 1992), 54.

22. Harold W. Noonan, *Personal Identity* (London and New York: Routledge, 1989), 1.

23. Ibid., 2.

24. Robert Nozick, "Personal Identity through Time," in *Personal Identity*, ed. Martin and Barresi, 92–114.

25. Derek Parfit, "Why Our Identity Is Not What Matters," in *Personal Identity*, ed. Martin and Barresi, 115–43.

26. Hubert J. M. Hermans and Harry J. G. Kempen, *The Dialogical Self: Meaning as Movement* (San Diego: Academic Press, 1993), xxii, 92.

27. The essays in Constantine Sedikides and Marilynn B. Brewer, eds., *Individual Self, Relational Self, Collective Self* (Ann Arbor: Sheridan, 2001), provide support for this complex way of looking at self-accounts. The editors argue that "the self-concept consists of three fundamental self-representations" (1). However, their three types differ from those I am presenting here in that I combine their first two, what they call the individual and "dyadic relationships" under "personal," and they do not include my third, the ontological arena. Also, many of the essays in this volume argue for the primacy of one or another of the three, and I argue that one of the three arenas is not necessarily primary in relation to the others.

28. For an excellent discussion of the interplay between similarity and difference in interpersonal relations, see C. R. Snyder and Howard L. Franklin, *Uniqueness: The Human Pursuit of Difference*. They say, for example, "People tend to experience a moderate degree of interpersonal similarity as positive, and when the degree of similarity becomes very high or very slight, then a more aversive emotional reaction occurs" (42).

29. Jopling, *Self-Knowledge and the Self*, 18, emphasis in original.

30. Ibid., 135, emphasis in original.

31. Ibid., 152.

32. Modell, *The Private Self*, 71.

33. Paul Ricoeur, *Oneself as Another*, trans. Kathleen Blamey (Chicago: University of Chicago Press, 1992), 193.

34. Arthur Aron and Tracy McLaughlin-Volpe, "Including Others in the Self," in *Individual Self, Relational Self, Collective Self*, ed. Sedikides and Brewer, 90.

35. See my discussion of Heidegger on these matters in Wesley A. Kort, *Modern Fiction and Human Time* (Gainesville: University of Florida Press, 1986), 152–65.

36. See G. Thomas Couser, *Recovering Bodies: Illness, Disability, and Life Writing* (Madison: University of Wisconsin Press, 1997). However, it should be noted that Couser points out how often attention in such writing is focused less on the body and the ailment or disability and more on how the culture constructs illness and disability, how the writer tries to retain personal integrity in relation to physical conditions, and the effort to retain identity in opposition to the depersonalizing effects of medical discourse and the relegation of the person, by reason of illness, to membership in an impersonal group of the similarly afflicted.

37. Jacques Lacan, "The Mirror Stage," in *Identity: A Reader*, ed. du Gay et al., 44–50.

38. Stuart Hall, "Who Needs 'Identity'?" in *Identity: A Reader*, ed. du Gay et al., 24.

39. Jopling, *Self-Knowledge and the Self*, 56.

40. Martin and Barresi, *Naturalization of the Soul*, 11.

41. Glover, *The Philosophy and Psychology of Personal Identity*, 62.

42. Galen Strawson, "The Self," in *Personal Identity*, ed. Martin and Barresi, 367, 368.

43. Noonan, *Personal Identity*, 41.

44. See my discussion of the linguistic turn in Wesley A. Kort, *Story, Text and Scripture: Literary Interests in Biblical Narrative* (State College: Pennsylvania State University Press, 1989), 61–71.
45. See my discussion of Derrida ibid., 114–17, 124–27.
46. Emile Benveniste, "Subjectivity in Language," in *Identity: A Reader*, ed. du Gay et al., 31–39.
47. Louis Althusser, "Ideology Interpellates Individuals as Subjects," in *Identity: A Reader*, ed. du Gay et al., 31–38.
48. Hermans and Kempen, *The Dialogical Self*, 32.
49. Terry Eagleton, "I Am, Therefore I Think: The Plight of the Body in Modern Thought," *Harper's*, March 2004, 90.
50. Ibid.
51. Albert W. Musschenga, "Personalized Identity in an Individualized Society," in *Creating Identity*, ed. Hermann Haring, Maureen Junker-Kenny, and Dietmar Mieth (London: SCM Press, 2000), 26.
52. Albert W. Musschenga, "Identity—Personal, Moral, and Professional," in *Personal and Moral Identity*, ed. Musschenga et al. (Dordrecht and London: Kluwer Academic, 2002), 186.
53. Augusto Blasi, "The Development of Identity: Some Implications for Moral Functioning," in *The Moral Self*, ed. Gil G. Noam and Thomas E. Wren (Cambridge: MIT Press, 1993), 107.
54. See Cavarero, *Relating Narratives*.
55. Jopling, *Self-Knowledge and the Self*, 84.
56. See David Kyuman Kim, *Melancholic Freedom: Agency and the Spirit of Politics* (New York: Oxford University Press, 2007).
57. Harry Frankfurt, "On the Necessity of Ideals," in *The Moral Self*, ed. Noam and Wren, 19.
58. Ibid., 25.

2. Narrative and Self-Accounts

1. Paul John Eakin, "Relational Selves, Relational Lives: The Story of the Story," in *True Relations: Essays on Autobiography and the Postmodern*, ed. G. Thomas Couser and Joseph Fichtelberg (Westport, Ct.: Greenwood Press, 1998), 74.
2. For a defense of this position, see the opening chapter of Wesley A. Kort, *Story, Text and Scripture: Literary Interests in Biblical Narrative* (State College: Pennsylvania State University Press, 1989), 6–23.
3. Galen Strawson, "The Self," in *Personal Identity*, ed. Martin and Barresi (Oxford: Blackwell, 2003), 353.
4. Ibid., 359.
5. David A. Jopling, *Self-Knowledge and the Self* (New York and London: Routledge, 2000), 55.
6. Sidonie Smith and Julia Watson, *Reading Autobiography: A Guide for Interpreting Life Narratives* (Minneapolis: University of Minnesota Press, 2001), 80.

7. Paul John Eakin, *How Our Lives Become Stories: Making Selves* (Ithaca and London: Cornell University Press, 1999), 21.

8. Arnold H. Modell, *The Private Self* (Cambridge: Harvard University Press, 1993), 183.

9. John Sturrock, *The Language of Autobiography: Studies in the First Person Singular* (Cambridge: Cambridge University Press, 1993), 258.

10. John Sturrock, "Theory Versus Autobiography," in *The Culture of Autobiography: Constructions of Self-Representation,* ed. Robert Folkenflik (Stanford: Stanford University Press, 1993), 25.

11. Jerome Bruner, "The Autobiographical Process," in *The Culture of Autobiography,* ed. Folkenflik, 38.

12. Shari Benstock, "Authorizing the Autobiographical," in *The Private Self: Theory and Practice of Women's Autobiographical Writings,* ed. Benstock (Chapel Hill: University of North Carolina Press, 1988), 11.

13. Felicity A. Nussbaum, "Eighteenth-Century Women's Autobiographical Commonplaces," in *The Private Self,* ed. Benstock, 150.

14. Robert Folkenflik, "The Self as Other," in *The Culture of Autobiography,* ed. Folkenflik, 234.

15. Adriana Cavarero, *Relating Narratives: Storytelling and Selfhood,* trans. Paul A. Kottman (London and New York: Routledge, 2000), 73.

16. Ibid., 90.

17. Robert Elbaz, *The Changing Nature of the Self: A Critical Study of the Autobiographic Discourse* (London and Sydney: Croom Helm, 1988), 44.

18. Georges Gusdorf, "Conditions and Limits of Autobiography," in *Autobiography: Essays Theoretical and Critical,* ed. James Olney (Princeton: Princeton University Press, 1980), 29.

19. Smith and Watson, *Reading Autobiography,* 84.

20. For a richly informative and accessible analysis of Augustine's contribution to autobiographical writing, see James Olney, *Memory and Narrative: The Weave of Life-Writing* (Chicago: University of Chicago Press, 1998).

21. Robert Folkenflik, "Introduction: The Institution of Autobiography," in *The Culture of Autobiography,* ed. Folkenflik, 6.

22. Ibid., 8.

23. Smith and Watson, *Reading Autobiography,* 84.

24. Laura Browder, *Slippery Characters: Ethnic Impersonators and American Identities* (Chapel Hill: University of North Carolina Press, 2000), 3.

25. Lawrence Buell, "Autobiography in the American Renaissance," in *American Autobiography: Retrospect and Prospect,* ed. John Eakin (Madison: University of Wisconsin Press, 1991), 48.

26. E. M. Forster, *Aspects of the Novel* (1927; New York: Harcourt, Brace, 1954), 86.

27. Sturrock, *The Language of Autobiography,* 3.

28. Ibid., 52.

29. Sturrock, "Theory Versus Autobiography," in *The Culture of Autobiography,* ed. Folkenflik, 25

30. Paul John Eakin, "Relational Selves, Relational Lives," in *True Relations,* ed. Couser and Fichtelberg, 75.

31. Larry Sisson, "The Art and Illusion of Spiritual Autobiography," in *True Relations,* ed. Couser and Fichtelberg, 103.

32. Sturrock, *The Language of Autobiography,* 50.

33. Linda R. Anderson, *Autobiography* (London and New York: Routledge, 2001), 123.

34. Mary Evans, *Missing Persons: The Impossibility of Auto/biography* (London and New York: Routledge, 1999), 1.

35. Smith and Watson, *Reading Autobiography,* 128.

36. Jean Starobinski, "The Style of Autobiography," in *Autobiography,* ed. Olney, 74–75.

37. Judith Butler, *Giving an Account of Oneself* (New York: Fordham University Press, 2005), 64.

38. Wayne C. Booth, *The Company We Keep: An Ethics of Fiction* (Berkeley and Los Angeles: University of California Press, 1988), 8. Hereafter this work is cited parenthetically in the chapter text.

39. See my *Modern Fiction and Human Time* (Gainesville: University Presses of Florida, 1986).

40. Sturrock, *The Language of Autobiography,* 14.

41. Sturrock, "Theory Versus Autobiography," in *The Culture of Autobiography,* ed. Folkenflik, 27.

42. Larry Sisson, "The Art and Illusion of Spiritual Autobiography," in *True Relations,* ed. Couser and Fichtelberg, 99.

43. Sturrock, *The Language of Autobiography,* 20.

44. Jerome Bruner, "The Autobiographical Process," in *The Culture of Autobiography,* ed. Folkenflik, 49.

45. Evans, *Missing Persons,* 4.

46. Anderson, *Autobiography,* 90.

47. Butler, *Giving an Account of Oneself,* 62.

48. Georges Gusdorf, "Conditions and Limits of Autobiography," in *Autobiography,* ed. Olney, 36.

49. Anderson, *Autobiography,* 72.

50. Smith and Watson, *Reading Autobiography,* 47.

51. Hubert Hermans and Harry Kempen, *The Dialogical Self: Meaning as Movement* (San Diego: Academic Press, 1993), 15.

52. Kathleen Woodward, "Simone de Beauvoir: Aging and Its Discontents," in *The Private Self,* ed. Benstock, 109.

53. Smith and Watson, *Reading Autobiography,* 132.

54. Hermans and Kempen, *The Dialogical Self,* xx.

3. Disclosing a Religious Identity

1. José Casanova, *Public Religions in the Modern World* (Chicago: University of Chicago Press, 1994), 142–45.

2. Ibid., 15.
3. Charles Taylor, *A Secular Age* (Cambridge: Harvard University Press, 2007), 592.
4. Robert D. Putnam and David E. Campbell, *American Grace: How Religion Divides and Unites Us* (New York: Simon and Schuster, 2010), 3.
5. For a clear and judicious treatment of the role of religion in public life from the founding of the Republic to the present day and of the dissatisfaction with that religion on both religious and nonreligious sides, see Jon Meacham, *American Gospel: God, the Founding Fathers, and the Making of the Nation* (New York: Random House, 2006).
6. See, for example, Talal Asad, *Genealogies of Religion: Discipline and Reasons of Power in Christianity and Islam* (Baltimore: Johns Hopkins University Press, 1993), 29.
7. Putnam and Campbell, *American Grace*, 148.
8. Casanova, *Public Religions in the Modern World*, 5.
9. Ibid., 64.
10. Ibid., 64–65.
11. Charles Taylor, *Varieties of Religion Today: William James Revisited* (Cambridge: Harvard University Press, 2002), 85.
12. Ibid., 86.
13. Putnam and Campbell, *American Grace*, 176.
14. Ibid., 539.
15. Ibid., 134.
16. Stewart Elliott Guthrie, *Faces in the Clouds: A New Theory of Religion* (New York: Oxford University Press, 1993), 10–11.
17. See R. Laurence Moore, *Selling God: American Religion in the Marketplace of Culture* (New York: Oxford University Press, 1994).
18. Gauri Viswanathan, *Outside the Fold: Conversion, Modernity, and Belief* (Princeton: Princeton University Press, 1998), xii.
19. Charles Taylor, *Varieties of Religion Today*, 101.
20. Claire Mitchell, *Religion, Identity and Politics in Northern Ireland: Boundaries of Belonging and Belief* (Burlington, Vt.: Ashgate, 2006), 12.
21. See, for example, Alasdair McIntyre, *Three Rival Versions of Moral Enquiry: Encyclopedia, Genealogy, and Tradition* (Notre Dame, Ind.: University of Notre Dame Press, 1990).
22. See, for example, Dan McAdams, *The Redemptive Self: Stories Americans Live By* (New York: Oxford University Press, 2006), 33.
23. On this distinction between religious people, see Stephen Sykes, *The Identity of Christianity* (Philadelphia: Fortress Press, 1984).
24. Richard King, *Orientalism and Religion: Postcolonial Theory, India, and "the Mystic East"* (London and New York: Routledge, 1999).
25. Terry Eagleton, *The Idea of Culture* (Oxford: Blackwell, 2000), 64–66.
26. This point constitutes the principal argument of my book, *Bound to Differ: The Dynamics of Theological Discourses* (State College: Pennsylvania State University Press, 1996).

27. Viswanathan, *Outside the Fold*, 38.
28. Michel Foucault, *Ethics, Subjectivity and Truth*, ed. Paul Rabinow, trans. Robert Hurley et al. (New York: New Press, 1994), 244.
29. Ibid., 228.
30. Casanova, *Public Religions in the Modern World*, 217.

4. Religious Debtors

1. Maya Angelou, *I Know Why the Caged Bird Sings* (New York: Bantam, 1993), 120. Hereafter this work is cited parenthetically in the chapter text.
2. It should be noted, regarding the detail with which early experiences are recalled, that Angelou seems not to draw a clear line in her autobiographical writing between the actual and the constructed or reconstructed. Of the many examples that could be given, one is her verbatim rehearsal of her grandmother's prayer on the occasion of Maya's having used the expression "by the way" (102). This blurring of distinction gives to her rendering of events, both personal and communal, a vivid and memorable quality they could not, I would think, otherwise have. I also think that this lack of distinction between the actual and the constructed, a distinction that is so important, for example, to Philip Roth, arises from or is fortified by a less deliberate preoccupation with her self-consciousness than one encounters in several other writers in this study, especially Roth.
3. While I think it can be said that Angelou directs her self-account noticeably to her black readers, especially regarding the point that their past should be viewed not only as something to be escaped but also as a resource to be retrieved and retained, it is important to note that she also writes for white readers, clarifying and defending aspects of black culture they may not otherwise understand. This is particularly evident in her several comments on the difficulties faced by black men in American society and the tactics they employ in response to them (see 221 and 224, for example).
4. Maya Angelou, *The Heart of a Woman* (New York: Random House, 1981), 56.
5. It should be added, however, that the extended and memorable narration of the revival and its results is not clearly separated at the chapter's conclusion from rollick in its more sensual forms enjoyed by the Saturday-night visitors to the house of the "good-time woman," Miss Grace (132).
6. Angelou implants in her narrative several indications that belief in a caring and just God, such as her grandmother had, is not something she herself readily or fully adopts. While, in Los Angeles, she says her prayers before going to sleep in the junkyard, she also thinks of the events of her life as directed by "Fate" (247). She sees her life as determined by arbitrary events to which she is forced to respond: "Life had a conveyor-belt quality. It went on unpursued and unpursuing, and my only thought was to remain erect, and keep my secret [her pregnancy] along with my balance" (286).
7. Angelou, *The Heart of a Woman*, 173.
8. Philip Roth, *The Facts: A Novelist's Autobiography* (New York: Penguin, 1989), 163. Hereafter this work is cited parenthetically in the chapter text.

9. Philip Roth, *Patrimony: A True Story* (New York: Simon and Schuster, 1991), 96.

10. Ibid., 98.

11. While Roth makes much of the highly unusual nature of the relationship he had with Josie, it also seems to be continuous with his relations with the other women he includes in his account, Polly, Gayle, May, and the Chinese prostitute he hires while in London with May. Female students in my class often object to Roth because of his attitudes toward women, attitudes that Zukerman, despite his and Maria's complaints on this point, does not for them sufficiently describe, perhaps because Zukerman himself, at the age of forty-five, is on his fourth wife. I think that the problem lies with Roth's assumption that if anything is significant, that significance must be imputed to it or constructed from it. Except for his home life, little seems for him to have an inherent significance. The women in his life—especially Josie, who does so explicitly and, for Roth, annoyingly—seem, in contrast, to recognize a significance in their relations to him that Roth does not or is not able to recognize. Instead, he gives to them, as Zuckerman says, "allegorical" roles. That is, he imparts or constructs a meaningful place for them in his self-account. But he can do so because they and the relationships he has with them lack inherent significance.

12. Dan Barry, *Pull Me Up: A Memoir* (New York and London: Norton, 2004), 9. Hereafter this work is cited parenthetically in the chapter text.

13. See, for example, Robert A. Orsi, "'Mildred, Is It Fun to be a Cripple? The Culture of Suffering in Mid-Twentieth-Century American Catholicism," *South Atlantic Quarterly* 93, no. 3 (Summer 1994): 547–90.

5. Religious Dwellers

1. Robert D. Putnam, *Bowling Alone: The Collapse and Revival of American Community* (New York: Simon and Schuster, 2000), 48.

2. Robert Wuthnow, *Loose Connections: Joining Together in America's Fragmented Communities* (Cambridge: Harvard University Press, 1998), 4.

3. John Sears, *Sacred Places: American Tourist Attractions in the Nineteenth Century* (New York: Oxford University Press, 1989).

4. Dan Wakefield, *Returning: A Spiritual Journey* (Boston: Beacon, 1997), 53. Hereafter this work is cited parenthetically in the chapter text.

5. Dan Wakefield, *New York in the Fifties* (New York: St. Martin's Griffin, 1992), 217.

6. Ibid., 125.

7. Letty Cottin Pogrebin, *Deborah, Golda, and Me: Being Female and Jewish in America* (New York: Crown, 1991), 24. Hereafter this work is cited parenthetically in the chapter text.

8. I agree with Pogrebin that religion provides many Americans with a way to set themselves off from other Americans, to identify as Americans of a particular kind, thereby placing themselves within a whole without being absorbed by it. But I also think that religious people tend to make religious

identity a special, even unique, case. I think it is important to recognize that this need or desire to be particular amidst a mass manifests itself in many other ways in the formation of American identities, and religious particularity, while by no means the same as other regional and institutional locations, also partners with them.

9. Kathleen Norris, *The Virgin of Bennington* (New York: Riverhead Books, 2001), 14.

10. Ibid., 93.

11. Ibid., 123.

12. Kathleen Norris, *Dakota: A Spiritual Geography* (Boston and New York: Houghton Mifflin, 2001), 1. Hereafter this work is cited parenthetically in the chapter text.

13. While I think that Norris is wholly justified in treating negatively the apparent unwillingness of Americans to attach themselves to particular locations—geographical, social, and organizational—and their penchant for mobility and self-containment, two points need to be added. First, Americans also continue to display a strong willingness to identify with places, groups, and institutions. Personal and national, as well as religious identities are very often tied to such locations. Second, there is in Norris a tendency to posit stability and mobility as contraries to one another. Indeed, there is in current cultural theory an opposition between the two, an advocacy either of rootedness or of a rhizome-like flexibility. What is especially worth noting is that these contraries are also embedded in identity theory, which needs to negotiate the relations between constancy or continuity and development or variation. This argues for a willingness to treat theories of human spatiality and temporality as related rather than as opposed to one another. A provocative point implied by Norris is her association of Christianity more with spatial than with historical or temporal considerations, a point she implicitly makes as well by distancing herself at least partially from Americans who are mobile and lack spatial commitments and by acknowledging favorably Native American and other traditional religious affirmations of rootedness and place-attachment.

14. I think it could be added to the contrast Norris creates between large urban centers, which she also blames for concealing from people their human limits (2), and small towns, which, because of their size, can become communities of people mutually concerned with one another, that recent urban geographers have pointed out that large cities can also be viewed as federations of institutions and small neighborhoods, groups of people who are aware of and even concerned for one another.

6. Religious Diviners

1. Courtney Bender, *The New Metaphysicals: Spirituality and the American Religious Imagination* (Chicago: University of Chicago Press, 2010).

2. Frederick Buechner, *Sacred Journey: A Memoir of Early Days* (New York: HarperCollins, 1991), 6. Hereafter this work is cited parenthetically in the chapter text.

3. In his *Telling Secrets* (San Francisco: Harper San Francisco, 1991), Buechner discloses more about where he was at the time of writing *The Sacred Journey*. He tells us that he was in a state of distress during this period in the early 1980s because of his daughter's protracted and life-threatening struggle with anorexia. This confession counters my comment in the first part of this study that self-accounts are usually given at the point of higher ground. It is clear here that Buechner describes and interprets his life and points to the future as a way also of providing for himself an alternative to the distress and even despair to which his daughter's illness, his inability to aid her, and his feeling of partial responsibility for it might lead him. I think that *The Sacred Journey* would have been a stronger self-account if Buechner, drawing attention to the time of writing as he does, had given us this part of the setting, thereby clarifying his eagerness in the account to see and to construct positive outcomes from negative events.

4. Mary Gordon, *Seeing through Places: Reflections on Geography and Identity* (New York and London: Simon and Schuster, 2001), 252. Hereafter this work is cited parenthetically in the chapter text.

5. For a fuller disclosure of her father and of her attitudes toward him, see Mary Gordon, *The Shadow Man* (New York: Random House, 1997).

6. Mary Gordon, *Circling My Mother* (New York: Pantheon, 2007), 145.

7. Gordon, *Shadow Man*, 208.

8. Gordon, *Circling My Mother*, 239.

9. Mary Gordon, *Reading Jesus: A Writer's Encounter with the Gospels* (New York: Pantheon, 2009), 176.

10. Ibid., 178.

11. Anne Lamott, *Traveling Mercies: Some Thoughts on Faith* (New York: Random House, 2000), 172. Hereafter this work is cited parenthetically in the chapter text.

12. Anne Lamott, *Plan B: Further Thoughts on Faith* (New York: Riverhead, 2005), 46.

9. Looking Ahead

1. John Updike, *Self-Consciousness: Memoirs* (New York: Knopf, 1989), 108.

2. See my *Story, Text, and Scripture: Literary Interests in Biblical Narrative* (University Park: Pennsylvania State University Press, 1989).

3. See my *"Take, Read:" Scripture, Textuality, and Cultural Practice* (University Park: Pennsylvania State University Press, 1996).

4. Ibid. See esp. chap. 2, "Modernity: Reading Other Texts As Though They and Not the Bible Were Scripture."

5. I argue the first point, that biblical wisdom texts can be seen as constants in American culture, in several places but especially in *Moral Fiber: Character*

and Belief in Recent American Fiction (Philadelphia: Fortress Press, 1982) and subsequently in *"Take Read:" Scripture, Textuality and Cultural Practice.* The point that Christianity is complicated by biblical texts that sponsor and warrant orientations that are in potential or actual conflict with one another is central to my *Bound to Differ: The Dynamics of Theological Discourses* (State College: Pennsylvania State University Press, 1992).

6. Joseph Haroutunian, ed., *Calvin Commentaries,* Commentary on John 5:39, Library of Christian Classics (Louisville, Ky.: Westminster/John Knox Press, 1979), 104.

7. For a discussion of the understanding of reading in these highly original and influential theorists, see my *"Take, Read": Scripture, Textuality, and Cultural Practice.*

8. *Calvin: Institutes of the Christian Religion,* ed. John T. McNeill, trans. Ford Lewis Battles, Library of Christian Classics, vols. 20 and 21 (Philadelphia: Westminster Press, 1960), 74.

9. See Hans Vaihinger, *The Philosophy of "As If": A System of the Theoretical, Practical, and Religious Fictions of Mankind,* trans. C. K. Ogden (New York: Harcourt, Brace, 1924).

INDEX